BEFORE THE
INDUSTRIAL REVOLUTION

European Society

and Economy,

1000-1700

BEFORE THE
INDUSTRIAL REVOLUTION

European Society and
Economy, 1000-1700

Carlo M. Cipolla

W · W · NORTON & COMPANY · INC ·

NEW YORK

FIRST EDITION

Library of Congress Cataloging in Publication Data
Cipolla, Carlo M
Before the Industrial Revolution.
Translation of Storia economica dell'Europa pre-industriale.
Bibliography: p.
Includes index.
1. Europe—Economic conditions. I. Title.
HC240.C49513   330.9′4′01   75–19366
ISBN 0–393–05538–8
ISBN 0–393–09255–0 pbk.

Cartography by Harold K. Faye

PRINTED IN THE UNITED STATES OF AMERICA

1 2 3 4 5 6 7 8 9

Contents

Illustrations

Maps

Figures

Tables

Preface

The world in which we live and the problems we face would be unintelligible without reference to that grandiose change which we label the Industrial Revolution. In its turn, the Industrial Revolution was but the ultimate phase, the historically coherent outcome of a development which took place in Europe during the first seven centuries of our millenium. The purpose of this book is precisely that of offering an up-to-date, documented synthesis of those human developments from which our world, with its blessings and its evils, eventually emerged.

The book addresses itself to both the student and the general reader; although fundamentally focused on social and economic problems, its approach is essentially interdisciplinary. This double ambivalence may help to explain some of its traits.

The style and the exposition have been kept at a level of reasonable simplicity but no efforts have been spared to provide the reader with precise references, abundant statistical material, and rich bibliographical information. Forbidding technicalities have been eliminated to the extent allowed by scholarly accuracy. At the same time the logical tools of economic and social analysis were clearly spelled out rather than being simply implied or altogether concealed in the prose of the narrative. This, hopefully, will help the economics student to see more clearly the connections between economic theory and economic history and, on the other hand, will help the layman to get acquainted with some of the basic tools of contemporary social sciences.

The book has been structured in two parts. In Part One the analysis is essentially static. It aims at clarifying the working of the society and of the economy of preindustrial Europe, placing the emphasis on some constant characteristics of both that society and that economy. Part Two illustrates instead the changes which took place within that framework and gradually transformed Europe from a primitive, uninteresting, underdeveloped corner of the world, constantly menaced by its more powerful neighbors, into a highly dynamic, developed, creative society which came to establish undisputed political, cultural, and economic predominance all over the globe.

Quite naturally, the nature of our inquiry is molded by values, mentalities, and beliefs which are peculiar to our age and society. When another society is under scrutiny, raising questions which bear little or no relation to the philosophy, values, and beliefs of that society inevitably poses difficulties. We would like to know the size of the population, the patterns of consumption, the level of production of, let us say, the province of Reims in France at the beginning of this millenium. The documents of the time give us instead detailed information of the miracles performed by St. Gibrian in the area. As the documentation left by the past reflects the interests and the values of the past, many of the problems raised in the following pages receive only tentative or approximate answers. The answers become more precise for centuries closer to our own, as men began to raise the questions which we raise.

Professor Marcella Kooy and Miss Alide Kooy translated the original Italian text into English. Mr. Robert E. Kehoe carefully edited the book and checked on its progress.

For the typing of the English manuscript I am indebted to the Institute of Business and Economic Research of the University of California. To all I wish to express my gratitude.

March 1974
Berkeley, California

PART 1

A STATIC
APPROXIMATION

CHAPTER ONE

Demand

Type of Analysis

The working of any economic system can be seen from two points of view, that of demand and that of supply. The two perspectives are intimately linked and reflect the same reality. When one describes them, however, the need to analyze first one and then the other arbitrarily accentuates the distinction between them.

Population

From the point of view of demand, the first element to consider is obviously population. If there were no people there would be no human wants. And if there were no human wants there would be no demand.

The study of population presupposes the collection of demographic data. Venice took censuses of its population at least since 1338. In the Grand Duchy of Tuscany censuses covering the whole state were taken in 1551, 1558, 1622, 1642, 1672, and several times thereafter. However, at national levels, reasonably accurate figures about the size as well as the structure of a population are not available before the nineteenth century, with the exception of Scandinavia, for which accurate data are available for the eighteenth century. The first English census took place in 1801.

For the period before 1800, demographic historians have tried to overcome the dearth of data by estimating population on the basis of indirect and heterogeneous information from fields as disparate as archeology, botany, and toponymy, as well as from written records of the most diverse kind, such as inventories of manors, lists of men liable to military service, and accounts of hearth taxes or poll taxes. Table 1-1 shows estimates of total population for the major areas of Europe. Such figures can be taken only as gross approximations.

Table 1–1
Approximate Population of the Major European Countries,
1000–1700 (In millions).

	c.1000	c.1300	c.1500	c.1600	c.1700
Balkans	—	—	7	8	8
Low Countries	—	—	2	3	3
British Isles	2	5	5	7	9
Danubian Countries	—	—	6	7	9
France	5	15	16	18	19
Germany	3	12	13	16	15
Italy	5	10	11	13	13
Poland	—	—	4	5	6
Russia	—	—	10	15	18
Scandinavian Countries	—	—	—	2	3
Spain and Portugal	—	—	9	11	10
Switzerland	—	0.8	0.8	1.1	1.2

The figures for the columns relating to the eleventh and fourteenth centuries are the fruits of hazardous hypotheses. Their margin of error is fairly high, hardly less than 20 percent and easily higher. Although the figures in the two last columns are more reliable, they also must not be taken as precise. More dependable figures are available for selected cities (see Appendix Table A-1), but they too are affected by large margins of error and must be taken only as orders of magnitude.

No matter how crude, however, all the figures in Table 1-1 consistently show that before the eighteenth century European population remained relatively small. For long periods it did not grow at all, and when it did, the rate of increase was always very low. Few cities numbered even more than one hundred thousand inhabitants (see Appendix Table A-1). When a city reached fifty thousand inhabitants, it was considered a metropolis. The preindustrial world remained a world of numerically small societies.

If a population does not increase or increases only slightly, in the absence of notable migratory movements the reason lies either in low fertility or high mortality or both. In preindustrial Europe fertility varied from period to period and from area to area, so that any generalization must be taken with more than a grain of salt. Celibacy was always fairly widespread, and when people married they generally did so at a relatively advanced age. These facts tended to reduce fertility; however, the prevailing birth rates were still very high, always above the 30-per-thousand level (see Appendix, Table A-2). While fertility rarely reached the biological maximum, it was nearer to this maximum than to the levels prevailing in the developed countries of the twentieth century.

If the population of preindustrial Europe remained relatively small, the reason was not so much low fertility as high mortality.[1] We shall return to this point later in the discussion.

It is worthwhile to distinguish between normal and catastrophic mortality. The distinction is arbitrary and in a way artifical, but it has the merit of facilitating description. We can broadly define *normal mortality* as the mortality prevailing in normal years—that is, years free from calamities like wars, famines, epidemics, and such disasters. As a rule normal mortality was below current fertility. *Catastrophic mortality* is the mortality of calamitous years and as a rule was far above current fertility. In years of normal mortality, the natural balance of the population (namely, the difference between the number of births and the number of deaths) was generally positive. In the years of catastrophic mortality, the natural balance of population was always highly negative. Owing to the recurrent ravages of catastrophic mortality linked to famines, wars,

---

1. One of the most sophisticated instruments of demographic analysis is the "life table." (Dublin, Lotka, Spiegelman, *Length of Life*.) A "life table" provides the most accurate statistical description of mortality and allows one to estimate life expectancy. Table A-4 (in the Appendix) shows that in the Sweden of 1778–82 a newborn male had a life expectancy of thirty-six years and newborn female thirty-nine years. The information is derived from a "life table" worked out by modern scholars on the basis of Swedish demographic data of the time. The technique of computing life tables was developed at the end of the seventeenth century.

and plagues, the populations of the various areas of preindustrial Europe were constantly subject to drastic fluctuations which, in their turn, were a source of instability for the economic system severely affecting both supply and demand.

Needs, Wants, and Effective Demand

All members of a society have "needs." The quantity and quality of these needs vary enormously in relation to numerous circumstances. Even those needs which seem most inelastic, like the physiological need for nourishment, vary considerably from person to person according to sex, age, climate, and type of work. In general, one can say that the quantity and quality of a society's needs depend on:

a. the size of population
b. the structure of the population by age, sex, and occupation
c. geophysical factors
d. sociocultural factors

The first point requires no comment. As to the second, it seems unnecessary to explain that old people and children do not have all the same needs, nor do men and women. As for the third, it should be obvious that a man living in Sweden or Siberia has many needs totally different from those of a man living in Sicily or Portugal. The relationship between needs and sociocultural conditions is of a more subtle character.

In preindustrial England people were convinced that vegetables "ingender ylle humours and be oftetymes the cause of putrified fevers," melancholy, and flatulence. As a consequence of these ideas there was a low demand for fruit and vegetables and the population lived in a pre-scorbutic state.[2] On the other hand, while many people refused to drink fresh cow's milk, many well-off adults paid wet nurses for the opportunity to suckle milk directly at their breasts. The old Dr. Caius maintained that his character changed according to the character of the wet nurse who nourished

---

2. Drummond and Wilbraham, *The Englishman's Food,* pp. 68, 69, 124, 125.

him. Whether his changes of disposition depended primarily on the quality of the milk or on hormonal secretions is not a question which should concern us here. The point is that there was a sustained demand for wet nurses not only to feed infants.

Other cultural factors can have an equally determining influence on needs, their nature, and their structure. For centuries Catholics made it a duty to eat fish on Fridays, while the men of the Solomon Islands forbade their women to eat certain types of fish. The Muslim religion forbids its followers to drink wine, while the Catholic religion created in all religious communities a need for wine to celebrate Mass. Extravagant ideas also contributed to the formation of needs held to be indispensable. The Galenic theory of humours created for centuries a widespread need for leeches.

These last examples have actually been chosen to prove that economists have good reasons for distrusting the word *needs*. The word implies "lack of substitutes," and is thus seriously misleading in economic analysis. One must also consider that the line of demarcation between the necessary and the superfluous is difficult to define. While daily bread clearly seems necessary and a trip to the Bahamas superfluous, between bread and a trip to the Bahamas there is a vast number of goods and services whose classification is problematical. Obviously the definition of need cannot be limited to the minimum amount of food indispensable for life. But as soon as the criterion is extended beyond that limit to include other elements, it is difficult to say where the line between the necessary and the superfluous should pass. Is one steak per week a need? Or is a need only a steak a month? We feel we need bathtubs, central heating, and handkerchiefs, but three hundred years ago in Europe these things were luxuries no one would have dreamed of describing as needs. Someone once wrote that we regard as needed what we consume and as superfluous what other people consume and we don't.

As long as a person is free to demand what he wants, what counts on the market are not the real needs but the wants. A man may need vitamins but may want cigarettes instead. The distinction is important, not only from the point of view of the individual, but also from the point of view of the society. A society may need more hospitals and more schools, but the members of that society may want, instead, more swimming pools, more theaters, or more freeways. There may also be dictators who impose or feed specific wants for military conquest, political prestige, or religious exaltation. For the market, what counts is not the objective need—which in any case no one can define except at minimum levels of subsistence—but the want as it is expressed by both the individual and the society.

In practice our wants are unlimited. Unfortunately, both as individuals and as a society, we only have limited resources at our disposal. In consequence, we must continually make choices, giving an order of priorities to our wants on the basis of economic as well as political, religious, ethical and social considerations.

Wants are one thing, effective demand is another. To count on the market, wants must be backed by purchasing power. When expressed through the expenditure of purchasing power, wants become effective demand and are registered by the market.

Since purchasing power is provided by income, it follows that, given a certain mass of wants, both private and public and given a certain scale of priorities, the level and the structure of effective demand are determined by:

a. level of income
b. the distribution of income (among individuals as well as institutions, and between the public and private sectors)[3]
c. level and structure of prices

Income and Its Distribution

The mass of incomes can be divided into three broad categories:

a. wages
b. profits
c. interest and rents

These different kinds of incomes correspond to different ways of participation in the productive process. They provide their recipients with purchasing power, thus enabling them to express their wants on the market in the form of effective demand. Obviously the

---

3. The distribution of income affects the level and the structure of demand because elasticities of demand vary at different levels of income.

person who generates and receives income spends it not only on himself but also on those he supports. In other words, the head of the family, who works and receives a wage, spends it to maintain not only himself or herself but also a spouse, children, and perhaps also an old mother or father if they are still alive. The earner of income, therefore, translates into effective demand not only personal wants, but also those of dependents. In other words, the income of the "active population" converts to effective demand the wants of the total population (active population plus dependent population).

Over the centuries, for the mass of the people, income was represented by wages, and up to the Industrial Revolution one can say that, given the low productivity of labor (see below) and other institutional factors, wages were extremely low in relation to prices; that is, real wages were extremely low. Reversing the above statement, we can say that current prices of goods were too high for current wages. In practical terms we would be saying the same thing, but we would be emphasizing that the basic problem was scarcity.

European society was fundamentally poor, but in every corner of Europe there were gradations of poverty and wealth. There were the poor and the very poor, and alongside them there were some rich and some very rich. Among the poorest, the peasants were overrepresented. At the end of the seventeenth century, the parson of the parish of Saint-Reim in Bordeaux noted that many of the artisans in his parish managed to survive only because they received from time to time the charity of the *"dames de charité."*[4] The artisans of more highly developed cities like Florence or Nuremberg however managed to lead a life which, if not comfortable, was at least not completely wretched. It was not unusual for an artisan in Nuremberg in the sixteenth century to have meat on his table more than once a week.[5] Several Florentine artisans were able to put aside small savings or to accumulate dowries for their daughters.[6] As always, reality can not be painted in black and white. However, it is undeniable that one of the main characteris-

---

4. Boutruche, *Bordeaux*, p. 504.
5. Strauss, *Nuremberg*, p. 201.
6. Fanfani, *Storia del lavoro,* pp. 421–22.

tics of preindustrial Europe, as of all traditional agricultural societies, was a striking contrast between the abject misery of the mass
and the affluence and magnificence of a limited number of very
rich. If with the aid of slides one could show the golden mosaics of
the monastery of Monreale (Sicily) side by side with a hovel of a
Sicilian peasant of the time, one would need no more words to
describe the nature of this phenomenon. It is useful to bear this
image in mind, but one should go further, attempting to complement the image with some measurements. Unfortunately, the data
available are few in quantity and poor in quality. According to
Tuscan fiscal assessments of 1427–29, wealth in the cities of Volterra and Pistoia was distributed approximately as shown in Table
1-2.

The fiscal assessments of 1545 for Lyon (France) indicate that
taxable wealth in that city was distributed as shown in Table 1-3.

In all three of these cases, 10 percent of the population con-

Table 1–2
Percentage Distribution of Population and
Estimated Wealth in Two Tuscan Towns, 1427–29

Pistoia		Volterra	
% Population	% Wealth	% Population	% Wealth
10	59	7	58
20	27	21	31
70	14	72	11
100	100	100	100

SOURCE: Herlihy, *Pistoia*, p. 188, and Fiumi, *Popolazione*, p. 94.

Table 1–3
Distribution of Population and
Wealth in Lyon (France), 1545

% Population	% Wealth
10	53
30	26
60	21
100	100

SOURCE: Gascon, *Grand Commerce*, Vol. 1, p. 370.

trolled more than 50 percent of the estimated wealth. In Lyon, however, if the assessment was correct, wealth was less inequitably distributed, because 60 percent of the population controlled 21 percent of the estimated wealth, while in Pistoia and Volterra about 70 percent of the population controlled less than 15 percent of the estimated wealth.

On the basis of the tax rolls of 1457, De Roover[7] classified the families of Florence for that year as follows:

    rich: 2 percent
    middle class: 16 percent
    poor: 54 percent
    destitute: 28 percent

Fiscal assessments are rarely reliable, and those of medieval and Renaissance times are particularly open to doubt. One may turn to other evidence. Frequently, the city authorities inquired about reserves of grain stored in private homes. Bags of grain were difficult to hide, and the quantity of grain stored was a function of the income as well as the size of the family. In a Lombard city at the middle of the sixteenth century the distribution of private grain reserves was shown as in Table 1-4.

Table 1–4

Distribution of the Grain Reserves in Pavia (Italy), 1555

Size of the Reserves of Grain per Family	*% Families*	*% Reserves*
More than 20 bags	2	45
More than 2, up to 20 bags	18	45
Up to 2 bags	20	10
None at all	60	—
	100	100

SOURCE: Zanetti, *Problemi alimentari*, p. 71.

Thus 2 percent of the families held 45 percent of the reserves, while 60 percent held no reserves at all.

In the period under discussion, the number of servants in a

---

7. De Roover, *The Medici Bank*, p. 30.

family was in obvious proportion to its income, and only the poorest did not manage to secure domestic help. At the middle of the sixteenth century the distribution of Florentine families according to number of servants was as in Table 1-5.

Table 1–5
Percentage Distribution of the Families of Florence (Italy)
according to Number of Servants, 1551

Number of Servants	% Families
With more than 5 servants	5
With 2 to 5 servants	18
With 1 servant	23
Without servants	54
	100

SOURCE: Battara, *La Popolazione di Firenze*, p. 70.

In general it is extremely difficult to evaluate adequately the distortions caused by inaccurate assessments, fiscal evasions, and so forth. Occasionally some individual of the time, on the basis of direct experience, tried to do what we cannot do. If that person was competent and had talent, his conclusions are invaluable. In 1698 Vauban classified the French population as follows:

rich: 10 percent
fort malaisé (very poor): 50 percent
near beggars: 30 percent
beggars: 10 percent

This estimate was no more than an educated guess.[8] Ten years earlier in England a man of genius, Gregory King, made more accurate calculations on national income, trade, and distribution of wealth, putting to good use all the material he had available in addition to his personal observations. The calculations he made are summarized in Table 1-6. If King's estimates are correct, in the England of 1688 about five percent of the population (classes A and B) controlled 28 percent of income, while the lower classes,

8. Vauban, *Project de dime royale*, pp. 2–4 (p. 6 in the edition by Coornaert)

which made up sixty-two percent of the population, received 21 percent of income. In Figure 1-1 King's data are contrasted graphically with comparable income distribution data for England in 1962.[9]

Although completely different in nature and origins, the above six estimates all point to an extremely inequitable distribution of

Table 1–6
Distribution of Income in England in 1688 according to the calculations of Gregory King

Socioeconomic Class	Number of Families (thousands)	Total Income in thousands of Pounds Sterling	% Families	% Income
A (temporal and spiritual lords; baronets; knights; esquires; gentlemen; persons in offices, sciences, and liberal arts)	53	9.816	4	23
B (merchants and traders by sea)	10	2.400	1	5
C (freeholders and farmers)	330	16.960	24	39
D (shopkeepers, tradesmen, artisans, and handicraftsmen)	100	4.200	7	10
E (naval and military officers and clergymen)	19	1.120	2	2
F (common seamen, laboring people and outservants, cottagers and paupers, common soldiers)	849	9.010	62	21
Total	1.361	43.506	100	100

SOURCE: King, *Natural and Political Observations*, p. 31.

---

9. A measure of relative inequality, Gini's coefficient of concentration, is calculated by determing the area between the actual Lorenz curve and the straight-line curve of perfect equality. This area as a ratio of the triangular area under the line of perfect equality is 0.551 for 1688 England according to King's data. See Figure 1-1, and Soltow, *Income Inequality*, p. 18.

both wealth and income.[10] However, they also suggest that, contrary to Pareto's statement, the distribution of wealth and income was not a constant.[11] In his report on Spain at the beginning of the sixteenth century, Francesco Guicciardini noted that "except for a few Grandees of the Kingdom who live with great sumptuousness, one gathers that the others live in great poverty."[12] The tone of this comment suggests that even a contemporary observer could not fail to notice that the distribution of income and wealth varied greatly from country to country. Wealth and income were inequitably distributed everywhere, but in some countries and/or at certain times they were much more inequitably distributed than in other countries and/or at other times.

The fundamental poverty of the preindustrial societies and the unequal distribution of wealth and income were reflected in the presence of a considerable number of "poor" and "beggars," (the two terms being then used as synonyms.) Next to the great mass of people who received minimal incomes there was a group of people who, because of lack of employment opportunities, incapacity, ignorance, poor health, or laziness, did not take part in the productive process and therefore did not enjoy any income at all. There is no chronicle or hagiography of medieval or Renaissance Europe which does not mention the beggars. Miniatures and paintings devote a good deal of space to these wretched characters. Travelers and writers make frequent reference to them. In 1601, Fanucci wrote, "In Rome one sees only beggars, and they are so numerous that it is impossible to walk the streets without having them around." In Venice the beggars were so numerous as to worry the government, and measures were taken not only against the beggars themselves, but also against the boatmen who carried them from the

---

10. Inequality of wealth distribution is normally greater than inequality of income distribution; in other words, holdings of wealth are more concentrated than incomes earned annually. To what degree the distribution of wealth differed from the distribution of income in preindustrial Europe is difficult to say, but one would have thought that the discrepancy was greater in those days than today because of the tremendous concentration of land and other property in the hands of the nobility and the Church.

11. Samuelson, "A Fallacy in the Introduction of Pareto's Law of Alleged Constancy of Income Distribution," p. 246.

12. Guicciardini, *Relatione*, p. 131.

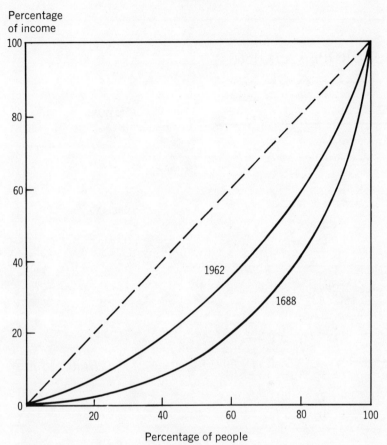

Percentage
of income

Percentage of people

Figure 1–1. Distributions of income in Great Britain in 1688 and 1962.
Source: L. Soltow, "Long-run changes in British income inequality," p. 20.

mainland. Such evidence easily creates the impression that the beggars were "many." But how many?

The existence of such a large number of destitute people was so troublesome that attempts were made to count them—if only to find, as in Florence in 1630—that "the number of poor was found to be greater than had been believed."

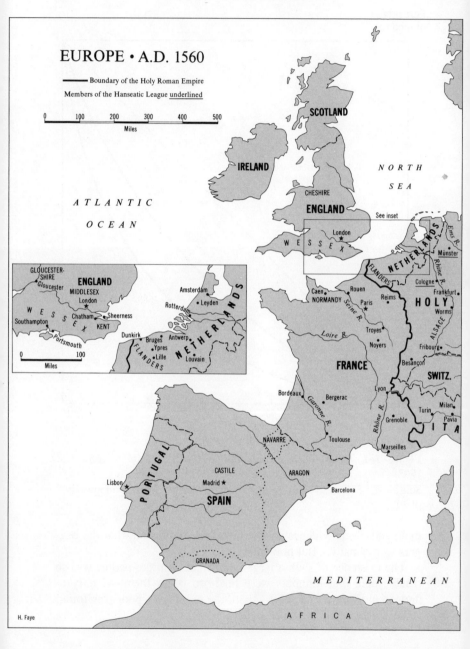

EUROPE • A.D. 1560

————— Boundary of the Holy Roman Empire

Members of the Hanseatic League <u>underlined</u>

0   100   200   300   400   500
Miles

H. Faye

As we have already seen, Vauban estimated that the beggars in France at the end of the seventeenth century made up about 10 percent of the population. The estimate does not sound absurd. Various surveys for different countries show that the "poor," the "beggars," the "wretched" represented a proportion that usually varied from 5 to 20 percent of the total population of the cities (see Table 1-7). The poor gathered in the cities because the rich lived there and alms were more easily available. However, even if one considers the populations of whole areas and not only those of the cities, one still finds that the poor comprised a significant segment of the society.

Table 1–7

The Poor as Percentage of the Total Population
in Selected European Cities, Fifteenth to Seventeenth Centuries

City	Years	% of Total Population
Louvain[a]	End of 15th century	18
Antwerp[a]	End of 15th century	12
Hamburg[b]	End of 15th century	20
Cremona[c]	c. 1550	6
Cremona[c]	c. 1610	15
Modena[d]	1621	11
Siena[e]	1766	11
Venice[f]	1780	14

SOURCES: (a) Mols, *Introduction*, vol. 2, pp. 37–39.
      (b) Bucher, *Bevölkerung*, p. 27.
      (c) Meroni, *Cremona fedelissima,* vol. 2, p. 6.
      (d) Basini, *L'uomo e il pane*, p, 81.
      (e) Parenti, *La popolazione della Toscana*, p. 8.
      (f) Beltrami, *Storia della popolazione di Venezia,* p. 204.

At the end of the seventeenth century in Alsace, in the area of Alençon, out of a total population of 410,000 inhabitants, 48,051 were beggars, that is, about 12 percent. In Brittany, out of a population of 1,655,000, there were 149,325 beggars, or about 9 percent.[13] At the beginning of the eighteenth century the Duke of Savoy could consider himself fortunate that in his states, out of a

---

13. Reinhard, Armengaud, Dupaquier, *Histoire générale de la population,* pp. 192–93.

total of 1.5 million inhabitants, only 35,492 or 2.5 percent were taken in the census as beggars.[14] In England the percentage of the poor was high enough to preoccupy the English monarchs from Henry VIII onwards, and to provoke specific custodial legislation which has gone down in history under the name of the Poor Laws. Of the end of the seventeenth century, Charles Wilson wrote:[15]

We need look no further than Gregory King's statistics for striking evidence of the magnitude of this problem at the end of the seventeenth century. Out of his total population of 5.5 million, 1.3 million—nearly a quarter—are described baldly as "cottagers and paupers." Another 30,000 were "vagrants or gypsies, thieves, beggars, etc. . . ." At a conservative estimate, a quarter of the population would be regarded as permanently in a state of poverty and underemployment, if not of total unemployment. This was the chronic condition. But when bouts of economic depression descended, the proportion might rise to something nearer a half of the population.

As implied at the end of the above quotation, the number of the poor fluctuated widely. Most people lived at a subsistence level. They had no savings and no social security to help them in case of distress. If they remained without work, their only hope of survival was charity. We look in vain in the language of the time for the term *unemployed*. The unemployed were confused with the poor, the poor was identified with the beggar, and the confusion of the terms reflected the grim reality of the times. In a year of bad harvest or of economic stagnation, the number of destitute people grew conspicuously. We are accustomed to the fluctuation in unemployment figures. The people of preindustrial age were inured to drastic fluctuations in the number of the poor. Tadino reported that in Milan (Italy) during the famine of 1629 in a few months the number of the poor grew from 3,554 to 9,715.[16] Gascon found that in Lyon (France) "in normal years the poor represented 6 to 8 percent of the population; in the years of famine their number grew up to 15 or 20 percent."[17]

The fundamental characteristic of the poor was that they had no

---

14. Beloch, *Bevölkerungsgeschichte*, vol. 3, p. 259.
15. Wilson, *England's Apprenticeship*, p. 231.
16. Tadino, *Raguaglio*, p. 11.
17. Gascon, *Grande commerce*, vol. 1, p. 404.

independent income. If they managed to survive, it was because income was voluntarily transferred to them through charity.

Income originates from the participation of labor and capital in the productive process. Income, however, can be transferred as well as earned, and the transfer of income is not necessarily linked with productive activity. In every society there are many forms of transfer of income (or of wealth). To simplify things, we can assemble them into two broad categories, voluntary transfers and compulsory transfers. Common forms of voluntary transfer of income (or wealth) are charity and gifts. A common form of compulsory transfer is taxation.

In the contemporary world we are accustomed above all to transfers in the forms of taxes and duties. As George Stigler has bluntly observed, "Charity and gifts are outside the logic of the system."[18] This, however, was not the case in preindustrial Europe. At that time charity and gifts were very much within "the logic of the system." Chronicles and documents continually refer to voluntary transfers of wealth on the part of the Church, the princes, the rich, and the ordinary people. The tradition of charity was strong and the act of charity an everyday affair. Certain events accentuated the phenomenon.

When death knocked at the door, people opened their purses more freely, for fear of the devil or for more reasonable sentiments. The chronicler Giovanni Villani relates that

in the month of September 1330, one of our citizens died in Florence who had neither a son nor a daughter . . . and among the other legacies he made, he ordered that all the poor of Florence who begged for alms would be given six pennies each. . . . And giving to each poor man six pennies, this came to 430 pounds in farthings, and they were in number more than 17,000 persons.[19]

When Francesco di Marco Datini, the great "Merchant of Prato," died in 1410, he left 100,000 gold florins to establish a charitable foundation and 1,000 florins to the hospital of Santa Maria Nuova

---

18. Stigler, *The Theory of Price,* p. 5.
19. Villani, *Cronica,* book 10, chapter 162. In fact, if six danari a head were given out and 430 pounds were spent, the total of beneficiaries was 17,200. Florence counted then about 90,000 inhabitants within the city walls.

in Florence for the construction of an orphanage. In Venice in 1501 the patrician Filippo Dron left rich legacies to the hospitals and other institutions of Venice, as well as a legacy with which to build one hundred small houses to give "for the love of God to the poor sailors."[20]

Disasters also served to accentuate the phenomenon of charity. In times of plague or famine, to appease God and the saints or from a natural spirit of solidarity, people donated more freely. In the eight years between the Easter of 1340 and June 1348, the parish of Saint German L'Auxerrois in Paris received 78 bequests. Then came the plague and in only eight months bequests reached the record figure of 419.[21] During the same plague of 1348 the hospital of Santa Maria Nuova in Florence received donations amounting to 25,000 gold florins, and the Compagnia della Misericordia received bequests worth 35,000 gold florins.[22] The donors did not come only from the ranks of the rich. An antiquarian who patiently compiled the list of benefactors of the Hospital of Santa Maria Nuova in Florence noted that "the list shows that every social class can boast generous souls full of charity for their brothers," among the donors one finds "the humble maidservant" leaving the few florins she has accumulated with the sweat and savings of many years, as well as powerful and rich citizens, owners of large estates, like Giovanni Pico della Mirandola.[23]

Apart from private largesse, there were the oblations of princes and public administrations. In the plague epidemic of 1580 the Commune of Genoa spent, between charity and health expenditures, about 200,000 ecus.[24] Very often food, and occasionally articles of clothing, were given to the poor. Henry III of England had a mania for distributing footwear.

Feasts were also suitable occasions for charity. In Venice the Doges made large donations to the poor at election time; in 1618,

20. Priuli, *Diarii*, p. 179.
21. Mollat, *La mortalité*, p. 505.
22. Carabellese, *La peste del 1348*, pp. 51 and 65.
23. Passerini, *Stabilimenti di beneficenza*, pp. 334–35. In pp. 873 *et seq.*, Appendix L, Passerini provides the list of names of benefactors of the hospital.
24. Paschetti, *Lettera*, p. 26.

Antonio Priuli distributed two thousand ducats in petty coins and a hundred in gold coins. In Rome at the election of a pope and subsequent anniversaries,

a half giulio was given to anyone who came to ask for it and the gift increased for each of the sons; pregnant women counted as two. People lent or hired each other their children, and pillows multiplied the pregnancies. The more opportunistic managed to present themselves more than once and to collect a good amount of money.[25]

While anecdotes and episodes of this kind can be interesting, they leave still unanswered the basic macroeconomic question, what order of magnitude did charity represent in relation to income?

It has been calculated that in England at the end of the Middle Ages in normal times the monasteries, holders of an immense fortune, gave between one and three percent of their income to the poor.[26] Various family budgets of the rich and the well-off in the sixteenth and seventeenth centuries show "ordinary charity" on the order of 1 to 5 percent of consumption expenditure, but, in addition to these gifts private individuals left to charity part of their wealth at death. Business enterprises regularly gave to charity; in the books of the Florentine mercantile companies, charity outlays are normally recorded in a special account under the heading "*conto di messer Domeneddio*" (literally, "account of Milord God"). Much of the "charity," however, was actually transfer of wealth to the Church, which then gave to the poor only a very small part of what it received.[27] Still, transfers to the poor normally must have amounted to noticeably more than one percent of gross national product (in the United States in about 1970, volun-

---

25. Gnoli, *Roma e i papi*, p. 123. For these and other examples of the kind, compare Fanfani, *Storia del lavoro in Italia*, pp. 430 *et seq*.

26. Snape, *English Monastic Finances*, pp. 112 *et seq*.

27. For this reason Abbot Muratori, *Della Caritá Cristiana*, p. 98, while urging people to charity, honestly advised them to give to charitable institutions rather than to religious orders. Things have not changed much since those days. In 1970 all forty-five Christian churches in the United States contributed together $764 million in benevolences, or 0.08 percent of GNP. However, they spent much more than this amount on new construction and four times this amount on congregational expenses. (Kohler, *Economics*, p. 220.)

tary interfamily transfer involved altogether "a tiny fraction of one percent of GNP"). Until recent times hospitals, houses for abandoned children, and foundations for the distribution of dowries to poor girls operated in Europe with the income accumulated over the years from private donations. Public authorities did intervene, especially in the Communes, but sporadically and in a minor way.

In the sixteenth century, England was exceptional because its government developed machinery for administration and enforcement of charity. In effect, then, England produced an effective national system of poor relief—the great Elizabethan Code of 1597 and 1601.[28]

The gift is, like charity, a transfer of wealth, but its motivation is not (or not necessarily) the poverty of the recipient. Like charity, the gift has not completely disappeared in industrial societies, but its economic importance has decreased considerably: all commodities and services have a price, and buying with money on the market is by far the most common way to acquire the desired commodities and services. In preindustrial Europe the situation was different and the further back one goes, the more important the role of the gift becomes in the system of exchanges. Often the motive behind the gift was not generosity, but either the compulsion to show off the donor's social status or the expectation of receiving in exchange another gift or the favors of someone in power. Traces of this tradition recur in industrial societies on the occasion of events like weddings or holidays like Christmas.

Gifts and charity do not exhaust the possible forms of voluntary transfers of wealth. In preindustrial Europe dowries and gambling had considerable importance. Although such transfers had no connection with productive activity, they could nevertheless affect it. As in all underdeveloped societies, people thought of dowries and of gambling as sources for financing business. Goro di Stagio Dati, for example, recorded:

On 31 March 1393, I was betrothed to Betta, the daughter of Mari di Lorenzo Vilanuzzi and on Easter Monday, 7 April, I gave her the ring

---

28. Elton, *An Early Tudor Poor Law;* Leonard, *Early History of English Poor Relief*, and Marshall, *The Old Poor Law.*

. . . I received a payment of 800 gold florins from the Bank of Gia-comino and Company. This was the dowry. I invested in the shop of Buonaccorso Berardi and his partners. . . .

Betta died in October 1402. In the trading accounts of 1403, Goro recorded:

When the partnership with Michele di Ser Parente expired, I set up a shop on my own. . . . My partners are Piero and Jacopo di Tommaso Lana who contribute 3,000 florins while I contribute 2,000. This is how I propose to raise them: 1,370 florins are still due to me from my old partnership with Michele di Ser Parente. The rest I expect to obtain if I marry again this year, when I hope to find a woman with a dowry as large as God be pleased to grant me.[29]

Buonaccorso Pitti tells in his *Cronica* how gambling brought him the necessary capital for a deal concerning horses:

they began to play and I with them and at the end I brought home from this twenty golden florins in winnings. The next day I returned and I won about eleven florins and so for about fifteen days, so that I won about twelve hundred florins. And having Michele Marucci con-tinually in my ears begging me not to play again, and saying, "Buy some horses and go to Florence." I, in fact, listened to his advice and I bought six good horses."[30]

Consider now the compulsory transfers of wealth. We think mostly of taxation, but plundering raids, highway robbery, and theft in the narrow sense belong to the same category. In medieval Europe political theorists saw a negligible demarcation between taxation and robbery. As for the distinctions among war, plunder, and robbery, they were very tenuous indeed. There is a curious clause in the laws of the Ine of Wessex which seeks to define the various types of forcible attack to which a householder and his property might be subjected: if fewer than seven men are involved, they are thieves; if between seven and thirty-five, they form a gang; if more than thirty-five, they are a military expedition.[31]

The relative importance of taxation on the one hand and plunder and theft on the other cannot be quantitatively assessed, but there

29. Dati, *Libro segreto*, p. 57. See also pp. 113, 114 and 116.
30. Pitti, *Cronica*, pp. 40–41.
31. Grierson, *Commerce in the Dark Ages*, p. 131.

is no doubt that the earlier the period in question the greater the importance of plunder and theft relative to taxation.

We shall discuss below the incidence of taxation in preindustrial Europe. Here it is worth spending a few words on plunder and theft. Much has been written about theft from the legal and judicial points of view, but little from the statistical. We know, however, that is was a very frequent event—which is not surprising if one considers the great proportion of poor in the total population, the inequality in distribution of income, the frequency of famine, and the limited capacity of preindustrial powers to control people and their movements. All this goes far to explain the frequency of theft and robbery on the part of common and low-class people. However, the noble and the wealthy also did their share, especially in the earlier centuries of the Middle Ages. In 1150 the Abbey of St. Victor of Marseille complained to Raymond Beranger, Count of Barcelona and Marquis of Provence, that Guillaume de Signes and his sons had robbed over the years 5,600 sheep and goats, 200 oxen, 200 pigs, 100 horses, donkeys and mules from the various possessions of the abbey. In 1314 a great quantity of timber had been stolen from a royal possession in the Craus valley (Haute-Provence, France). An inquiry showed that the robbery had been perpetrated by the men of the Count of Beuil, under his orders: the count traded in timber.[32] About war-plunder, one may mention that at the beginning of the fifteenth century the sire d'Albret admitted to a Breton knight that "Dieu mercy" war paid him and his men well, but that it had paid still better when he fought on the side of the King of England, because then "riding *à l'aventure*," he could often "get his hands on the rich traders of Toulouse, Condon, La Réole or Bergerac."[33] The leader of the *lansquenets*, Sebastian Schertlin, who fought in Italy from 1526 to 1529 and took part in the sack of Rome, returned to Germany with a booty of money, jewels, and clothing valued at approximately 15,000 florins. A few years later, the good Sebastian bought himself an estate which included a country house, furniture, and cattle at a price of 17,000 florins. Among the Swedish commanders who participated in the Thirty Years' War, Kraft von Hohenlohe amassed

---

32. Sclafert, *Cultures en Haute-Provence*, p. 11, 37.
33. Wolff, *Toulouse*, p. 61, n. 189.

war booty of about 117,000 thalers, Colonel A. Ramsay about 900,000 thalers in cash and valuables, and Johan G. Baner, a fortune estimated at something between 200,000 and a million thalers which he deposited in banks in Hamburg.[34]

Ransom is a form of plunder. We are best informed on conspicuous ransoms paid by princes and high dignitaries for their release. When Isaac Comnenus, duke of Antioch, was captured by the Seljuqs in the reign of Michael VII, the sum of 20,000 gold besants had to be paid for his release.[35] In 1530 King Francis I of France had to pay the enormous ransom of 1.2 million gold ducats to Emperor Charles V for the liberation of his two children.[36] Individuals of lesser importance were worth a great deal less. But the total amount of ransoms paid by travelers captured by pirates, soldiers and citizens captured in war, and towns captured by the enemy represented at all times a continuous large transfer of wealth.

We have absolutely no way to measure the relative importance of unilateral transfers (including charity, gifts and dowries, as well as plunderings, ransoms, and thefts) on the one hand and exchanges on the other. But it appears that the earlier the period under examination, the greater is the relative importance of transfers compared to that of exchanges. Indeed, for the Dark Ages Grierson has asserted that "the alternatives to trade (gift and theft) were more important than trade itself."[37] Another authority has aptly observed, "Savage society was dominated by the habit of plundering and the need for giving. To rob and to offer: these two complementary acts covered a very large portion of exchanges."[38] Such was the logic, as it were, of *that* system. As time progressed and civilization developed, the system slowly changed, and so did its logic, but the world in which exchanges are by far the predominant type of transaction emerged only in the last few centuries.

Transfers of income or wealth, whether voluntary or compulsory, mean redistribution of income or wealth. In general, charity

34. For these and other examples, compare F. Redlich, *De Praeda Militari,* pp. 54 ff.
35. For this and other examples see Grierson, *Commerce in the Dark Ages,* p. 135.
36. Mignet, *Rivalité de François I et de Charles V,* vol. 2, pp. 452–61.
37. Grierson, *Commerce in the Dark Ages,* p. 140.
38. Duby, *Guerriers et paysans,* p. 60.

works in favor of a more equal distribution. Through charity, income or wealth is transferred from the rich to the poor. In Europe, however, during the Middle Ages and the Renaissance, every donation to the Church was regarded as charity. To the extent to which charity to the Church was kept by the Church and not redistributed among the poor, it favored the concentration of wealth (in this case in the hands of the Church) rather than a more equitable distribution of it.

Similarly, taxation could be ambivalent. Inasmuch as tax revenues were used to maintain hospitals, to pay communal teachers or community doctors, or to finance free distributions of food, taxation meant a more equitable distribution of income. If, however, taxation was used to concentrate a larger share of available resources in the hands of the prince, the imbalance in the distribution of wealth was made worse, especially when the burden of taxation fell proportionately more heavily on the lower orders.

Types of Demand

Total effective demand can be divided into

  a. demand for consumption goods
  b. demand for services
  c. demand for capital goods

This division intersects another, inasmuch as demand can also be divided into

  a. private internal demand.
  b. public internal demand
  c. foreign demand

Each section a, b, c, can be subdivided into subsections 1, 2, and 3 or vice versa.

Private Demand

Let us begin with internal demand for consumer goods and services in the private sector. The lower the disposable income is, the higher the proportion spent on food. The reason for this phenomenon—in technical terms—is that the demand for food has an income elasticity lower than unity. It sounds forbidding, but all it means is that people cannot easily cut down on food expenditure when their income diminishes, and they cannot expand their food intake beyond a certain point when their income grows.[39]

In 1950 expenditures on food made up 22 percent of total consumption expenditure in the United States, 31 percent in the United Kingdom and 46 percent in Italy (see Table 1-8). Clearly, the

Table 1–8

Percent Composition of Private Consumption
in Selected Countries, about 1950

	United States	United Kingdom	France	Italy
Food	22	31	38	46
Alcoholic beverages	1	2	9	7
Clothing and household textiles	14	13	11	15
Housing, light, water and fuel	10	14	8	6
Household goods	15	10	8	1
Others	38	30	26	25
	100	100	100	100

SOURCE: Gilbert, *Comparative National Products,* p. 60.

poorer the country is the greater will be the proportion of available income its inhabitants have to spend on food. An analogous argument applies to the relation between expenditure on bread and total expenditure for nourishment. The lower the income, the

---

39. All studies of family living expenditures have confirmed Engels's law: outlays for food increase proportionately and outlays for other goods and services decline as the level of total expenditure declines. According to H Working, " . . . the relation between expenditure on food and total expenditure, presents a marked uniformity and comes close to this type of relation:

$$F/T = a - b \log T$$

where F represents expenditure on food and T total expenditure," (Working, *Statistical Laws,* p. 45).

higher will be the percentage spent on "poor" items such as bread and other starchy foods.[40]

In sixteenth-century Lombardy a memorial on the cost of labor and the cost of living stressed that:

the peasants live on wheat, . . . and it seems to us that we can disregard their other expenses because it is the shortage of wheat that induce the laborers to raise their pretensions; their expenses for clothing and other needs are practically irrelevant.[41]

Early in the seventeenth century, a keen and well-informed English traveler commented upon the poor diet of the continental peasant, making interesting international comparisons:[42]

As for the poore *paisant* (in France), he fareth very hardly and feedeth most upon bread and fruits, but yet he may comfort himselfe with this, that though his fare be nothing so good as the ploughmans and poore artificers in England, yet it is much better than that of the *villano* in Italy.

Peasants were relegated to the lowest income groups in preindustrial Europe. The mass of the urban population was better off, but whenever extant documents allow some tentative estimates on the structure of expenditure, one generally finds that, in normal years, even in the towns, 60 to 80 percent of the expenditure of the mass of the population went for food. (see Table 1-9).

Though ordinary people spent about 60 to 80 percent of their income on food, this does not mean that they ate and drank well and plentifully. On the contrary, the masses ate little and poorly, but the average man's income was so low that even a poor diet, absorbed 60 to 80 percent of that income—this in good times. Untroubled years, however, were not the norm in preindustrial Europe. Plants were not selected, people did not know how to fight

---

40. The ultimate reason for which grains are the food of the poor must be sought in the ecological chain of energy. The wheat plant transforms solar energy directly into chemical energy. Animal meat, instead, is the product of a double transformation process in which are added the "losses" of the primary process, connected with the growth of forage, and the "losses" of the secondary process connected with the development and growth of the animal.
41. Cipolla, *Prezzi e salari in Lombardia*, p. 15.
42. Dallington, *The View of France*, T3 v.

Table 1–9

Estimated Composition of Private Expenditure of the Mass of the Population, Fifteenth–Eighteenth Centuries

	England (15th century)	Lyon, France (c. 1550)	Antwerp— Low Countries (1596–1600)	Holland (middle 17th century)	Northern France (before 1700)	Milan, Italy (about 1600)	England— non-agricultural Labor (1794)
			Percent of Expenditure				
Food	≈80	≈80	≈79	≈60	≈80		74
Bread (percent of food)	(≈20)	(≈50)	(≈49)		(≈25)	(≈30)	
Clothing and textiles		≈5	≈10		≈12		5
Heating, light, and rent	≈8	≈15	≈11		≈8		11
Various							10

SOURCES: Phelps Brown and Hopkins, *Wage Rates and Prices*, p. 293; Phelps Brown & Hopkins, *Seven Centuries of Building Wages*, p. 180; Gascon, *Grand Commerce*, vol. 2, p. 544; Schollier, *De Levensstandard in de 15 en 16 Eeuw te Antwerpen*, p. 174; Eden, *The State of the Poor*; Posthumus, *Geschiedenis der Leidsche Lakenindustrie*.

pests, fertilizers were scarce. As a result, crop failures were exceedingly frequent. In addition, a relatively primitive system of transportation made any long-distance supply of foodstuffs impossible, unless by sea. Consequently, the prices of foodstuffs fluctuated wildly, reflecting both the inelasticity of demand and man's limited control over the adverse forces of nature. Between 1396 and 1596, in a port such as Antwerp, easily supplied by sea, the price of rye showed yearly increases of the order of 100–200 percent in eleven years and in nine other years showed yearly jumps of more than 200 percent.[43]

As has been observed, "the buying power of the working classes depended essentially on climate conditions.[44] When there was a poor harvest and prices of foodstuffs soared, even the expenditure of 100 percent of a worker's income could hardly feed him and his family. Then there was famine, and people died of hunger.

The lower orders lived in a chronic state of undernourishment and under the constant threat of starvation. This explains the symbolic value that food acquired in preindustrial Europe. One of the traits which distinguished the rich from the poor was that the rich could eat their fill. The banquet was what distinguished a festive occasion—the village fair, the celebration of a wedding—from the daily routine. The generous offer of food was the sign of hospitality as well as a token of respect: university students had to offer a lavish dinner to their professors on the day of their graduation; a visiting prince or a foreign emissary was always greeted with sumptuous banquets. On these occasions, as a reaction to the hunger that everyone feared and saw on the emaciated faces of the populace, people indulged in pantagruelic excesses. The degree of hospitality, the importance of a feast, the respect toward a superior—all were measured in terms of the abundance of the fare and of the gastronomic excesses which resulted from it.

After having bought their food, the mass of the people had little left for their wants, no matter how elementary they were. In preindustrial Europe, the purchase of a garment or of the cloth for a

---

43. Van der Wee, *Antwerp Market*, vol. 2, p. 391.
44. Foursatié, *Machinisme et bien-être*, p. 61.

garment remained a luxury the common people could only afford a few times in their lives. One of the main preoccupations of hospital administration was to ensure that the clothes of the deceased "should not be usurped but should be given to lawful inheritors."[45]

A Country Wedding. A painting by Pieter Brueghel the Elder, about 1565. In this glimpse of peasant life a wedding takes place in a barn sparsely furnished with rough stick furniture and crude clay bowls, and jugs. Kunsthistorisches Museum, Vienna.

During epidemics of plague, the town authorities had to struggle to confiscate the clothes of the dead and to burn them: people waited for others to die so as to take over their clothes—which generally had the effect of spreading the epidemic. In Prato (Tuscany) during the plague of 1631 a surgeon lived and served in the pest house for about eight months lancing bubos and treating sores,

---

45. See the *Ordinationi per il buon governo di tutti li Hospitali del Contado di Perugia*, Perugia, 1582, p. 3.

catching the plague and recovering from it. He wore the same clothing throughout. In the end, he petitioned the town authorities for a gratuity with which to buy himself new apparel: it cost fifteen ducats, which was as much as his monthly salary.[46]

Among the ordinary people, lucky was he who had a decent coat to wear on the holy days. Peasants were always clothed in rags. All this led to a status symbolization process. As Louis IX of France used to say, "It is just right that a man should dress according to his station." Since the price of cloth was high in relation to current incomes, the very "length of the coat depended to a large extent on social position."[47] Nobles and rich men were noticeable because they could afford long garments. In order to save, the common people wore garments which reached only to their knees. As the length of the coat acquired symbolic value it became institutionalized. In Paris, the surgeons were divided into two groups, the highly trained surgeons, who had the right to wear long tunics, and the low-class barber-surgeons, who did not have the right to wear a tunic below the knee.

Having spent most of their income for food and clothing, the lower orders had little to spend for rent and heating. In the large towns rents were exceedingly high in relation to wages. In Venice in the second half of the seventeenth century, the rent for one or two miserable rooms amounted to more than 12 percent of the wage of a skilled worker.[48] Thus housing often consisted of a hovel shared by many, a condition that favored the spread of germs in times of epidemics. Commenting on the high death rates which prevailed among the lower classes during the plague of 1631 in Florence, Rondinelli recorded that

when the counting of the population took place, it was found that 72 people lived crowded together in an old ugly tower in the courtyard of de' Donati, 94 were crowded in a house on street dell'Acqua and about 100 in a house on San Zanobi Street. If by mischance only one had fallen pray to the disease, all would probably have been infected.[49]

---

46. Cipolla, *Cristofano*, pp. 117–18.
47. Lebarge, *A Baronial Household*, p. 141.
48. Beltrami, *Popolazione di Venezia*, p. 222.
49. Rondinelli, *Relazione*, p. 59.

The physician G. F. Fiochetto, in his report on the 1630 epidemic in Turin, recorded that one of the first cases of infection was that of Francesco Lupo, shoemaker, who stayed in a house "where sixty-five people, men and women, all artisans, were living."[50] In Milan during the plague epidemic of 1576, in the poorer sections of the city 1,563 homes were regarded as infected. In these homes containing 8,956 rooms lived 4,066 families.[51] This gives an average of six rooms per house and two rooms per family. The Milanese Public Health Board issued an ordinance in 1597 to the effect that

no matter how poor and how low their status, people are not allowed to keep more than two beds in one room and no more than two or three people should sleep in one bed. Those who claim that they have rooms large enough to contain coveniently more than two beds, must notify the Health Board which will send an inspector for control.[52]

This was wise, but poverty stood in the way of wisdom. When the plague hit Milan in 1630, a clergyman reported that

the poor are the most harmed by the plague because of the confined living conditions in houses vulgarly called stables, where every room is filled with large families, where stench and contagion prevail.[53]

In Genoa, during the epidemic of 1656–57 a nun reported that

a very great number of poor people live in crowded conditions. There are ten to twelve families per house and most frequently one finds eight or more people sharing one room and having neither water nor any other facility available.[54]

Of course not all laborers lived under such appalling conditions. As already noted, there were differentiations within the lower orders. Also, in the smaller centers the situation was not as bad as in the larger cities. In the small town of Prato in 1630 there were on average three to four persons per house, and rarely more than five or six.[55] In the countryside, however, most peasants lived crowded in conditions very similar to those prevailing in the poor-

50. Fiochetto, *Trattato*, p. 19.
51. Besta, *Vera narratione*, p. 31.
52. Archivio di Stato di Cremona, Arch. Comunale, Inv. 4, t. 3.
53. Archivio di Stato di Milano, Fondo Sanitá, Parte Antica, b. 278.
54. Presotto, *Genova*, p. 385.
55. Cipolla, *Cristofano*, p. 156 ff.

est quarters of the larger cities. As life at home was so unpleasant, whenever possible the men moved to the tavern.

As indicated above, the well off and the rich ate adequately. In fact, in reaction to the hunger that surrounded them, they ate too much, as a result of which they suffered from gout and had to have recourse to the barber-surgeons for frequent blood-letting. The estimate of the food consumption in the homes of the rich is complicated by the continuous presence of domestic staff and the frequent presence of guests. A further difficulty in estimating food consumption is the fact that the rich and the well off were usually land owners: at least part of the food they consumed was grown on their lands and often does not appear in their bookkeeping.

Precise calculations are often impossible, but on the basis of existing family accounts one can hypothesize orders of magnitude. For the sixteenth and seventeenth centuries, one is inclined to believe that the rich spent 15 to 35 percent of their total consumption for food and the well to do 35 to 50 percent (see Table 1-10). These percentages, however, are not comparable to the 70 to 80 percent that has been calculated for the budget of the lower orders. Whereas for the bulk of the population income and consumption practically coincided (saving being a negligible amount), in the case of the rich income was much higher than consumption by an amount difficult to define and which, in any case, would have little meaning in terms of averages. When compared to total income rather than to consumption, expenditure on food by the rich and well to do would thus represent a lower percentage than the 15 to 50 percent mentioned above.

The same psychological force that induced the rich to overeat drove them to make an excessive display in their dress. The public authorities had to intervene with the sumptuary laws to restrain wealthy citizens from overostentation and prevent them from squandering wealth on conspicuous clothing. The acquisition of jewelry was partly exhibitionism, but also a form of hoarding. Expenditure on clothes and jewelry, however, could often not be separated, and one can conjecture that in the sixteenth and seventeenth centuries this type of expenditure absorbed, according to the situation, from 10 to 30 percent of consumption of the rich and the well to do (see Table 1-10). At the end of the fifteenth century,

Table 1–10

Structure of Expenditure on Consumer Goods and Services
of Three Families of Middle-Class and Princely Rank
in the Sixteenth and Seventeenth Centuries

	% of Expenditure		
	I *(Well-to-do* *Middle* *Class)*	*II* *(Wealthy* *Middle* *Class)*	*III* *(Princely)*
(a) Food[1]	47	36	34
(b) Clothing	19	27	8
(c) Housing	11	3	27
Subtotal: a + b + c	[77]	[66]	[69]
(d) Wages of servants	1		10
(e) Hygiene and medicines	2	1	3
(f) Entertainment	6	5	
(g) Purchases of jewelry and works of art	2.5	27	
(h) Taxes	1		Exempt
(i) Charities	0.5		6
(j) Various	10	1	12

SOURCES: I—Expenses of the notary Folognino of Verona in 1653–57 from
Tagliaferri, *Consumi di una Famiglia borghese del Seicento.*
II—Expenses of the middle-class burgher Williband Imhof of Nurem-
berg, about 1560, from Strauss, *Nuremberg,* p. 207.
III—Expenses of the Odescalchi family in 1576–77, from Mira, *Vicende
economiche di una famiglia italiana,* Chapter 5.

1. In the expense accounts of the noble English families of the Sixteenth
and Seventeenth centuries collected by L. Stone, food accounted for 10
to 25 percent of consumption expenditure. Expense on food of the wealthy
Cornelis de Jonge van Ellemeet of Amsterdam, at the end of the 17th
century, amounted to about 35 percent of total annual expenditure (exclud-
ing taxes). Account must be taken of the fact that for the well to do,
expenditure on food included food for the servants and that abundantly
offered to many guests.

the expenditure of the king of France for jewelry and clothing
amounted to no less than 5 to 10 percent of all the royal
revenues.[56]

Then there was the household expenditure of the time on heating,

---

56. Piponnier, *Costume,* p. 95.

candles, furniture, gardening, and so on. When a person overspent
on one category he naturally saved on another. On the whole, food,
clothing, and household expenses usually involved a good 60 to 80
percent of the expenditure on current consumption of the rich and
the well to do.

The combination of pronounced inequality of income distribution and a low level of real wages favored the demand for domestic
services. This demand was highly elastic in relation to income as
the number of servants was a symbol of opulence. Even at the end
of the eighteenth century, a girl like Mary Berry, who belonged to
a well-off but not very rich English family, in planning with her
fiancé the balance sheet of their future household, came to the con-
clusion that provision had to be made to cover "the wages of four
women servants—a housekeeper, a cook under her, a housemaid
and a lady's maid—three men servants and the coachman."[57]

As we shall see later, the number of servants in relation to
population was very high and, of course, domestics were concentrated in the houses of the rich and the well to do. (see Table 1-5).
Nevertheless, given the low average level of wages, servants' pay
did not generally represent more than 1 to 2 percent of the consumption expenditure of moneyed families, although in exceptional
cases it could reach 10 percent. One should add, however, that the
money wages actually paid to the servants did not represent the
total effective expenditure on their account. In order to evaluate
this expenditure, one should take into account the costs of food,
lodging, heating, and other items provided for servants by their
employers. Toward the end of the seventeenth century, the very
wealthy Cornelis de Jonge van Ellemeet of Amsterdam spent about
forty florins a year to clothe each one of his ten servants. In addition Van Ellemeet spent on each servant also about seventeen
florins for meat, eighteen florins for butter, and unspecified
amounts for drinks, heating, accommodation, and other facilities.
The average individual wage of the servants was some seventy
florins a year.[58] Clearly the wages represented only a minor part of

---

57. Strachey, *Portraits,* p. 111.
58. De Muinck, *A Regent's Family Budget,* p. 229. Each servant consumed,
on an average, 187 pounds of meat and 77 pounds of butter a year.

the expenditure on servants. The situation was not appreciably different in the homes of the less wealthy. If the maid of the Florentine craftsman Bartolomeo Masi was able to save fourteen florins in five years, it was because her food, accommodation, and probably some clothing were provided by her employer's family.

It would be a serious mistake to believe that the demand for services by the wealthy classes was limited to the demand for domestic servants. The variety of service personnel in demand included lawyers and notaries; teachers for children; persons performing religious ministrations; various workers and artists who maintained and embellished the living quarters; in the case of the nobility, various types of entertainers, such as musicians, poets, dwarfs and jesters, falconers, and stable boys; and last, but not least, doctors, in connection with which, early in the eighteenth century, the famous physician, Dr. Bernardino Ramazzini commented,

If the laborer does not recover rapidly he returns to the workshop still ailing and he neglects the doctor's prescriptions, if they stretch over a long period. Certain things can only be done for the rich who can afford to be ill.[59]

Of all these types of services, only the medical and legal were expensive. The other services were about as accessible as the domestic ones.

The consumption of the wealthy, even when it had overtones of extravagance, never showed much variety. The economic system and the state of the arts did not offer the consumer the great variety of products and services which characterize industrial societies. Food, clothing, and housing were by far the major items of expenditure of the rich. The difference between the rich and the poor was that the rich spent extravagantly on all three items, while the poor often did not have enough to buy food. Moreover, the mass of the populace had no opportunity to save, while the rich, although indulging in conspicuous consumption, did.

Not all income received is necessarily spent on consumer goods and services. Income not spent on such goods and services is natu-

---

59. Ramazzini, *Le malattie dei lavoratori*, p. 27.

rally saved. This is the first obvious truth which emerges from the definition of saving. Another obvious truth is that everyone does not save to the same extent. Saving is a function of

a. psychological and sociocultural factors
b. the level of income
c. income distribution

In Turin in 1630, when because of the plague all the people were quarantined within their houses, the Town Council noted that the bulk of the workers "lived from day to day,"[60] that is, they had no savings to fall back on and therefore, when restricted to their houses, had to be subsidized by the city.

As we have repeatedly pointed out, however, even among the lower orders there were gradations of poverty, and if there were those who "lived day to day," there were also those who, by tightening their belts and limiting their wants, managed to set aside a few coins.

If for the majority the saving of small sums implied heroic sacrifice, income for some was sufficiently high to easily allow a substantial accumulation of wealth. According to Hilton, in the fourteenth and fifteenth centuries in certain years, the Dukes of Cornwall succeeded in saving and investing up to 50 percent of their income. In 1575–78, in Rome, the princely Odescalchi family, which enjoyed a very high standard of living, spent, on the average, some three thousand lire of the time annually on current consumption. A remarkable figure, but the family's average income was about thirteen thousand lire, out of which a saving of ten thousand lire per annum was possible—that is, 80 percent of their income.[61] Cornelis de Jonge van Ellemeet, one of the five or six richest people in Amsterdam at the end of the seventeenth century, saved, on the average, from 50 to 70 percent of his annual income.[62] In a predominantly poor society lacking corrective means (taxation and/or rationing), a high concentration of wealth is an indispensable condition to the formation of saving. Let us refer briefly to Gregory King's estimates for England in 1688. The reliability of the

---

60. Cipolla, *Cristofano*, p. 31, n. 1.
61. Mira, *Vicende Economiche*, p. 208.
62. De Muinck, *A Regent's Family Budget*, p. 224.

figures themselves is irrelevant to the matter under discussion. Even if they were pure invention, they would still serve as a hypothetical example. The total annual income of England was estimated at 43.5 million pounds. The fact that 28 percent of this income was concentrated in the hands of only five percent of families (see above, Table 1–6) meant that these families had an average annual income of 185 pounds and therefore a marked possibility of saving. In fact, Gregory King estimated that these families saved 13 percent of their annual income. Their total saving of 1.3 million pounds represented 72 percent of national saving (1.8 million pounds). If the national income of 43.5 million pounds had been subdivided in a perfectly egalitarian way among the 1.36 million families which made up the English population, each family would have received an income of 32 pounds. At that level, no family would have been in a position to save, and national saving would have been reduced practically to zero.

According to Gregory King, national saving in England at the end of the seventeenth century amounted to less than 5 percent of national income. England at this time was one of the richest preindustrial societies that ever existed, but it was not characterized by a particularly high concentration of income; quite the contrary. A poorer economy with a higher concentration of income could have had saving above the 5-percent level.[63]

Imposing cathedrals, splendid abbeys, sumptuous residences, and huge fortifications are there to testify that at certain times in certain societies a marked surplus must have been available for substantial investments. The generally low level of incomes impeded the accumulation of savings, but the concentration of income facilitated it. The proportion of income saved was the resultant of these two opposing forces. Taking all factors into consideration, one can assume that, according to locally prevailing conditions, European preindustrial societies managed in "normal" years to save between 2 and 15 percent of income. An industrial society in "normal" years saves from 5 to 20 percent of its income. The substantial difference, however, is that an industrial society can attain such levels of saving while still providing the masses with a high level of con-

---

63. Gould, *Economic Growth,* p. 154.

sumption, while the preindustrial societies were in a position to save only if they succeeded in imposing miserably low standards of living on a large proportion of the population. Moreover, "normal" years are the standard for industrial societies, but the word "normal" acquires an ironic flavor when applied to preindustrial Europe. In those days life had rough overtones: tears followed laughter, tragedies followed feasts with great frequency and intensity. The violent fluctuations in human mortality were a reflection of this general variability. Years of fat cattle, during which it was possible to save, were followed by years of lean cattle, during which saving took on negative value. Averaging would make little sense, because it would cancel out one of the main characteristics of the period, namely, the violent contrasts from one year to the next.

Income is spent on the acquisition of goods and services. In turn, expenditure creates new income in the form of wages, profits, interest, and rents. Thus the flow of income becomes circular. The flow has a critical point at which a mechanism must ensure its continuity. The mechanism must ensure that income not spent on consumption will be spent for capital goods, in other words, that saving will be converted into investment. Monetary saving which is not invested is defined as hoarding. In preindustrial Europe three sets of circumstances favored the freezing of saving in the form of hoarding: (a), Institutions to collect savings and to direct it to productive uses were either lacking or inadequate; (b), The opportunities for turning saving to productive purposes were limited; and (c), Money in circulation consisted of pieces of metal. Gold and silver always had a special fascination for man, and the temptation to hoard gleaming pieces of gold and silver is stronger than the temptation to hoard printed paper.

To get an idea of the amount of purchasing power frozen in hoarding over the centuries, it is sufficient to look at the numismatic collections in museums and in private hands. There one can see physically the pieces from a wide range of treasures which were hidden and rediscovered by accident centuries later. In addition to archeological evidence, there are also written testimonials. One could quote the cases of impressive treasures accumulated by this or that monarch, this or that pope, or this or that abbot; but the cases of ordinary well-to-do people are perhaps more significant. When Pasino degli Eustachi, a rich merchant and at the same time an official in the administration of the Duke of Milan, died in Pavia (Lombardy) in 1445, his estate included:[64]

	VALUE IN GOLDEN DUCATS	PERCENTAGE OF WEALTH
Cash	92,500	77.6
Jewels	2,225	1.9
Provisions	150	0.1
Clothing	1,495	1.3
Apparel and household goods	483	0.4
Buildings	5,000	4.2
Land	12,300	10.3
Capitalized value of rents	5,000	4.2
	119,153	100.0

Coins represented in relative terms about 78 percent of the value of the estate. As the golden ducat weighed 3.53 grams, in absolute terms the coins hoarded amounted to about 720 pounds of gold— and in those days, the purchasing power of gold was much higher than it is today. Pasino was an extreme case because as a government official he enjoyed an extraordinarily high income and Pavia, the small town in which he lived, did not offer great opportunities for investment. In contrast, Vincenzo Usodimare, a silk manufacturer in Genoa, in 1537 had only 4 percent of his wealth in cash.[65] However, even in the bustling, mercantile London of the seventeenth century, Pepys kept a sizable amount of his wealth in liquid form: on September 28, 1664, he had nearly 1,000 pounds in cash in his house.

Hoarding can be regarded as a leak which reduces the volume of the flow of monetary income. If the hoarding process continues, it eventually reduces the flow to a level at which no further net hoarding is possible.

Of course, if there were people who hoarded wealth there were others who dis-hoarded it. At the beginning of the 11th century the

---

64. Aleati, *Una dinastia di magnati medievali,* p. 753.
65. Massa, *Un'impresa serica,* p. 23.

Archbishop of Cologne used up all the treasure accumulated by his predecessors to help the poor in time of famine. When the Bishop of Worms, Burkard, died in 1025, he left behind some books and three pennies, having lavished on the poor all the treasure he had inherited. The sacking and robberies of armed bands alternatively served to build up treasures and to put them back in circulation. When Charlemagne succeeded in penetrating the intricate fortifications of the Avars, he found there riches accumulated over centuries. Fifteen big wagons, each drawn by four oxen, were needed to carry the gold, silver and gems back to Aachen.

From a macroeconomic point of view the relevant point is whether, during a given period, the total amount of hoarding is greater, equal or smaller than the total amount of dis-hoarding. Historically there have been periods when hoarding clearly prevailed and periods of net dis-hoarding. In Italy in the 10th and 11th centuries, bishops and monasteries emptied their treasuries during their struggle against the German emperors.[66] The bishops across the Alps did the same for the benefit of various reform movements.[67] Throughout Europe the feverish activity in religious building which characterized the 11th and 12th centuries was seemingly financed through a massive process of dis-hoarding.[68] When wealth is hoarded it is not available for investment. On the other hand, hoarding may occur because investment is not attractive. When in preindustrial Europe investment was at low levels, the reason was not necessarily that the potential sources of saving were insufficient but rather that the opportunities for turning saving to productive purposes were very few and/or that a high level of uncertainty discouraged expenditure on capital goods.[69] Conversely, dis-hoarding was generally related to periods of investment euphoria and all the reclamations of land which were accomplished —the cathedrals, the castles, the palaces which were built, the canals which were excavated, the ships which were launched— clearly show that periods of investment euphoria were not so rare in preindustrial Europe.

---

66. Violante, *I Vescovi dell'Italia Centro-settentrionale, p.* 201.
67. Herlihy, *Treasure Hoards in the Italian Economy*, p. 5.
68. Duby, *Guerriers et paysans*, p. 183.
69. See Postan, *Investment in Medieval Agriculture*, pp. 579 and 581 and Deane, *Capital Formation*, p. 115.

Public Demand

So far we have dealt with private demand. Let us now consider public demand.

It is necessary to state in advance that, before the 18th century, public and private sectors are difficult to distinguish, and the earlier the period in question, the more artificial and antihistorical the distinction becomes. The fact is that in the feudal world of the eighth to eleventh centuries there was no distinction between public and private. With the emergence of the city-states and then the absolute states, the distinction between public and private reemerged, but these two concepts asserted themselves very slowly and not contemporaneously in the various sectors.

Until recent times European monarchs made no distinction between their private patrimonies and the treasuries of the states. In fourteenth- and fifteenth-century France, even the seigneurs of the kingdom thought "that they had rights to the financial resources of the state and that it was legitimate for them to get hold of a large part of such resources."[70]

Another factor that helped to obscure the distinction between the private and public domains was the powerful presence of the Church as a patrimonial and economic entity. Was the Church a private entity, or was it, rather, a public body? Any answer would be arbitrary, for although we raise this question today, it did not exist in the minds of the people at that time. In the following pages, we shall consider the Church as distinct from both the private and the public sectors. This distinction is also arbitrary; but as stated above, any alternative solution would be equally arbitrary.

The level and the structure of public demand depends on
  (a) the income of the public power
  (b) the "wants" of those in power and of the community which they control or represent
  (c) the price structure
Point (a) needs some comment. While in the case of private people income, in a sense, is given, public powers have the potential to increase taxes so that up to a certain point their income is also a

---

70. Rey, *Finances Royales*, p. 608.

function of their "wants." "Up to a certain point" only, because beyond that point fiscal pressure can dry up the sources of income; in other words, you cannot eat the cow and then hope for milk. The protests and complaints of taxpayers are the most frequently encountered items in the documents of every age and country. In the Middle Ages, the chorus of protestations was joined by the moralists and the political theorists (the two groups being scarcely distinguishable), who never lost an opportunity to point out that any prince who fleeced his subjects so that he might live in pomp or wage a war was committing a deadly sin. If one were to take the content of all these documents and texts literally, one would conclude that people were constantly being bled to death by greedy and bloody rulers.

There is no doubt that throughout the late Middle Ages and the Renaissance the public powers managed to broaden the tax base, to eliminate the constitutional obstacles to taxation, and to raise the rates of imposts. They also constantly devised new and ingenious fiscal expedients. In France after 1522 the Crown's efforts to increase the number of fiscal windfalls and to search out additional expedients was institutionalized in the form of a fiscal bureau with the superbly well-chosen name of the office of *parties casuelles*. All this reflected the emergence of the modern state from the ruins of the feudal world, and the progressive enlargement of its functions. The revenues of the republic of Siena at the beginning of the thirteenth century were about 1,000 lire a month in tributes and loans; by midcentury they were about 20,000 lire a month, and at the end of the century about 50,000 lire.[71] The total revenues of the Republic of Venice increased from about 250,000 ducats around 1340 to about 1.15 million ducats around 1500, to about 2.45 million ducats around 1600.[72] The revenues of the papal government grew from 118,000 ducats for Rome and 236,000 for the rest of the state in 1526 to 408,000 for Rome and 687,700 for the rest of the state in 1600.[73] In Spain the income drawn with two taxes, the *alcabala* and the *millones*, increased by more than 500 percent between 1504 and 1596. Moreover, while in 1504 the rev-

---

71. Fiumi, *Fioritura e decadenza*, p. 455.
72. Lane, *Venice*, p. 426.
73. Delumeau, *Vie économique et sociale de Rome*, pp. 841–42.

enue from the *alcabala* represented 85 percent of the state's revenues, in 1596 it represented only 25 percent.[74] In England the revenues of the Crown grew from about 140,000 pounds a year around 1510 to about 860,000 pounds a year around 1640.[75] In France the revenues of the Crown rose from about 4 million livres around 1500 to about 31 million around 1610.[76]

Information of this kind strikes the imagination, but we must beware of appearances: the figures quoted above have to be seen against the background of growing prices, growing population, and growing wealth. Similarly, the hue and cry of the moralists and the political theorists must be interpreted in the light of the prevailing view that a well-ordered state should be funded without taxation.

The fact of the matter was the fiscal pressure on the part of the public administration always met with resistance, often strong and sometimes insuperable. The preindustrial state did not have at its disposal the techniques and the means of investigation available to the industrial state, and the concealment of wealth was relatively easy. Moreover, the nobles and the clergy normally enjoyed fiscal immunity. As late as 1659 in the territory of Ravenna (Italy), clergy, nobility, and foreigners were exempt from paying taxes, and they held 35, 42, and 15 percent of the land, respectively.[77] Some professional groups, such as university professors in Renaissance Italy and lawyers and doctors in fourteenth century France, were also normally excused from paying taxes. Such privileges did not, like a talisman, protect the recipients for evermore. In the course of time both the Church and the nobility lost ground in their effort to escape taxes, and at times exceptionally energetic rules brushed aside existing privileges. Still, over most of Europe for most of the time, fiscal privileges were a reality that created delays, reduced receipts, and complicated the tax-raising process. Worst of all, fiscal privileges also forced the public power to turn to indirect taxation, which fell heavily on the consumption of necessities. Consequently the fiscal burden hit the poor proportionally harder, which

---

74. Vicens Vives, *Economic History of Spain,* chapter 30.
75. Dietz, *English Government Finance,* p. 190.
76. Clamageran, *Histoire de l'impôt,* vols. 1 and 2.
77. Porisini, *La proprietá terriera nel comune di Ravenna,* pp. 31, 75–76.

in turn explains the complaints, protests, and lamentations mentioned above.

All in all, one must admit that the portion of income drawn by the public sector most certainly increased from the eleventh century onwards all over Europe, but it is difficult to imagine that, apart from particular times and places, the public power ever managed to draw more than 5 to 8 percent of national income.[78]

As has been said above, given the size of public revenues and the structure of price, the level and structure of public demand depend on the wants of the public powers and the community they control or represent. In preindustrial Europe the wants that counted were, of course, the wants of those in power. These wants were generally related to war and defense, civil administration, court life, and festivities.

Publicly organized feasts had both a practical purpose and a symbolic value. They amused the populace, pacifying it with diversions and charity.[79] At the same time, they were intended to represent symbolically a certain commonness of interests and sentiments between the people and the prince—thus the festive celebrations after a military victory, the birth of an heir, the recovery of a prince, and the end of an epidemic. Some of these celebrations cost enormous fortunes. According to contemporary newsletter accounts of the feast arranged in 1637 by the king of Spain for the entertainment of the visiting Bourbon Princess of Carignano, there were seven thousand wax lights, which alone cost over 8,000 ducats. The cost of this one day's feast amounted to 500,000 ducats. This enormous expenditure shocked everyone who thought about the matter.

To facilitate description, we have distinguished between expenditures on festivities and those for administration, but the people of the time would have wondered at this distinction. The administra-

---

78. At the middle of the nineteenth century in most European states, public expenditure still represented only 2 to 6 percent of national income. 79. Feasts and days of rejoicing were the occasion for distributions of charity, processions, tournaments, and—at least by our standards—less cheerful kinds of shows. In Spain, the marriage in 1680 of Charles II to Marie-Louise was celebrated by the public execution of 118 accused persons—some of them sentenced to perish in the flames.

tive tasks of the state were very few and simple, and the organization of public festivities was regarded as one of them. A major item of expenditure was embassies and other forms of representation. Part of this money was spent, again, on pomp, banqueting, and festivities, and part went for informers and spies. For the rest, little was spent. It is true that from the twelfth century onward the bureaucrats became progressively more numerous, but many administrative tasks continued to be performed by noblemen who—in deference to the principle of *noblesse oblige*—received no salary for their activity, though they often found other and not always reputable ways to obtain some compensation.

One type of public demand deserves special consideration, although it did not represent a large figure in the budgets. Given the low level of income, the mass of the population could hardly satisfy the most elementary wants for food, shelter, and clothing. A series of other wants, especially for medical and education services, while strongly felt, could not be satisfied because people did not have the income necessary to translate them into effective demand.

In the communes of Italy and Flanders, it was speedily recognized that some of these wants qualified as necessities with an ethical and social value that could not be ignored. Thus a system of paying doctors, surgeons, and teachers with "public money" was devised so that any sick person, even if he was poor, could be treated, and the children of common people could go to school. In 1288 Milan (Italy), with approximately 60,000 people, had three surgeons "receiving salary from the community" who had to treat "all the poors who needed care." In 1324 Venice (Italy), with a population of about 100,000, had thirteen physicians and eighteen surgeons who were on the payroll of the community to serve the poor. In 1630 in the smaller centers in the provinces of Florence and Pisa (Italy), 30 physicians out of 55 and 24 surgeons out of 62 were "municipal." Outside Italy, there were municipal doctors in Bruges in the thirteenth century; in Lille, Ypres, and Dunkirk in the fourteenth; and later in Bordeaux, Freibourg, Basel, Colmar, Paris, Lyon, and other cities.[80] In education also, public demand acquired progressively more importance. In the early Middle Ages

---

80. For the above, compare Cipolla, *Public Health*, chapter 1.

the very few who received an education received it from convents or from private teachers. With the emergence of the communes, the practice of paying teachers with public money spread. Private teaching never disappeared completely and until recently continued to play an important role, particularly in the education of the children of the upper class. But public teachers and schools spread fairly rapidly after the eleventh century. It is worth recalling the wise words with which the administrators of a modest Tuscan community—Casteldelpiano—decided in 1571 to allocate part of the modest funds of the community to the employment of a schoolteacher:

That for no other reason nor occasion could they make as convenient and lawful use of the funds of their community to the benefit of the community and the citizens as in this, namely, in hiring a schoolteacher.

Education may be viewed not as consumption but as investment in human capital. As to public investment of a more conventional type one must mention military construction like city walls, fortifications, castles, and so on. Other kinds of public construction included communal buildings, hospitals, and bridges. Finally, there was construction of a conspicuous type, such as the royal palaces. In Renaissance Italy, the more illustrious princes invested considerable resources also in the embellishment of the cities. Guns and warships are an unattractive form of capital, but they are capital goods, and from the middle of the fifteenth century they absorbed rapidly increasing amounts of public expenditure.

We shall see below that in the private sector part of the available resources were always used to build up and maintain food reserves. The same is true of the public sector. The public authorities were doubly interested in the problem of food supplies: first, for humanitarian reasons and for good administration; second, for reasons of political stability, because hunger was the most frequent cause of popular revolts and insurrections. Florence, Pisa, Lucca, Siena, and other cities established *"Uffici dell"Abbondanza"* (Offices of Abundance) between the end of the twelfth and the beginning of the thirteenth centuries. These *Uffici* were entrusted with the task of overseeing food supply and building up public stores for distribution in time of scarcity. Grain purchases on the part of the Commune of Florence *pro annona publica* are mentioned in documents as early as 1139.[81] Another case of acquisition of grain on the part of the Commune of Florence for the building up of public reserves is recorded in a document of May 1258.[82] By the beginning of the fifteenth century the municipality of Frankfurt-am-Main (Germany) had an elaborate system of reserves fed by taxes in kind. Occasionally the community resorted to market operations as in 1437 when it purchased up to 28,380 bushels of grain to be stored.[83] At Bassano (Italy) in the second half of the fifteenth century, the town administration built a *fondaco* (depot) in which it stored grains against future needs.[84] At Modena (Italy), there was a public body for the establishment and maintenance of food reserves. Besides the public body, however, in 1501 a *Santo Monte della Farina* (Holy Mountain of Flour) was set up on the initiative of Father Girolamo da Verona. It was designed to store grains, but it was administered by the guilds of the city.[85] Obviously, the faith in state bureaucracy was shaky.

Where enlightened administrations held power, public investments of a more productive nature were also undertaken. Between 1168 and 1191, Philippe d'Alsace, count of Flanders, opened canals linking the valley of Escaut with the coast and created the new harbors of Gravelines, Nieuport, and Damme. About the same time the Bishops of Bremen-Hamburg organized the reclamation of the marshy lands called *Stauffen*. In 1230–31 the Commune of Bologna spent considerable sums on the purchase of machinery which was freely given to immigrant craftsmen for the development of woolen and silk manufactures. In Florence during the depression that accompanied the plague of 1631,

The Grand Duke made eighteen-month interest-free loans for a total amount of 150,000 *scudi* to the wool and silk workshops, so that they could continue to work and thus support the labor force of these principal crafts in the city. He also ordered the start of construction of the

---

81. Fiumi, *Fioritura e decadenza*, vol. 117, p. 467.
82. Carabellese, *La peste del 1348*, pp. 7 *et seq.*
83. Wolff, *Prix et marché*, p. 465.
84. Lombardini, *Pane e denaro a Bassano*, pp. 29 *et seq.*
85. Basini, *L'Uomo e il pane*, p. 39.

façade of Santa Maria del Fiore and the completion of the Pitti Palace. All this was done to support more craftsmen and laborers. And since the farm laborers are the backbone of the state, he also provided for them by making them dig ditches and canals to draw plenty of water for the use and beautification of the city.[86]

The relative importance of the various kinds of public expenditures varied noticeably from place to place and from time to time, so that any attempt to reconstruct the patterns of typical budget would have little or no meaning. One should also distinguish between demand of the central administrations and the demand of the local administrations.

However, whether one considers the north or the south of Europe, bad or good times, local or central administrations, one finds that the largest portion of public expenditure was always devoted to military affairs. The fact that so many developments of a technological nature, from the casting of iron to the emergence of schools of veterinary science and engineering, had military beginnings indicates clearly the sector favored by public spending.

Commenting on the budget of the Venetian republic, Fabio Besta concluded that public spending on public works was "not high" (with the exception of outlays for the defense of the lagoon against the damages done by the sea and the rivers), interest paid on public loans "appears in all the budgets to be high," spending on embassies and representatives "was always considerable," but military expenditure "surpassed by far all the other expenditures and at times reached extraordinary levels."[87] It has been estimated that at the end of the sixteenth century in Venice expenditures on the fleet and the arsenal alone amounted to 25 to 30 percent of revenues,[88] to which must be added the expenditure for the army on land. This was in times of peace. In time of war the standard revenues were not sufficient, and it was necessary to resort to voluntary and/or forced loans and/or to the depreciation of the currency to pay for military expenditures. In England, Henry V spent about two-thirds of his budget plus nearly all of the revenues from his French pos-

86. Catellacci, *Ricordi,* pp. 384–85.
87. *Bilanci della repubblica di Venezia,* vol. 1, book I, pp. ccix–ccxv.
88. Romano, *Economic Aspects,* p. 80.

sessions for military purposes. Three-quarters of the public expenditures in the last five years of the reign of Elizabeth I were for war or war-related activities. In the first years of the reign of James I the proportion was cut to one-third, but it rose later in his reign.[89] Things have not changed much since those days. Today military expenditures may represent a smaller share of public expenditure, but public expenditure accounts for a higher percentage of national income.[90]

What has been said so far in regard to public expenditure can be usefully complemented with the presentation of a few selected public budgets. Table 1-11 summarizes the annual average public expenditure of Perugia (Italy) in the first half of the fourteenth century. Perugia was then a free commune, that is, a city-state: Military expenditure accounted for one-third of the budget. Table

Table 1–11
Annual Average Expenditure Provided in the Budgets of the Commune of Perugia in the First Decade of the Fourteenth Century

Type of Expenditure	Lire	Percent of Budget
Wages	21,299	34
Military	21,022	33
Embassies	2,420	4
Public Works	5,050	8
Charity	3,600	6
Miscellaneous	10,184	15
	63,575	100

SOURCE: Mira, *Le Entrate Patrimoniali di Perugia*, p. 21.

---

89. Bean, *War*, p. 216.
90. Supposing the public revenues amounted to 5 percent of national income; if military expenditures were as high as 50 percent of the public budget, they still amounted to only 2.5 percent of national income. In 1961, 1965, and 1970, military spending as a percent of GNP at factor cost was:

	1961	1965	1970		1961	1965	1970
Argentina	3	2	2	Israel	7	12	25
Australia	5	3	4	Jordan	16	13	21
Canada	4	3	2	Saudi Arabia	12	7	13
Cuba	8	7	6	Sweden	4	4	4
Czechoslovakia	6	6	5	Switzerland	3	3	2
Egypt	6	7	9	U.K.	6	6	5
France	6	6	4	U.S.	9	8	8
Iran	4	4	8	U.S.S.R.	6–10	6–10	6–10

1-12 summarizes the budget of the Kingdom of Naples for the 1591–92 fiscal year. As the figures show, military expenditure amounted to 55 percent of the total.

Table 1–12
Expenditure Provided in the
Budget of the Kingdom of Naples, 1591–92

Type of Expenditure	Ducats	Percent
Dues to the Apostolic See	12,632	1
Honorarium to the Viceroy	10,000	1
Court Expenditure	10,021	1
Embassies and Secret Expenditure	187,690	9
Wages and Salaries	66,696	3
University	2,256	—
Head Physician (Health)	145	—
Mail and Couriers	22,000	1
Police	38,557	2
Charity	2,556	—
Army and Navy	1,091,299	55
Outstanding Interests	485,172	25
Miscellaneous	48,752	2
Total	1,977,776	100

SOURCE: Amodeo, *A proposito di un antico bilancio*; compare also Coniglio, *Il viceregno di Napoli*, pp. 123 *et seq.*

In assessing the expenditure of the central administrations of the states of preindustrial Europe, one must bear in mind that the central authority at that time was infinitely less encroaching and pervasive than in the industrial state. Several activities were left to the competence of the local administrations, which also contributed, with their expenditure, to the public demand. In general, in the budgets of the local authorities, administrative outlays made up a bigger share of the whole, but not much bigger. Even in the budgets of the local administrations, military spending often weighed excessively, in the form of forced lodging of troops, contributions to the purchase of arms, and repairs of city walls. In the budget of the City of Como (Italy) for 1610, outlays connected with military affairs represented 53 percent of the total expenditure of the community.[91]

91. Caizzi, *Il Comasco*, p. 40.

Demand of the Church

One can hardly overstate the importance of the Church as an economic entity in preindustrial Europe. The Church was always ready to condemn those who pursued Mammon, but it never applied to itself the advice it preached to others.

The income of the Church derived partly from the administration of its estates, and partly from transfers of income to it. The wealth of the Church increased either through new acquisitions or through donations from people seeking a passport to Paradise. Donations to the Christian Church were never so abundant as in the fifty or sixty years around the year 1000.[92] In that period the Church amassed an immense fortune. In the following centuries, the process continued at a much slower pace (see Table 1-13) but

Table 1–13
Size of the Ecclesiastical Property in Selected Areas
of the Florentine Territory in the Fifteenth and Sixteenth Centuries

Territory	Size of the Territory in Acres	Percentage of Lands Owned by the Church		
		1427	1498	1508–12
Acone (Valdisieve)	319	14	13	27
Gaville (Valdarno)	1,986	10	23	24
Macioli (Valli del Mugnone and della Carza)	3,684	7	15	15
Monteceraia (Mugello)	2,249	2	7	7
Montulivi (Valdipesa)	907	2	24	
Mosciano (Florence)	385	9	33	36
Panzano (Valdigreve and Valdipesa)	2,852	19	21	19
Passignano (Valdipesa)	1,804	46	60	64
Paterno (Florence)	692	6	31	27
Pulica (Valdipesa)	1,124	15	26	28
Le Rose (Florence)	504	23	18	16
Rostolena (Mugello)	3,197	8	6	6

SOURCE: Conti, *La formazione della struttura agraria*, vol. 3, part 2, pp. 26 ff.

---

92. Duby, *Guerriers et paysans*, p. 187.

accelerated in times of disaster and castastrophe. When the Black Death devastated the Iberian Peninsula in 1347–51, the nobles and the rich of Castile outdid themselves in donating lands and buildings to the Church. At the end of the epidemic, the dislocation of wealth was such that in 1351 King Pedro I (probably entreated by those survivors to whom, *ex post*, the price paid for the help of Providence must have seemed excessive) ordered the Church to return at least part of the donations it had received.

Every now and then, however, the Church fell upon hard times, times in which bad administration or individual cunning unfavorably affected its property. Before the eighteenth century, the worst period was perhaps the Reformation. The secularization of the English monasteries by Henry VIII in the first half of the sixteenth century is deservedly famous. About 1430 the English monasteries owned about 15 percent of the English land while the rest of the Church owned another 10 percent and the Crown only 6 percent. In 1530 there were about 825 monasteries in England with about 9,300 monks and nuns. The total annual net income of the religious orders amounted to about 175,000 pounds, or nearly three-quarters as much again as the average annual income of the Crown at the same date.[93] By 1550 nothing was left of the English monasteries and their immense estates. Not only were their lands confiscated and sold, but their furniture, silver, libraries, jewels, and other holdings were also dispersed. In Yorkshire alone, the revenues to the Crown from this despoliation were as follows:[94]

YEAR OF ACCOUNT	VALUE OF JEWELS AND PLATE AND PROCEEDS FROM SALE OF GOODS (Pounds)	INCOME FROM RENTS (Pounds)	TOTAL INCOME (Pounds
1536	3,102	186	3,288
1538–39	1,639	3,200	4,839
1541–42	158	11,061	11,219
1544–45	149	8,837	8,986

In Sweden, Gustav Vasa was no less formidable than Henry

---

93. Woodward, *The Dissolution*, p. 122; Cooper, *The Social Distribution of Land*, pp. 108–9; Youings, *The Dissolution,* passim.
94. Woodward, *The Dissolution*, p. 130.

VIII was in England. Between 1500 and 1550 ecclesiastical property in Sweden was literally liquidated for the benefit of the Crown (Table 1-14).

Table 1–14
Percentage Distribution of Land in Sweden
Between 1500 and 1700

| | Year | | |
	1500	1560	1700
Crown	5	28	36
Church	21	—	—
Nobles	22	22	33
Peasants	52	50	31
	100	100	100

SOURCE: Hecksher, *An Economic History of Sweden,* pp. 67 and 126.

What the Reformation did in these areas was done in Lombardy by bad administration, nepotism, and the policies of the dukes. In fact, in Lombardy the ruin of the ecclesiastical estate began well before it began in the countries affected by the Reformation. The erosion became evident in the second half of the fourteenth century and progressively accelerated during the fifteenth century and the first half of the sixteenth. By 1555, in the State of Milan, the Church held only about 15 percent of the land.[95] We do not know precisely what it held one and a half centuries before, but we have reason to believe that its property was much greater. Lombardy was not unique. In the Piacentino, at the end of the sixteenth century, the Church was left with only about 9 percent of the land.[96] In the territories of the Republic of Venice, according to Stella, the size of the ecclesiastical land holdings was a constant concern to the administration in the sixteenth and seventeenth centuries.[97] If one were to judge only on the basis of such concern one would

---

95. Cipolla, *Propríeté ecclésiastique,* p. 326. In a vast area (about 115,000 acres) of the irrigated plain, the Church held more than 25 percent of the land while the nobility held about 60 percent. Compare Coppola, *L'Agricoltura,* p. 218.

96. Romani, *La gente e i redditi del Piacentino,* p. 88.

97. Stella, *La proprieta ecclesiastica.*

conclude that ecclesiastical property continued to grow. But if the figures assembled by Beltrami are correct, one must admit that the concern of the Venetian nobility was not well founded: for example, in the territory of Padua at the middle of the seventeenth century, the nobles held 71 percent of the land and the Church only 7 percent.[98] In the province of Ravenna, however, the ecclesiastical property continued to increase. In 1569 the clergy held about 27 percent of the land; they held 30 percent by 1612–14, 35 percent by 1659, and 36 percent by 1731.[99] But Ravenna was part of the Papal State.

Evidently, where the socioeconomic structure moved in a more or less modern direction, the landed property of the Church was reduced to limits ranging from 20 to 25 percent of the land. On the other hand, where medieval conditions prevailed, as in the Kingdom of Naples, ecclesiastical property continued to predominate.

As indicated, the current income of the Church did not come only from revenues from its estates, but also from transfers of income. Such transfers were in part voluntary (charity, offerings, and such) and in part forced (tithes). The Reformation cut into this source as well. In Geneva, for example, in 1544 alone, 12,000 florins in papal tithes were appropriated by the Commune, which spent 4,000 for the Protestant pastors and 1,500 for the hospital.[100]

It is easy and in a sense justifiable to speak of the Church, but economically speaking the Church was an abstraction. The reality was represented by a vast array of economic units endowed with vastly different amounts of wealth and income. There were the pope, the cardinals, the bishops, the wealthy monasteries whose economic condition was in all respect comparable to that of the richest nobles.[101] But there were also country priests and the mendicant orders, and they shared the fate of the humblest and poorest classes.

---

98. Beltrami, *Saggio di storia dell'agricoltura*, p. 66.
99. Porisini, *La proprietá terriera*, p. 19. The nobility held 53 percent in 1569, 49 percent in 1612–14, and 42 percent in 1659. *(Ibid.* pp. 23–31.)
100. Monter, *Calvin's Geneva*, p. 156. On secularization in Berne see Feller, *Geschichte Berns*, pp. 314–21.
101. The comparison was made even in the period in question. Cf. Woodward, *The Dissolution*, p. 4.

The distribution of wealth within the Church reflected the unequal distribution of wealth in the society as a whole. Conti has
highlighted the ruin, of the lower and middle clergy, and the
enrichment of the monasteries, in the territory of Florence in the
eleventh and twelfth centuries.[102] In the seventeenth century in
the district of Ravenna, according to G. Porisini, 70 percent of the
Church's enormous property was held by the four wealthy abbeys
of Ravenna, while the remaining 30 percent was divided among
many parishes, chapters, and secular clergy.[103] In the territory of
Cannes (France) in 1772, the Church held about 10 percent of the
landed property, but most of this property was concentrated in the
hands of the abbey of Lerins; the other priests of the area had a
very small share.[104]

The aggregate effective demand of the Church was the sum of a
vast range of different schedules of demand. The demand of the
poorer units was directed above all to food and clothing, their
demand schedule closely resembling that of family units in the
poorer classes. The demand of the bishops, cardinals, and monasteries paralleled, instead, the structure of demand of the upper
classes. At the apex of the imposing structure, the demand of the
papal court had all the characteristics of the conspicuous demand
of a lavishly rich princely court.

Foreign Demand

So far we have dealt with internal demand. Every economic system
has, however, a network of exchanges with other economic systems.
These exchanges include exchanges of goods and services, transfers
of wealth, and movements of capital and precious metals.

The foreign trade of a given country consists of its imports and
exports. Exports are the response to foreign demand, while imports
are determined by internal demand.

As indicated above, the demand of the mass of the populace was
largely centered on food, while the consumption expenditure of the

---

102. Conti, *La formazione della struttura agraria*, vol. 1, pp. 215–16.
103. Porisini, *Proprietá terriera*, p. 20.
104. Derlange, *Cannes*, p. 30.

wealthy was largely—and conspicuously—directed toward food, clothing, and housing. In view of this fact, it is not surprising that the great bulk of foreign trade consisted of foodstuffs and textiles. As late as the end of sixteenth century, cloth accounted for about 80 percent of the total exports of England while textile materials, groceries, timber, and wine were the four main categories on the imports side. Owing to the high costs of transportation, especially during the Middle Ages, foreign trade was largely—though by no means exclusively—concerned with high-quality products; hence the large share of spices and expensive wines in the international exchange of primary products and the large share of luxury cloths in the international exchange of textiles. It also followed that the mass of the people generally had to content itself with local products and that only the well to do could afford the exotic. The ability of the average man in the street to walk into a shop in Milan or in London to buy something produced in Hong Kong or Tangier is a recent development made possible by the Industrial Revolution.

In order to measure the importance of foreign trade, one can add the values of imports and exports and relate the total to the Gross National Product. The result is influenced by the volume and the value of imports and exports, but also by other factors, such as the physical size of the country and the size of its population which are relevant in determining the size of the Gross National Product. A country like the United States might have considerable foreign trade, but given the vastness of the country, the greater part of economic activity exhausts itself within its boundaries, where a wide variety of resources is found. For a little country like Luxembourg, on the other hand, nearly every exchange is an international exchange, and, therefore, in relation to the Gross National Product, the value of foreign trade represents a much higher percentage. In recent years, the ratio was about 5 percent for the United States and about 160 percent for Luxembourg.

The number of studies devoted to international trade in medieval and Renaissance Europe defies imagination, but the focus has been almost exclusively on commercial techniques and the behavior and fortunes of individual firms. The lack of statistical material worthy of the name has perpetuated the lack of interest in certain macroeconomic relationships. England is perhaps the country for which the best statistics on foreign trade exist for the preindustrial era (see Table 1-15).

Table 1–15

Approximate Value of English Imports and Exports, 1500–1750

	Exports	Re-exports	Total Exports	Imports
		(million of current pounds)		
c. 1490	0.3			0.3
c. 1600	1.0			
c. 1640	2.8	0.1	2.9	
c. 1660	3.2	0.9	4.1	
c. 1685			6.5	
1700–09	4.5	1.7	6.2	4.7
1700–49	6.5	3.6	10.1	7.3

SOURCES: Davis, *Commercial Revolution;* Minchinton, *English Overseas Trade*, pp. 9–15; Schumpeter, *English Overseas Statistics*; Gould, *Economic Growth*, p. 221n. Between 1500 and 1700 the general level of prices rose about 400 percent.

One can estimate that at the beginning of the reign of Henry VII English imports and exports balanced at the level of about 300,000 pounds a year; by the end of the seventeenth century, exports (of locally produced goods) had increased to about 4.5 million pounds a year and imports to about 4.7 million pounds a year. This increase reflected in part a rise in prices but was mostly due to a remarkable increase in the volume of foreign trade.

At the end of the seventeenth century, exports of domestic goods alone must have come to 10 percent of the national product.

For states territorially much smaller than England, such as the Communes of Florence and Genoa or the Republic of Venice, in the thirteenth and fourteenth centuries the ratio of foreign trade to the national product must have been nearer to the level of Luxembourg today than to that of England at the end of the seventeenth century. As for other countries, it is difficult to say. Moreover, while it makes some sense to consider England as a whole, since the country was fairly well integrated economically, it would be stretching history too much to consider, for example, fourteenth-century France or sixteenth-century Germany as economic units.

From a general point of view, there is no doubt that the development of international trade brought positive net global effects. But from the point of view of single regions, or even of single states or nations, the problem is not so simple.[105] The idea of trade as an "engine of growth" is a gross oversimplification. For any given society, the long-run consequences of foreign trade depend largely on the qualitative structure of that trade and the effects of foreign demand on both patterns of employment and capital formation in the society in question.

The economic development of the Italian communes was largely related to the development of foreign trade. But examples to the contrary are not difficult to find, even without turning to the cases of colonies or of certain countries in Latin America today. The strong Dutch demand for grain on the Polish market in the sixteenth and seventeenth centuries; the Dutch, English, and French demand for oil and silk on the Italian market in the seventeenth century favored the involution of the economies of Poland and Italy along feudal-agricultural lines and created the preconditions for the long-term stagnation of these countries. In Portugal, about half a century after the Methuen Treaty of 1703, the Marquis of Pombal could justifiably complain that "two-thirds of our necessities are now supplied by England. The English produce, sell, and resell everything which is needed in our country. The ancient manufactures of Portugal have been destroyed." Port wine and the gold of Brazil paid for the imports, and the pressure of foreign demand kept Portugal's human and physical resources strictly tied to the agricultural and mining sectors.

---

105. On this important point see Gould, *Economic Growth*, chapter 4.

CHAPTER TWO

The Factors of Production

Classes of "Inputs"

A productive system can be fancifully described as a huge box: certain things flow in one side and other things flow out the other side. What flows in, we call *input*, and what flows out, we call *output*.

Input is made up of heterogeneous elements called *factors of production*. Traditionally economists group the innumerable and heterogeneous factors of production under three broad headings, called, respectively, *labor, capital,* and *natural resources* (the last category including land as well as water supply, iron ore, coal deposits, and so forth). Like most classifications, the tripartition is arbitrary and oversimplifies matters, but as it has proven useful for analytical purposes, we shall follow it in the historical analysis below. However, it is essential to sound a warning.

One of the major difficulties in historical reconstruction is that, in order to express ourselves, we must make use of the current language. Unfortunately, the words we use daily evoke in our minds pictures of the contemporary world. Expressions such as *labor* and *capital*, automatically evoke in our minds the picture of the factory, with its high concentration of managers, wage laborers, and complex machinery. An effort of imagination is required to recapture, behind the modern spoken expression, the very different reality of the past. In this attempt, one must be careful not to go to the other extreme, to fall victim to stereotyped, fanciful typologies.

The factory in the modern sense did not exist; the corresponding reality was the small workshop. The equivalent of the modern businessman was the merchant, but he was not what we mean by the word *merchant*. Specialization had not yet developed to the degree that characterizes industrial societies, and a merchant was very often the head of a manufacturing enterprise, a money lender, and a trader, all at the same time. As a trader he generally dealt in a variety of products in cloths as well as spices, cereals as well as metals. Even the distinction between wholesale and retail trade did not exist. The one recognizable difference among merchants was that some operated on an international scale with substantial capital, while others were petty, local merchants of limited means and horizons.

Similarly, for the term *labor* we must try to recapture a different reality from that which we associate with the term today. Wage labor did exist in preindustrial Europe, but it was not as preponderant as in the modern world. In agriculture, wage labor played a minor role. Sharecroppers were, instead, very numerous and in some parts of Europe they were the predominant form of agricultural labor. As for the manufacturing sector, all textbooks emphasize that, before the Industrial Revolution, the artisan was the most common type of worker. This is true, but the artisan was far from being a stereotype. There were many craftsmen who worked with the help of an apprentice. There were workshops with a number of aritsans joined in a society. And there were even more complex units in which craftsmen actually employed both wage-earners and apprentices and, in retrospect, functioned as proto-capitalists.

Labor

All members of a population are consumers, but not all of them are producers. Apart from the parasites and the infirm, the youngest and oldest members of a population consume but do not produce. In any society, once population totals have been established, it is important to identify (a) the economically active population (those who produce and consume), (b) the dependent population (those who consume but do not produce), and (c) the relation between the two (dependency ratio).[1]

Prevailing birth and death rates and, in cases of significant migratory movements, immigration and emigration, determine the age structure of a given population. Preindustrial European societies were characterized by high fertility and high mortality rates. Consequently, the so-called age pyramid of European preindustrial populations normally presents a relatively wide base as against an acutely angled apex. (see Figure 2-1). Consider the structure of two populations when both were at a preindustrial stage, namely, the Swedish population in the second half of the eighteenth century and the Italian population soon after the middle of the nineteenth century—the one Nordic and Protestant, the other Mediterranean and Catholic. The percentage distribution of the two populations divided into broad age groups is shown in Table 2-1.

Table 2–1
Percentage Age Distribution of Two Preindustrial
Populations, Sweden (1750) and Italy (1861)

Age Groups	Sweden 1750 %	Italy 1861 %
65 and over	6	4
15–64	61	62
0–14	33	34
Total	100	100

Despite wide differences in latitude, climate, color of eyes and hair, food, religion, and culture, in both cases the population in the fifteen–to–sixty-four age group represented little more than 60 percent of the total while the group under age fifteen made up almost a third. The dependency ratio in both populations was at about 60

---

1. If we assume conventionally that age 15 separates children from adults and age 65 separates the labor force from the old, then the children are designated as $_{15}P_0$, the labor force as $_{50}P_{15}$ and the old as $_{\infty}P_{65}$ (in this typical notation the beginning age interval is shown by the subscript on the lower right of the letter P and the length of the interval by a subscript on the lower left). Thus: the dependency ratio may be written:

$$\frac{_{15}P_0 + _{\infty}P_{65}}{_{50}P_{15}} \times 100$$

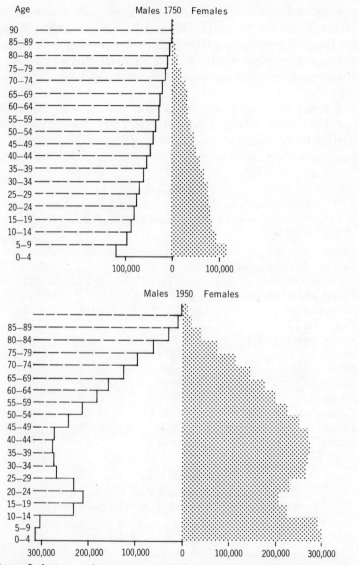

Figure 2–1. Age and sex structure of the population of Sweden in 1750 and 1950.

Source: *Historisk Statistik för Sverige*, Stockholm, 1955, vol. 1, Appendix fig. 4 (1750) and fig. 5 (1950).

percent (i.e., 60 "dependents" for every 100 economically "active"). Before the nineteenth century, national censuses were not taken in Italy but available data on the population of various Italian cities confirm that the population under fifteen years of age always made up a third or more of the total population (see Table 2-2).

Before proceeding, it may be useful to make a comparison with the structure of industrial populations. Table 2-3 contains data relating to the Swedish and English populations in 1950–51. As one can see, in an industrialized society, the population in the

Table 2–2
Adolescents as Percentage of Total Population
in Selected Italian Areas (1427–1642)

City	Year	Age Group	Percent of Total Population
Arezzo and surrounding countryside	1427–29	0–14	32
Pistoia and surrounding countryside	1427–29	0–14	37
Parma (city)	1545	0–14	32
Parma (countryside)	1545	0–14	41
Brescia	1579	0–18	40
Siena	1580	0–10	23
Vicenza	1585	0–15	42
Milan	1610	0– 9	24
Carmagnola	1621	0–15	41
Padua	1634	0–15	30
Venice	1642	0–18	46

Table 2–3
Percentage Age Distribution of Two Industrial
Populations, Sweden (1950) and England (1951)

Age Groups	Sweden 1950 %	England 1951 %
65 and over	10	11
15–64	66	67
0–14	24	22
Total	100	100

fifteen–to–sixty-four age group represents about two-thirds of the total population, that is, little more than in the preindustrial society. The most striking difference between the societies of preindustrial Europe and those of contemporary Europe lies in the composition of the dependent population. While in modern Europe children of zero to fourteen years make up from 65 to 70 percent of the dependent population, in preindustrial Europe they represented about 90 percent. In other words, the burden of dependence in preindustrial Europe was almost totally represented by children. The gravity of the problem is measured by the number of abandoned children.

In Venice in the sixteenth century, the *Ospedale della Pietà* usually cared for an average of 1,300 foundlings, which, out of a total population of 130,000 to 160,000, represented almost 1 percent.[2] In Florence in 1552, in the *Ospedale degli Innocenti*, there were 1,200 foundlings; out of a total population of about 60,000 the foundlings made up 2 percent. In Prato (Italy) in 1630 the *Ospedale della Misericordia* cared for 128 young girls, 54 boys, and 98 babies, a total of 280 foundlings. Prato then had a population of approximately 17,000, and the foundlings were, therefore, about 1.6 percent of the total population.[3] It must be noted that values of the order of 1 or 2 percent of total population meant, in a preindustrial society, some 3 to 7 percent of the children in the age group zero to fourteen. It must also be remembered that the figures above refer in large measure to the number of foundlings who survived. According to a Venetian estimate in the sixteenth century, 80 to 90 percent of the foundlings died in their first year of life.[4] If one relates the number of those "admitted to the Ospedale della Pietà" to the number of births in the city, one finds that in Venice, in the second half of the eighteenth century, foundlings represented 8 to 10 percent of all births (see Table 2-4). In Milan at the end

---

2. Beltrami, *Popolazione di Venezia*, p. 143, n. 17.
3. For the figures above, compare Battara, *Popolazione di Firenze,* p. 34, and Cipolla, *Cristofano*, pp. 35 and 44. It must be noted that, out of the total number of foundlings, females often exceeded males by a long way. Even in faraway China, females were predominantly the victims of infanticide.
4. Beltrami, *Popolazione di Venezia*, p. 143, n. 17.

Table 2–4
Foundlings in Venice, 1756–87

Year	Foundlings			No. Births	% Foundlings Over Births
	M	F	MF		
1756	199	210	409	5246	7.8
1759	204	201	405	5172	7.8
1765	192	233	425	5090	8.3
1776	230	248	478	5243	9.1
1782	229	238	467	5166	9.0
1783	235	244	479	5077	9.4
1785	228	233	461	5074	9.1
1787	231	250	481	5220	9.2

SOURCE: Beltrami, *Popolazione di Venezia*, p. 143, n. 18.

of the seventeenth century the number of foundlings was on average 450 per year (Table 2-5), and this figure represented more
than 12 percent of the estimated births in the city.[5]

Such high percentages must be viewed with caution. We know
from various sources that those who wished to rid themselves of
newly born babies often came from far away to abandon them in

Table 2–5
Foundlings in Milan, 1660–1729

Decade	M	F	MF
1660–69	1967	2090	4057
1670–79	1802	1913	3715
1680–89	1774	1816	3590
1690–99	2616	2699	5315
1700–09	2697	2610	5307
1710–19	2479	2625	5104
1720–29	2250	2172	4422

SOURCE: Buffini, *Ospizio dei Trovatelli*, Vol. 1, Appendix, Tables 1 and 2.

---

5. Between 1680 and 1715 the population of Milan and its suburbs was
about 120,000. In one large parish the birth rate was about 30 per thousand.
Adopting this rate for the whole city, one may assume that in the city and
its suburbs the births numbered approximately 3,600 per year. See Sella,
Popolazione di Milano, pp. 471 and 478.

the city. The number of foundlings, therefore ought to be related to a larger population than the local one. This would lower the percentages mentioned above, but even so, it would be difficult to deny that the practice of abandoning newborn babies was tragically widespread.

In our industrial societies, we consider as economically active the population in the age group fifteen to sixty-four. It is an arbitrary assumption based on the rationales that (a) in many countries compulsory education for the young continues to the age of fifteen and (b) the age of sixty-five is, in many professions, the limit for retirement. In reality, however, there are individuals who start working long after their fifteenth year of age and others who start earlier. There are people who retire before sixty-five and others who are still working at a later age. There are adults who have never worked and there are people who regularly collect a salary but whose inclusion among the active population is the result of gentle violence worked by statistics upon reality. To consider as active all those in an industrial society who fall in the fifteen–to–sixty-five age group and as dependent all the remainder probably overestimates the percentage population which is effectively productive and thus underestimates the real dependency ratio. Productivity in industrial societies is so high that it is not difficult for such societies to afford dependency ratios of over 50 percent. In fact, it is the high industrial productivity that has allowed the introduction of compulsory education up to fifteen years, allows many to continue their education until the age of twenty-five or twenty-eight, allows most people to retire at sixty-five, allows many women of working age not to participate in productive activities, and allows many to figure in statistics of active population while doing nothing more than keep their chairs warm.

The conditions prevailing in preindustrial Europe were vastly different. Those who were economically "active" worked from dawn to dusk, but given the low average of productivity they could not support many dependents. It followed that normally the few old people had to work until the end of their days (which, incidentally, was psychologically good for them), and the young people had to be set to work long before the age of fifteen.

In general, child labor is described as a ghastly by-product of the

Industrial Revolution. The truth is that in preindustrial society, children were as widely employed as at the time of the Industrial Revolution. The difference was that in the preindustrial society, the mass of children was employed in the fields and, therefore, only during the summer and autumn months (hence the tradition of long school holidays during summer and autumn), while with the development of the factory system, the children were employed the whole year around. Life in the fields was perhaps not so unhealthy as in the factories of the early Industrial Revolution, but the hardships to which children were subjected were not more tolerable. A Lombard ordinance of the late sixteenth century pointed out:

At the time when the weeds are pulled from the rice patches, or other work is performed in the rice fields, some individuals called "foremen of the rice workers" manage in various ways to bring together a large number of children and adolescents against whom they practice barbarous cruelties. Having brought the children with promises and inducements to the chosen place, the foremen then treat them very badly, do not pay them, do not provide these poor creatures with the necessary food, and make them labor as slaves by beating them and treating them more harshly than galley slaves are treated, so that many of the children, although originally healthy, die miserably in the farms or in the neighboring fields. As His Excellency the Governor does not want these foremen of the rice workers to act in the future as they did in the past or to continue to slaughter children, he orders this traffic to be stopped.[6]

In the eighteenth century the Austrian physician J. P. Frank wrote that:

In many villages the dung has to be carried on human backs up high mountains and the soil has to be scraped in a crouching position; this is the reason why most of the young people are deformed and misshapen.[7]

Preindustrial Europe also made widespread use of female labor in areas other than domestic service. First of all, women produced

---

6. Archivio Mensa Vescorile di Pavia, b. 123, decree of the 22nd March, 1590.
7. Frank, *Medicinische Polizey*, Vol. 1, p. 16.

many commodities at home which today are produced industrially and exchanged on the market (bread, pasta, woolens, socks, and so on). Miniatures of the fourteenth, fifteenth, and sixteenth centuries show us, however, that women were also regularly employed in agricultural work, and documents show that, in the major manufacturing centers, women were widely employed in spinning and weaving in the workshops. In Florence, among wool weavers, women workers made up 62 percent of the labor force in 1604 and 83 percent in 1627.[8]

Textile manufactures were often organized on the basis of the putting-out system; that is, a merchant gave out raw wool, for example, to workers who worked in their own homes, and later collected the product from them for sale or for further processing. This system facilitated the employment of women who, between one task and another at home, busied themselves with work for the merchants. In 1631, when plague struck San Lorenzo a Campi, in Tuscany, and many houses were quarantined, a health inspector reported that he had "found a greater amount [of wool] than anticipated" and provided his superiors with a list of twelve houses in each of which a woman was working wool for some merchant.[9]

Women were also employed in work which we usually consider to be the preserve of men. In Toulouse, between 1365 and 1371, in the building yard of the Périgord College, men and women were employed in almost equal numbers, and the women carried stones and bricks in baskets, which they placed on their heads.[10] The French miniature reproduced here depicts women employed in metallurgical works. In Venice women were largely employed in the arsenal in the manufacturing of sails.[11]

For a correct evaluation of female employment in the preindustrial era, one must also take into account wet nurses. The wet nurse is a person who, for a monetary reward, sells food (mother's milk) and a service (care of the infant). The economic and

---

8. See below, p. 124.
9. Archivio Stato Firenze, *Sanità*, Negozi, b. 161, c. 40 2nd September, 1631.
10. Wolff, *Toulouse*, p. 441.
11. Beltrami, *Popolazione di Venezia,* p. 201.

A French metallurgical works. This sixteenth-century French miniature shows that women were employed also in metallurgical works where the skills they practiced in the kitchen were put to use in operating small furnaces.

social importance of the wet nurses in preindustrial Europe compared with the importance of the baby-food industry in our contemporary society.

The "active" population can be usefully analyzed in relation to its distribution by productive activity.

Generally speaking, statisticians and economists like to distinguish among three broad categories of occupations, corresponding to the three sectors of activity respectively termed primary, secondary, and tertiary. The primary sector normally includes agricultural activities and forestry. Sometimes fishing and mining are also included. The secondary sector consists of manufacturing. The tertiary sector includes the "remainder." Like all residual categories, this one is a source of ambiguity and confusion. In industrialized societies, the tertiary sector is mainly represented by the production of services such as transport, banking, insurance, the liberal professions, advertising, and the like. Some years ago, an Australian economist, Colin Clark, put forward the theory of a highly positive correlation between the general level of development of an economy and the relative size of the tertiary sector. But other economists with firsthand knowledge of certain primitive societies have shown that in a preindustrial society, the tertiary, or "residual" group, is also fairly large, with the difference that, instead of including bankers and insurance agents, it includes a picturesque variety of people with trades ranging from dealers in stolen goods to gatherers of used items.

Because of the lack of statistical data, no one will ever know with any degree of accuracy what percentage of the European population was employed in the primary sector at various times before the eighteenth century. Only for the middle of the eighteenth century are there some reasonable estimates relating to England, France, Sweden, and the Republic of Venice (see Table 2-6). They still are far from precise, but they can be taken as broad indications of orders of magnitude.

On this basis it does not seem absurd to maintain that in the centuries preceding 1700, in every European society, the percentage of population actively employed in agriculture varied, as a rule,

Table 2–6

Estimates of Population Employed in Agriculture as
Percentage of Total Labor Force, about 1750

Country	Percent
England	65
France	76
Sweden	75
Republic of Venice	75

between 65 and 90 percent, reaching minima of 55 to 65 percent
only in exceptional cases. The reason for this concentration lay in
the low productivity of agriculture.

Seven or eight peasants succeeded with difficulty in producing
(over and above what was necessary to maintain themselves and
their families) the surplus necessary to maintain two or three other
people. In particularly favorable circumstances, especially when
water routes made the supply of cereals from abroad economical, a
country could reduce the percentage of population actively
employed in agriculture to below traditional levels. A typical case is
that of Venice, which regularly imported grain from Lombardy,
Southern Italy, and the Black Sea, while the local population was
engaged in everything but agriculture. A document dating from the
end of the tenth century described the Venetians with amazement:
et illa gens non arat, non seminat, non vindemiat (that nation does
not plow, sow, or gather vintage). Venice's case was exceptional,
but between 1400 and 1700, marked developments in maritime
transport made it possible for some countries with favorable geographical positions to depend considerably on the supply of grain
from abroad. This was certainly the case with seventeenth-century
Holland, which imported large quantities of cereals from eastern
Europe via the Baltic-Sund-North Sea, not only for her own consumption, but also for re-export. Undoubtedly seventeenth-century
Holland employed a much lower percentage of its population in
agriculture than other European countries did, but even in Holland's case, it is doubtful that the percentage ever fell below 50 percent. On the other hand, if the imports of the Dutch contributed to
reduce the fraction of those employed in the primary sector in certain areas of western Europe, they favored an increase of the same

fraction in the countries of eastern Europe. For every ten who ate bread, seven or eight had to produce wheat, and if these seven or eight were not all in one geographic area, they had to be in another.

The large percentage of the population employed in the primary sector, can easily lead one to overestimate the percentage of effective labor put into this sector. For a more precise assessment of the labor input, one has to take into account that for climatic reasons, during long periods of the year the peasant did not work; he was there, but he was not active, while most handicraftsmen were active all months of the year. Furthermore, peasants' wives, normally regarded as being employed in agriculture, in addition to their agricultural activities, generally contributed to the manufacturing sector (especially in weaving) and to the services sector (as domestic servants or as wet nurses) during the winter months.

Table 2-7 shows the occupational distribution of the population in selected European cities. The first thing to emphasize is the correlation between what emerges from these figures and what has been said in the preceding chapter about the structure of demand. The bulk of demand was concentrated on food, clothing, and housing. The structure of demand influences the price structure, which, in turn, determines the structure of production. It is, therefore, not at all surprising that in Table 2-7 the three sectors—food, textiles, and construction—account for the greater part of the active population under consideration—that is, broadly, from 55 to 65 percent. Those employed in the food sector represent a relatively small percentage because the data refer to urban populations, and the bulk of those employed in the production of food lived in the country. Only those employed in the distribution of foodstuffs lived in the towns. For Gloucestershire, in 1608, a census is available that includes not only three major cities (Gloucester, Tewkesbury, and Cirencester), but also the surrounding rural areas.[12] Putting together both townsmen and country dwellers, one sees (Table 2-8) that those employed in the production and distribution of food represented by far the largest group (46 percent) and that the combined group of those employed in the three sectors

---

12. The census does not, however, include the town of Bristol.

Table 2–7

Occupational Distribution of the Population of Selected European
Cities, Fifteenth to Seventeenth Centuries

	Verona 1409	Como 1439	Frankfurt 1440	Monza 1541	Florence 1552	Venice 1660
a. Food distribution and agriculture	23	21	21	39	13	17
b. Textiles and clothing	37	30	30	25	41	43
c. Building	2	4	8	1	6	4
Subtotal: a + b + c	[62]	[55]	[59]	[65]	[60]	[64]
d. Metalwork	5	8	8	10	7	5
e. Woodwork	5	4	5	2	2	8
f. Leather	10	7	4		7	7
g. Transport	2	3 }	22	{ 1	1	9
h. Miscellaneous	6	17 }		{ 21.5	21	2
i. Liberal professions	10	6	2	0.5	2	5
	100	100	100	100	100	100

SOURCES: For Verona: Tagliaferri, *Economia Veronese*; for Como: Mira, *Aspetti dell'Economia Comasca*; for Frankfurt: Bucher, *Die Bevölkerung von Frankfurt*; for Monza: Cipolla, *Per la Storia della Popolazione Lombarda*; for Florence: Battara, *Popolazione di Firenze*; for Venice: Beltrami, *Composizione Economica e Professionale*. Domestic servants were not always included in the censuses on which the table is based.

of food, clothing, and construction represented about 73 percent of the working male population. However high the subtotals, a + b + c in Table 2-7 and a + b + c + d in Table 2-8, they still underestimate the relative importance of the mixed food-clothing-construction group, because, for example, many of those included in the category "leather" produced shoes and sandals and therefore should be added to the "clothing" sector, and many of those in the category "woodwork" produced goods and services connected with housing and therefore should be added to the "building" sector.

In the discussion of the level and structure of demand, it was mentioned that the great disparity between the wealth of a few and the low average level of wages logically stimulated demand for

Table 2–8

Occupational Distribution of Males, Aged 20–60, in Gloucestershire, by Percentages, 1608

	Cities	Countryside	Cities and Countryside Together
a. Agriculture	4	50	46
b. Food and drink	7	2	2
c. Textiles and clothing	26	23	23
d. Building	2	2	2
Subtotal: a + b + c + d	[39]	[77]	[73]
e. Metalwork	6	3	3
f. Woodwork	6	4	4
g. Leather	5	1	1
h. Transport	3	2	2
i. Professionals and gentry	6	3	3
j. Servants	3	7	7
k. Miscellaneous	32	3	7
	100	100	100

SOURCE: Tawney, *An Occupational Census*, p. 36.

domestic services. Princes were not the only ones to have a rentinue of servants. Neither well-to-do people nor clergymen lagged far behind. In the monastery of Evesham, in England in 1096, there were fifty-two servants for sixty-six monks, and the former figure did not include gardeners, a blacksmith, a mason, and other laborers of various kinds. In the monastery of Meaux, also in England, in 1393, twenty-six monks were served by forty domestics.[13]

Domestic personnel are not always easily pinpointed in the demographic and fiscal records of the time, because either the listings in the documents were limited to heads of families, or the service staff was mixed in with members of the family. In some urban censuses, however, domestic servants were listed separately (see Table 2-9). Whenever the available figures allow some calculations, the result is that in the European cities of the fifteenth, six-

---

13. Snape, *English Monastic Finances*, pp. 13–14.

teenth, and seventeenth centuries domestic servants represent about
10 percent of the total population, which means about 17 percent
of the population in the age group fifteen to sixty-five.

Table 2–9

Domestic Servants as a Percentage of Total Population
in Selected European Cities, 1448–1696

City	Year	%
Fribourg	1448	10
Bern	1448	9
Nuremberg	1449	19
Basel	1497	18
Ypres	1506	10
Parma	1545	16
Florence	1551	17
Venice	1581	7
Bologna	1581	11
Rostock	1594	19
Bologna	1624	10
Florence	1642	9
Venice	1642	9
Münster	1685	15
Lille	1688	4
Ypres	1689	7
London (40 parishes)	1695	20
Dunkirk	1696	6

Devoutness and superstition strengthened each other in creating
and supporting the demand for religious services. On the other
hand, diffuse devoutness led many individuals of both sexes into
the ranks of the clergy. Other elements also favored the increase in
the ecclesiastical population. The institution of the dowry was an
incubus for most families and a danger to the integrity of the family
inheritance. To avoid the problem, the Chinese traditionally
resorted to infanticide. In Europe, especially among the well to do,
the custom was to confine the daughters to a convent.

Table 2-10 provides some data on the ecclesiastical population
in selected European cities from the fifteenth to the seventeenth

Table 2–10

Ecclesiastical Population in Selected European Cities, 1400–1700

City	Date	Total Population (thousands) (a)	No. of Priests (b)	No. of Monks & Nuns (c)	Total No. of Priests, Monks, & Nuns (d)	Clergy as % of Total Population		
						$\frac{b}{a} \times 100$	$\frac{c}{a} \times 100$	$\frac{d}{a} \times 100$
Toulouse	c.1400	c.23			c.1000			4.3
Frankfurt	1440	10			225			2.3
Nuremberg	1449	20			250			1.3
Bologna	1570	62			3310			5.3
Venice	1581	135	586	3553	4139	0.4	2.6	3.1
Naples	1599	233		5702			2.4	
Besançon	c.1600	11			600			5.5
Rome	1603	105	1241	4512	5753	1.2	4.3	5.5
Cremona	1621	40	150	1852	2002	0.4	4.6	5.0
Florence	1622	66		4917			7.5	
Pisa	1622	15		951			6.3	
Bologna	1624	62	138	3431	3569	0.2	5.5	5.7
Venice	1642	120	735	4171	4906	0.6	3.5	4.1
Siena	1670	16		1755			10.9	
Pistoia	1672	8		726			9.1	
Besançon	1709	17	275	571	846	1.6	3.4	5.0

centuries. Viewing a region as a whole, one finds that in 1745 the Great Duchy of Tuscany had 890,605 inhabitants, including

Clerics: 3,955
Priests: 8,095
Monks: 5, 482
Hermits: 168
Nuns: 9,736

The 27,436 ecclesiastics represented about 3 percent of the total population.[14] Beloch has estimated that, at the middle of the eighteenth century, in all of Italy the ecclesiastical population represented about 2 percent of the total population.[15] In 1591 Spain, with a total population of about 8.5 million people, had about 41,000 priests, 25,000 friars, and 25,000 nuns.[16] Thus the clergy represented about 1.1 percent of the total population. About France we know that in Alsace and the area of Alençon, at the end of the seventeenth century, of a total of 409,822 inhabitants the clerical population numbered 4,609 individuals, or about 1.1 percent. In Brittany in 1696, the ecclesiastical population amounted to 18,889 in a total population of 1,654,699—again about 1.1 percent. In the area of Caen, out of 609,203 inhabitants, the clergy totaled 5,225—that is, nearly 1 percent.[17] In England and Wales in 1377 the priests numbered about 24,900 and the monks and nuns about 10,600. In a total population of some 2.2 million people the clergy represented about 1.5 percent. In the first decades of the sixteenth century in England and Wales there were about 9,300 monks and nuns in a population of approximately 3.5 million inhabitants.[18] In Poland around 1500 there were about 6,900 monks and nuns and about 15,000 priests. The population of Poland numbered about 4.5 million, thus the clergy represented

14. Parenti, *Popolazione della Toscana*, pp. 73 and 126.
15. Beloch, *Bevölkerungsgeschichte Italiens*, vol. 1, pp. 73–79.
16. Ruiz Martin, *Demografia ecclesiastica*, p. 685.
17. Reinhard, Armengaud, Dupaquier, *Histoire Générale de la Population*, pp. 192–93.
18. For the data for 1377 see Russell, *The Clerical Population*, pp. 177–212. For the data relating to the first decades of the sixteenth century see Woodward, *The Dissolution of the Monasteries*, p. 2. See also Knowles, *Religious orders*, vol. 2, pp. 256–57.

about 0.5 percent.[19] In considering these figures one has to keep in mind that, given the age composition of preindustrial populations, 1 or 2 percent of the total population meant respectively 1.5 or 3 percent of the population above age fifteen.

From an economic point of view the clergy can be seen as producers of a particular type of service, and, inasmuch as there is a demand for this service (a demand which, like all other producers, the clergy does its best to stimulate) the clergy have the right to be considered part of the economically active population. In most respects the contribution of the clergy to a community is not different from that of the psychiatrists in modern societies, and it has been observed that in the countries where people have no recourse to the confessor, they end up by having recourse to the psychiatrist (with the disadvantage that individually they pay much more for the service). In addition, in preindustrial Europe, and especially in the rural areas, the parish priest often also performed those functions which we now regard as belonging to the schoolteacher and the doctor. Obviously, hermits present a special case, but to the extent that people believed these strange creatures to intercede with God, by means of their prayers, for the remissions of the sins of the world, and to the extent that people were ready to pay for the service, even hermits had every right to be included in the category of producers. From an economist's point of view, a good or service has no absolute utility, only the utility attributed to it, rightly or wrongly, by the consumer.

One of the major drawbacks of the traditional textbooks is that they identify the active population of preindustrial Europe with the *merchants,* the *craftsmen,* the *landlords,* and the *peasants* and they neglect the professionals, in particular the notaries, lawyers, and physicians. There was considerable demand from the private sector as well as the public sector for the services of the professionals, and this aspect of the problem has been discussed above in Chapter 1. Tables 2-11 and 2-12 provide some data relating to the size of the major professions in selected European cities. The Italian cities of the thirteenth and fourteenth centuries stand out for the size of the

---

19. Kjoczowski, *La population ecclesiastique*, passim.

Table 2–11

Number of Notaries, Lawyers, and Physicians in Relation
to Total Population in Selected Italian Cities, 1268–1675

City	Year	Notaries	Lawyers	Physicians
		Per 10,000 Inhabitants		
Verona	1268	124		
Bologna	1283	212		
Milan	1288	250	20	5
Prato	1298	278		
Florence	1338	55	9	
Verona	1409	70	6	3
Pisa	1428	90		
Como	1439	17	12	2
Verona	1456	54	4	9
Verona	1502	40	6	5
Verona	1545	26	7	5
Verona	1605	8	17	4
Carmagnola	1621	21	14	3
Florence	1630			5
Pisa	1630			9
Rome	1656			12
Rome	1675			13

SOURCE: Cipolla, *The Professions*, p. 43.

professional group and especially for the size of the notarial profession. Table 2-12 shows also that the number of the physicians was generally relatively higher in Italian cities than in other European towns, at least until the end of the seventeenth century. Whether this was beneficial to the people's health is another matter altogether. Most likely it was harmful,[20] but if people were prepared to pay for doctors' services, the supply of such services satisfied psychological needs, and, therefore, the availability of doctors, regardless of what they were able to do, must be put in the same plane as the availability of priests and hermits.

From the economic and social points of view, the importance of notaries, lawyers, and doctors can hardly be exaggerated and most certainly it was far out of proportion to their numbers. To

---

20. Cipolla, *Public Health*, chapter 2.

Table 2–12
Number of Physicians in Relation to Total Population
in Selected European Cities, 1575–1641

City	Year	Physicians	Population (thousands)	Doctors per 10,000 Inhabitants
Palermo	1575	22	70	3.1
Florence	1630	33	80	4.1
Pisa	1630	12	13	9.2
Pistoia	1630	5	9	5.5
Rome	1656	140	120	11.6
Rome	1675	164	130	12.6
Antwerp	1585	18	80	2.2
Rouen	1605	16	80	2.0
Lyons	1620	20	90	2.2
Paris	1626	85	300	2.1
Amsterdam	1641	50	135	3.7

SOURCE: Cipolla, *Public Health,* chapter 2.

begin with, members of the medical, legal, and notarial professions usually belonged to the small circle of the well to do, many of them as affluent as the rich merchants. Enjoying high incomes, physicians, lawyers, and notaries originated a demand for distinctive clothing, beautiful houses and land, as well as for books, spectacles, and scholastic services for their children. Moreover, since physicians, lawyers, and notaries represented the respectable element of the middle class, they gave this class a strength and prestige greater than that which would have accrued to it from its affluence alone.[21]

Economic history, in order to be comprehensible, must also be social history, taking into account values and factors which cannot be measured in solely economic terms. The history of the professions is an essential part of the story of the "intangible" values. Scholarly prestige, restrictive practices through the enforcement of licensing, relatively high personal income—all these factors individually reinforced each other and in combination made possible the social ascent of the professionals. In this respect medieval and Ren-

---

21. Cipolla, *The Professions,* pp. 37–52.

aissance Europe stands out as a unique example in world history. In other parts of the world, such as China, the providers of medical and legal services never succeeded in asserting themselves socially as well as economically. In certain other societies they did, but as members of a priestly caste. Only in western Europe, during the Middle Ages, did the professionals clearly separate themselves from the clergy and still move to the higher steps of the social ladder. The preeminence acquired in medieval western Europe by the professionals is at the origin of many institutions and characteristics of our industrial societies.

Obsessed with merchants, craftsmen, landowners, and peasants, economic historians have usually ignored the representatives of "the oldest profession in the world." A distinction must obviously be made between general prostitution and legalized prostitution. As regards the first, one cannot hope to have adequate information, but as regards the second, enough is known to justify the statement that, squalid though it may be, this sector always had great economic relevance. Moreover, it is easy to show that there is some positive correlation between the economic development of a given center and the presence of women of easy virtue. The fairs that were held in the province of Scania (southern Sweden) between August 15 and November 9 in the thirteenth and fourteenth centuries (the famous *nundinae Schanienses*) were well known not only for the number of merchants and fishermen who met there, but also for the number of *fahrende Frauen*.[22]

In the sixteenth and seventeenth centuries, the two major centers of prostitution in Europe were Venice and Rome, a primacy which, with the Industrial Revolution, was to be taken over by London and Paris. The gamesome ladies of Venice, called courtesans, were famous for their refinement and culture and, as Thomas Coryat wrote, "the name of a Cortezan of Venice is famous all over the Christendome."[23] In the sixteenth century, Montaigne, who was a great mind but also a great gossip, relates that the Cardinal d'Este regularly traveled to Abano for the baths, but even

---

22. Gade, *Hanseatic Control*, p. 16.
23. Coryat, *Crudities*, vol. 2, p. 38.

more to visit the "lovelies" of the Serenissima.[24] In fact, the courtesans were one of the major attractions of Venice for tourists and traders, and the English travelers of the early seventeenth century have left valuable information on the subject.

To establish numbers of prostitutes is a difficult task. First of all, the category does not lend itself to an exact definition, because between the two extremes of "honest woman" and "public prostitute" there is a vast range of intermediate conditions with blurred outlines. Second, whoever wishes to make a survey of the subject inevitably finds himself faced with reticence of every type and kind. Finally, the topic is such as to lend itself easily to the most fanciful tales. In Florence in the sixteenth century it was held that "about 8,000 courtesans" plied their trade,[25] but the 1551 census recorded only three.[26] The first figure is certainly an exaggeration, but the second does not reflect the truth, as witnessed by a poem of 1533 that lists forty women of easy virtue, describing them by name, surname, and various qualities.[27] In sixteenth-century Venice, those interested in "all that the brigand apple brought" could buy at little expense a booklet containing the "tariff of all prostitutes in which one finds the price and the qualities of all courtesans of Venice." According to two chroniclers of the early sixteenth century, there were then in Venice about 12,000 official prostitutes, but the figure is probably an exaggeration.[28]

In Rome, in the sixteenth and seventeenth centuries, it was said that there were 10,000 to 40,000 prostitutes.[29] Possibly this figure too was an exaggeration. Official figures are of course, as Table 2-13 indicates, much lower, ranging from 7 to 9 per thousand of total population. In assessing such figures, however, one has to keep in mind that in Rome, with its exceptional preponderance of priests, monks, and cardinals, women were underrepresented. In 1600, out

---

24. Montaigne, *Journal*, p. 142.
25. Dallington, *Survey of Tuscany*, p. 48.
26. Battara, *Popolazione di Firenze*, pp. 58 and 66.
27. Graf, *Il Cinquecento*, p. 265.
28. For the catalogue see Bloch, *Die Prostitution*, vol. 2, part 1, p. 123. On the estimates of the number of official prostitutes see Beloch, *Bevölkerungsgeschichte*, vol. 3, p. 101.
29. Bloch, *Die Prostitution*, vol. 2, part I, p. 254; and Delumeau, *Rome*, p. 420.

Table 2–13
Number of Officially Recognized Prostitutes
in Relation to Total Population of Rome, 1598–1675

Year	Total Population	Prostitutes	Prostitutes per 1,000 Inhabitants
1598	97,743	760	8
1600	109,729	604	6
1625	115,444	940	8
1650	126,192	1148	9
1675	131,912	889	7

SOURCE: Schiavoni, *Demografia di Roma.*

of 109,729 inhabitants, there were only 46,596 females, and the women in the fifteen-to-sixty-five age group must have numbered approximately 30,000; thus the 604 women of easy virtue listed in the census of that year represented about 2 percent of the adult female population of Rome. For a holy city, the percentage looks high especially if one considers that the figures refer only to those prostitutes who were officially recognized as such.

The economic importance of this social group was more than proportional to its numerical size. Thomas Coryat, at the beginning of the seventeenth century, wrote of Venice:

Some of them [the courtesans] having scraped together so much pelfe by their sordid facultie as doth maintaine them well in their old age: for many of them are as rich as ever was Rhadope in Egypt, Flora in Rome or Lais in Corinth. One example whereof is Margarita Aemiliana that built a faire monastery of Augustinian monkes.[30]

About the same time, Fynes Moryson wrote:

Each cortizan hath commonly her lover whom she mantaynes, her *ba-lordo* or gull who principally mantaynes her, besides her customers at large, and her *bravo* to fight the quarrells. The richer sorte dwell in fayre hired howses and have their owne servants but the common sorte lodge with bandes called ruffians, to whome in Venice they pay of their gayne the fifth parte, as foure shillings in twenty, paying besides for

---

30. Coryat, *Crudities*, vol. 2, p. 46.

their beds, linnen and feasting, and when they are past gayning much, they are turned out to begg or turne bandes or servants.

Since official prostitutes were taxed for their trade, in the larger towns they represented an important source of income for the public finances. According to Robert Dallington, at the end of the sixteenth century the Grand Duke of Tuscany "hath an income out of the brothel stewes which is thought at the least thirty thousand crownes a yeare in Florence onely"[31] In Rome, the attempt made by Pius V in 1566 to expel prostitutes from the Holy City failed because, in the words of the Venetian ambassador, Paolo Piepolo,

to send them away would be too big a thing, considering that, between them and others who for various reasons would follow them, more than 25,000 people would leave this city; and tax-farmers in Rome let it be understood that (if the prostitutes were expelled) they would either renounce their contracts or ask for a compensation amounting to 20,000 ducats a year.[32]

Italy has always been the country of the oddest compromises. We have already seen in the passage by Coryat that a monastery of the Augustinians in Venice was built with funds provided by a prostitute. In Rome, prostitutes were under obligation to bequeath part of their possessions to the Monastery of the Converted. When Pius V dedicated himself to the building and beautifying of the Civitas Pia, one of the expedients to which he had recourse in order to raise funds was to release the prostitutes from the obligation to bequeath part of their possessions to the monastery as long as they contributed at least 500 scudi toward his holy building.[33]

It would be wrong to identify the rural population wholly with the agricultural population, and the urban population entirely with the active population in the secondary and tertiary sectors. In the suburbs of the cities lived laborers who grew vegetables or performed other essentially agricultural activities. On the other hand, one encountered artisans and a few professional people also in small rural and semi-rural communities. In the village of Lomello

---

31. Dallington, *Survey of Tuscany*, p. 48.
32. D'Ancona, in Montaigne, *Journal*, pp. 303 n.
33. Scavizzi, *Attività edilizia*, p. 175, n. 7.

(Lombardy) around 1435, out of a population of about five or six hundred, there were at least two tailors, one weaver, a schoolteacher, and other artisans.[34] In 1541 in the area of Monza (Lombardy), in the rural centers numbering fewer than two hundred inhabitants each, those engaged in agriculture made up about 75 percent of the population; the remaining 25 percent consisted of craftsmen, traders, cart drivers, boatmen, and the like.[35] In the small rural parish of Ealing in Middlesex (England) in 1599, out of 426 inhabitants there were three tailors, one smith, one carpenter, one wheelwright, and four clerks.[36] In France in 1691 in the small rural parish of Laguiole, among 990 people were found one lawyer, six barber-surgeons, one schoolteacher, five master cobblers and eight journeyman cobblers, four master tailors and three journeyman tailors, one architect, three master masons and three journeyman masons, two carpenters, eight weavers, one glazier, three locksmiths, one wool-draper, and other craftsmen.[37]

In spite of these figures, however, skilled labor was concentrated in towns, where the organized apprenticeship greatly contributed to the development of highly qualified craftsmen. This fact is important in gauging the economic effects of epidemics. Given the high concentration of population in an environment that was hardly hygienic, towns usually suffered a much higher mortality than the rural areas. Thus, differential mortality between town and countryside implied a selective elimination to the disadvantage of skilled labor. According to King Charles IX, the plague of 1564 killed "three-quarters of the craftsmen and laborers" of the silk manufactures in Lyon.[38] According to Father Antero, in the plague epidemic of 1657, "out of two thousand or more weavers who were in Genoa, not more than fifty-nine are alive, and out of four hundred spinners, only forty remain."[39] These losses were especially serious because the training of a professional man or of a skilled

---

34. Cipolla, *Storia delle epidemie*, pp. 117–18.
35. Cipolla, *Popolazione Lombarda*, p. 152.
36. Allison, *Elizabethan Village*, pp. 91–103.
37. Noel, *Paroisse de Laguiole*, pp. 199–223.
38. Gascon, *Grand Commerce*, vol. 2, p. 495.
39. Antero, *Lazzaretti*, p. 294. See also the sources quoted by Presotto, *Genova*, p. 431.

worker involved a high "cost;" and the disappearance of specialized labor, leaving aside the human aspects of the tragedy, meant
loss of scarce capital.

The presence of skilled labor was a decisive factor for the fortunes of manufacturing activity. Current economic analysis tends to
stress the importance of human capital, but this is not a modern
discovery. If anything, it is a rediscovery. In the Middle Ages and
in the Renaissance, the relevance of human capital to economic
prosperity was taken for granted. Governments and princes were
active in trying to attract artisans and technicians and in preventing
their emigration. We shall return to this point in Part 2, when deal-
ing with diffusion of technology. Here, however, it is worth men-
tioning a significant example.

In 1230, the Commune of Bologna launched a definite policy of
economic development. The idea was to encourage the setting up
and development of textile manufactures, particularly wool and
silk. To achieve its aim, the Commune announced that those artisans who would move to Bologna and start an enterprise would
enjoy the following advantages:

a. they would receive free, from the city, a *tiratorium* (or the
    equivalent value of 4 lire) and two looms (or the equivalent
    value of 2 lire each)
b. a loan of 50 lire for five years free of interest, to cover the
    expenses for the initial installation, the cost of raw materials,
    upkeep of the family, and so forth
c. exemption from all taxes for 15 years
d. immediate grant of citizenship

In the two years 1230–31, 150 artisans with their families and
their assistants settled in Bologna. (At that time Bologna numbered
at most 25,000 inhabitants.) In its undertaking, the Commune of
Bologna freely distributed some nine thousand lire of the time, a
very large sum.[40] The operation turned out to be very successful
for the woolens sector.

Bologna's case is particularly interesting because of the early

---

40. For all above, see Mazzaoui, *Veronese Textile Artisans.*

period in which it took place, because of the size of the operation in both human and monetary terms, and for the excellent documentation which has survived but, as we shall see in Chapter 6, one encounters many similar cases in the following centuries. They show that everywhere in Europe public powers were very much aware of how important the availability of skilled labor was to economic progress.

The number employed in a particular sector of the economy tells something, but not everything, about the effective quantity and quality of the labor in that sector, both in an absolute sense and in relation to labor inputs in other sectors, A lot depends on the number of working days effectively put in, the number of working hours per working day, the physical and psychological condition of the workers, and the workers' level of education and technical training.

A Lombard document dated 1595 recorded that

the year consists of 365 days, but 96 are holy days, and thus one is left with 269. Of these, a great many are lost, mostly in wintertime and even at other times, because of rain and snow. Another part of the year is lost because everyone does not always find work, except in the three months of June, July and August.[41]

The document in question refers to agricultural labor and points out that religious festivities and climatic and seasonal conditions had a marked effect on the amount of labor effectively put into productive activities. The holidays were traditionally numerous. The above document cites a total of ninety-six a year in Lombardy. In Venice, the guilds imposed abstention from work in 80 to 90 holidays a year.[42] Elsewhere, holidays were no less frequent, although in Protestant Europe the Reformation noticeably reduced their number.[43]

Climatic conditions and seasonal fluctuation of demand hit agricultural and building activities especially hard. Consequently, the percentages of those employed in agriculture and construction tend

---

41. Cipolla, *Prezzi, salari,* p. 14.
42. Sella, *Commerci e industrie a Venezia,* p. 124.
43. Hill, *Puritanism,* p. 43.

to overestimate the proportion of labor inputs in these sectors in relation to the labor inputs in the other sectors of the economy.[44]

We know very little about the physical and psychological conditions of the labor force before the Industrial Revolution. We do know that the mass lived in a state of undernourishment. This gave rise, among other things, to serious forms of avitaminosis. Widespread filth was also the cause of troublesome and painful skin diseases. To this must be added in certain areas the endemic presence of malaria, or the deleterious effects of a restricted matrimonial selection, which gave rise to cretinism. Finally, one can add the effects of occupational diseases due to the appallingly unhealthy conditions under which certain trades were conducted and to the handling of toxic substances.

Separately or together, these factors had a negative influence on the quantity and quality of effective labor inputs. On the other hand, the beauty and perfection of many products of European preindustrial craftsmanship give the inescapable impression that the craftsman of the time found in his work a satisfaction and a sense of dignity which are, alas, foreign to the alienating assembly lines of the modern industrial complex.

Little or nothing is known of the level of education of the masses before the Industrial Revolution. The urban revolution of the eleventh and twelfth centuries opened a new era with the introduction of public schools, and many a city witnessed a noticeable development of elementary education. In Florence, around 1330, Giovanni Villani recorded: "There are from 8,000 to 10,000 boys and girls who are at school learning how to read and from 1,000 to 1,200 boys who learn abacus and arithmetic" in the schools.[45] We know from other sources that Florentine youths went to school to learn reading and writing at the age of five or six. At the age of eleven, those who were both willing and able continued their education in one of the six schools of arithmetic where they remained for 2 to 3 more years. About 1338, Florence had a population of roughly 90,000 inhabitants. Given the age structure of populations in those days, the age group between five and fourteen must have consisted

---

44. Gould, *Economic Growth*, pp. 75 and ff.
45. Villani, *Cronica*, book 11.

of about 23,000 children. If Villani's data are correct, more than 40 percent went to school. A document dated 1313 shows that in Florence it was taken for granted that an artisan should be able to "write, read, and keep accounts," and it is known that a good many humble Florentine artisans wrote extremely readable, and, for us, instructive, family histories.[46]

Florence was in the vanguard of Europe in the fourteen century. During the fifteenth and sixteenth centuries, one city after another followed her example, but the diffusion of elementary education among the masses long remained a typically urban characteristic. In the Protestant countries the Reformation succeeded in spreading the rudiments of reading and writing among the rural population but in Catholic countries, the bulk of the peasants remained illiterate until the modern era. About the middle of the seventeenth century, less than 50 percent of the adult population of the major western European cities were illiterate; elsewhere, the figure ranged from 50 to 95 percent.[47]

These observations lead us to discuss education and professional training in an economic context.

To raise and educate a child costs money. If the young person is of working age and is instead sent to school, the person also costs the economy what he does not produce. That which the young person could produce if he was sent to work and does not because he is at school is income foregone for the economy and represents an opportunity cost.

These costs are borne by the family and the society, in expectation of future incomes. What is spent in raising and educating a person is a form of investment, which is directly comparable to the building of a factory. While it is being built, the factory, too, does not produce and the cost of construction is borne in expectation of future incomes. In the training of a person, as in the building of a factory, the investment can be a good one or a bad one. A student who studies little and badly during his school years is the equiva-

---

46. For above, compare Cipolla, *Literacy*, pp. 45–47.
47. Cipolla, *Literacy*, pp. 60–61.

lent of a factory which is badly built: the defects will become evident when production starts.

The poverty of preindustrial societies did not allow large investments in human capital. A few years at school were a luxury that not many could afford, especially in the country. Apprenticeship offered the advantage that the young people produced while they learned; thus the opportunity cost of their education was practically eliminated. In fact, all professional and technical training was given by way of apprenticeship.

Table 2–14

Age Limits for Acceptance into Apprenticeship
in Selected Trades in Seventeenth-Century Venice

Trade	Age Limit	
	Minimum	*Maximum*
Tinkers		16
Dyers		20
Weavers	12	17
Stonecutters	11	13
Caulkers	10	20
Painters	14	16
Goldsmiths	7	18
Sausage makers	16	18

SOURCE: Beltrami, *Popolazione di Venezia*, pp. 198–99.

In Venice, at the beginning of the seventeenth century, the ages for acceptance into apprenticeship in certain trades varied from ten to twelve years (see Table 2-14). The average duration of apprenticeship varied according to trades; for instance:

> victualling and sale of products of the soil: 5 years
> production of clothing or personal services: 3 years
> other trades: 5 years

The guilds regulated professional education in every detail, and in some cases, to the benefit of the children of their own members, they even organized school courses to teach the rudiments of reading and writing.[48]

---

48. Unwin, *Economic History*, pp. 92–99.

Originally, training for the higher professions—jurisprudence, medicine, and notarial art—also took place through various forms of apprenticeship. But from the end of the twelfth century, and more decidedly in the thirteenth century, special schools were created, from which the universities emerged.

One of the fundamental characteristics of the urban societies of preindustrial Europe was the tendency toward association, which manifested itself increasingly from the end of the twelfth century. If in the preceding centuries men had sought protection and the safeguard of their own interests in a relationship of subordination to the powerful (feudalism), with the emergence of urban societies the safeguard of personal interests was sought mainly in associations among equals. This was the essence of the urban revolution. The commune was initially nothing more than the sworn association of citizens—the super-association, above and beyond the particular associations which took the name of Arti, guilds, companies, confraternities, societies, or universities.

Class and group conflicts played a fundamental part in determining who could and who could not form a guild, and the dominance or decline of a group signified the opportunity (or lack of it) for rival groups to unite in a legally recognized guild. Within the guilds, a definite order of precedence faithfully reflected the distribution of power. For the whole of the thirteenth century, merchant guilds remained unchallenged in dominating the European scene. In the ensuing centuries, various occupational categories gradually acquired the right to constitute themselves into autonomous associations, and the craft guilds became increasingly influential.

The guilds satisfied a number of requirements. Among the various tasks of the guilds, there was usually that of collective organization of religious ceremonies, charity, and mutual assistance. These tasks were not a smokescreen. For a craftsman of the time, participation by his own guild in the town's procession in honor of the patron saint or the Virgin Mary was as important as, if not more important than, a discussion of wages and production. And the guilds effectively played an important role in providing social assistance to their own members and education for their members' children as well as in setting and enforcing quality controls in production.

All these functions should not be underestimated. But neither should one underestimate the fact that one of the fundamental aims of all guilds was to regulate and reduce competition among their own members. With regard to the supply of labor, a guild aimed at exercising strict control over the admission of new members and their entry into the labor market. On the other hand, when competition among employers was in question, the corporate body always served to control and strictly regulate competition among its members as far as demand for labor was concerned. Consequently, in any study of the level and structure of employment and wages in centuries preceding the eighteenth, guilds' action must of necessity occupy a position of the first importance.

Capital

Physical capital is represented by goods which are produced by man and are not consumed, being either used as productive inputs for further production or stored for future consumption. Capital can be usefully divided into *fixed capital* and *working capital*.

Fixed capital consists of those economic goods produced by man which are repeatedly used in the course of a number of productive cycles. Machine tools are the classical type of fixed capital, but the shovel, the plow, and the barrel, as well as the ship, the cart, and the bridge are also fixed capital.

Sir John Hicks wrote a few years ago:

What is the essential mark by which we are to distinguish modern industry from the handicraft industry? . . . This is a clue to the distinction between the two kinds of industry for which we are looking.

The capital of a merchant is, mainly, working or circulating capital—capital that is turned over. A particular merchant may indeed employ some fixed capital, an office, a warehouse, a shop or a ship; but these are no more than containers for the stock of goods on which his business centres. Any fixed capital that he uses is essentially peripheral.

As long as industry remained at the handicraft stage the position of the craftsman or artizan was not so very different. He did indeed have tools, but the tools which he used were not usually very valuable; the turnover of his material was the centre of his business. It is at the point when fixed capital moves, or begins to move, into the central position that the revolution occurs. In the days before modern industry, the only fixed capital goods that were being used, and which absorbed in their production any considerable quantity of resources, were buildings and vehicles (especially ships).[49]

The thesis that fixed capital acquired a degree of importance only with the Industrial Revolution and, even then, only in the final stages of the Revolution, has never been questioned and has, indeed, been reasserted emphatically by a number of scholars.[50] As a first approximation it is undoubtedly valid, but if one wants to move away from broad, sweeping generalizations, one must put forward a number of important qualifications.

In agriculture fixed capital has always been relatively important. The working or circulating capital consisted of seeds, fertilizers, and reserves. Fixed capital consisted of barns, houses for the workers, implements (shovels, plows, pitchforks, barrels, presses, etc.), cattle, irrigation canals, water mills, and windmills. In the eleventh century, of the twenty-nine farms of the Abbey of St. Germain des Prés outside Paris, only eight had water mills (though these totaled fifty-nine); and at the beginning of the tenth century, the records of the Abbey of St. Bertin pointed to the construction of a mill as an admirable event.[51] But from the eleventh century onward, water mills and windmills multiplied and became a common feature of the rural landscape. Toward the end of the eleventh century in England in the region of the Trent and Severn rivers, 5,624 mills were in operation—that is, one mill for every fifty families. In 1350 in the territory of Pistoia (Italy) 250 mills were in operation—that is, approximately one mill for every twenty-five families.[52] In the course of time, not only did the number of mills continue to increase, but their average power per unit also increased. Toward the end of the eighteenth century, more than half a million water mills operated in Europe, and many of them had more than one wheel.

---

49. Hicks, *A Theory,* pp. 141–42.
50. See for all Pollard, *Fixed Capital.*
51. Duby, *L'Economie Rurale,* vol. 1, p. 74.
52. For eleventh-century England see Hodgen, *Domesday Water Mills.* For fourteenth-century Pistoia see Muendel, *The Horizontal Mills.*

Hogs and poultry can be classified as circulating capital (even though a hen kept alive because of its egg production is fixed capital), but horses, cattle, and sheep were fixed capital. At the end of the thirteenth century in the territory of Chieri (Piedmont) over an area of about 20,000 acres, there were 1,200 sheep and 850 head of cattle. The ratio of animals to area was, therefore, a little more than one ox and about 1.5 sheep for every 25 acres.[53] In 1336 on about 1,900 acres owned by Merton College (England), of which about two-thirds were arable land, there were 69 horses, 228 cattle, and 1,276 sheep.[54] The ratio of animals to land was, therefore, about one horse, three head of cattle and fifteen sheep for every 25 acres. In 1530 in six country parishes in Brianza, north of Milan (Italy), there were 11,058 persons above seven years of age, 762 children below seven years of age, and 1,823 animals. For every 100 persons older than seven, there were, therefore, about 7 children and 16 animals.[55] In 1574 on the properties of the Hospital at Imola (Italy), there were 96 persons. Of these, thirty-three were workingmen who made use of 51 head of cattle and 37 sheep, with a ratio of animals to laborers of about 1.5 head of cattle per laborer.[56] An inquiry made in 1471 in the regions of Grasse, Castellane, Guillaume, and Saint-Paul-de-Vence in Haute-Provence (France) yielded the following results:[57]

	NO. OF LOCAL- ITIES	NO. OF HOUSE- HOLDS	NO. OF DONKEYS, MULES AND HORSES	NO. OF SHEEP AND GOATS	HEAD OF CATTLE
Totals	70	3,167	2,494	114,837	5,498
Averages:					
Per locality		45	36	1,641	78
Per household			0.8	36	2

In western Finland in 1719 for a population of 14,975 peasant families, ther were 9,918 horses, 49,018 cattle, and 53,845 sheep.[58]

---

53. Rotelli, *Economia agraria*, p. 20.
54. Slicher Van Bath, *Agrarian History,* pp. 180–81.
55. Beretta, *Pagine,* p. 84.
56. Galassi, *Campagna Imolese,* p. 112.
57. Sclafert, *Cultures en Haute-Provence,* pp. 140–48.
58. Slicher Van Bath, *Agrarian History*, p. 291.

As one can see from these figures, the ratios of animals to land, of animals to laborers, and of animals to population varied greatly from one area to another and from one period to another. But always and everywhere animals were a form of fixed capital which was far from peripheral in the productive system. Toward the end of the seventeenth century, William Petty calculated that, if the value of all agricultural land in England could be estimated at about £144 million, the animals could be valued at a quarter of that sum, that is, at about £36 million.[59] In many areas, livestock was much more abundant in the Middle Ages and the Renaissance than in modern times. For six of the seventy localities in Haute-Provence covered by the inquiry of 1471 mentioned above, the following comparison has been made:[60]

	NO. OF HOUSEHOLDS	NO. OF SHEEP AND GOATS	HEAD OF CATTLE
in 1471	863	25,050	1,451
in 1956	12,834	471	407

Horses, cattle, and sheep were capital not only for agriculture. Sheep provided the raw material for the woollens industry. Horses and oxen were indispensable for transport. Also, the military sector relied heavily on this sort of capital. From the fifteenth century onward, armies tended to move with greater speed as horses and mules gradually replaced oxen as a means of transport in military operations. As late as the second half of the nineteenth century in several European countries, the census tabulations included not only people, but also horses and mules; and the object of the enumeration was essentially military. Toward 1845, the number of horses and mules available in the major European nations was estimated as shown in Table 2-15.

Animals as a form of capital were highly vulnerable in preindustrial society. In medieval and Renaissance Europe, epizoötic diseases were no less frequent or less disastrous than epidemics.[61]

---

59. Petty, *Verbum sapienti*, p. 106.
60. Sclafert, *Cultures en Haute-Provence*, p. 148.
61. On the history of epizoötics see the works cited in Haeser, *Bibliotheca epidemiographica*, p. 17.

Table 2–15

Number of Horses and Mules in Selected European
Countries, about 1845

Country	Horses and Mules
Austria (Empire)	2.7 million
France	2.7 million
England	2.3 million
Italy	1.0 million
Prussia	1.5 million
Russia	8.0 million

SOURCE: Balbi, *l'Austria*, p. 165 and *Annuario Statistico Italiano*, 1857, p. 554.

At times, these diseases assumed international political significance, as when in Pannonia, in 791, nine-tenths of Charlemagne's horses died and the Frankish king found himself in great military difficulties.[62] More often, an epizooty was of purely local significance, but not infrequently it brought tragedy to entire regions. In 1275, "A rich man of France brought into Northumberland a Spanish ewe, as big as a calfe of two yeares, which ewe being rotten infected so the country that it spread over all the realme; this plague of murrain continued for 28 years."[63] Between 1713 and 1769 in Frisia, major epizootics caused the following losses:[64]

December 1713–February 1715: 66,000 head of cattle
November 1744–August 1745: 135,000 head of cattle
November 1747–April 1748: 23,000 head of cattle
May 1769–December 1769: 98,000 head of cattle

When cattle died, the consequences for the economy of the time were comparable to the consequences of large fires which would destroy machines and power stations in a modern industrial economy. Moreover, replacement was made difficult by the fact that among horses, cattle, and sheep, sterility was very widespread. For the territory of Montaldeo (Italy), a survey of forty-nine cows during the period 1594–1601 shows an index of sterility of about

62. *Annales Laurissenses vel Einhardi*, a. 791.
63. Stow, *Annales*, p. 200.
64. Faber, *Cattle-plague*.

50 percent, with only twenty-five calves born; the sterility of sheep in Montaldeo, was even higher, about 70 to 75 percent.[65]

Despite being small, hungry, and often sterile, horses, oxen, and sheep were extremely valuable form of capital. Supply was limited and demand was high. In Montaldeo in the seventeenth century, one had to accumulate the wages of 100 ten-to-twelve-hour work days in order to buy one cow. At the beginning of the eighteenth century, it was necessary to sell over 50 liters of wine to buy one small pig.[66]

The value of this form of capital was a temptation to the mass of the poor. Fernand Braudel wrote that ". . . in England at the beginning of the nineteenth century, thieves and horse-thieves were a class of their own."[67] The fact is that cattle thieves were a thriving and numerous class not only in England, but in all European countries.

In the transport sector, one must distinguish between water transport and overland transport, and for the latter between long-distance and local transport. In water transport, boats and ships were fixed capital. In long-distance overland transportation until the sixteenth century, horses and mules were the predominant form of fixed capital employed—not until the second half of the sixteenth century were there enough roads to allow the extensive use of carts and carriages for long-distance travel. On the other hand, carts were used very early for local overland transport, especially for agricultural products. From whatever point of view one looks at things, it is obvious that fixed capital, in the form of draught animals, beasts of burden, ships, boats, carts, and carriages, was not peripheral in transport services.

The thesis that fixed capital had a purely peripheral importance in the productive process before the Industrial Revolution is most valid for the manufacturing sector. As discussed above, when, in

---

65. Doria, *Uomini e terre*, p. 52.
66. *Ibid.*
67. Braudel, *Civilisation matérielle*, p. 267.

The Great Crane at Bruges. This machine is a typical example of fixed capital in preindustrial Europe. As one readily notices the main problem was the power source; the crane had to be operated with human energy. Bayerisches Statsbibliothek, Munich.

1230–31 the Commune of Bologna invited a number of foreign artisans to set up manufactures of silk and wool, the city administration provided each artisan with a *tiratorium* worth four Bologna lire of the time and two looms worth two lire each. The fixed capital considered necessary for a productive unit was, therefore, valued at eight lire. At the same time, the Commune loaned each artisan fifty lire for the expense of setting up and starting the plant, for raw materials and for the upkeep of his family. The artisans undertook to repay the fifty-lire loan over a period of five years. This fact suggests that, under normal conditions, the fixed capital necessary to an enterprise, valued as we have seen at eight lire, could be amortized in less than a year. Other examples of this kind can be easily assembled, but only with some qualifications. In the case of the textile manufactures of Bologna, the entire productive process was not completed in the houses of the artisans. From an early date, mills were used for the fulling of cloth, and they represented a considerable investment in fixed capital. Over the centuries in Bologna itself, special mills were built for the manufacture of silk. By the seventeenth century these mills has reached an exceptional level of mechanical sophistication and represented an important investment. The mill set up in early eighteenth-century England by Sir Thomas Lombe in imitation of the Bologna silk mills consisted of 25,586 wheels and 97,746 pieces and could produce 73,726 yards of silk yarn for every revolution of the enormous driving wheel.[68] In the mining sector, machines were needed for pumping water and for lifting and carrying ore; during the fifteenth and sixteenth centuries, this machinery often acquired notable dimensions. In the shipbuilding sector, basins, docks, workshops, implements, and cranes represented considerable fixed capital. The Arsenal of Venice was deservedly famous throughout the later Middle Ages and the early modern period for its size, its installations, and the stocks of materials. In England at the end of the seventeenth century, the fixed assets of the Kentish shipyards at Chatham, Deptford, Woolwich, Sheerness, and Portsmouth were valued at about £76,000 (Table 2-16). If we accept Gregory King's estimates of the English national income for 1688 (43.5

---

68. Poni, *Archéologie*, p. 2.

Table 2–16

Fixed Plants in Four Major English Naval Shipyards, 1688

	Docks	Work-shops	Depots	Workers' Houses	Cranes	Value of Plant (pounds)
Chatham	5	24	10	10	4	44,940
Deptford	1	17	2	7	2	15,760
Woolwich	2	5	1	7	2	9,669
Sheerness	1	3	1	8	12	5,393

million pounds, according to Table 1-6) the sum of 76,000 pounds was equivalent to almost 0.2 percent of the annual English national income.

There is no doubt, however, that apart from specific industries, normally in the manufacturing sector, fixed capital was of limited size. Moreover, since machinery and equipment were relatively simple, the greatest part of the fixed capital sunk in most manufactures was represented by buildings. In five factories operating in the Republic of Genoa (Italy) near the end of the eighteenth century, the composition of fixed capital was as follows:[69]

	Value of Building (%)	Value of Equipment (%)	Total
Silk-throwing factory	87	13	100
Paper mill	87	13	100
Paper mill	85	15	100
Paper mill	85	15	100
Furnace	100	—	100

One important form of fixed capital was represented by weaponry. The armament of a preindustrial state looks ridiculously small in comparison to the weaponry of a modern industrial state, but in relation to the Gross National Product of the time it represented quite an investment. Moreover, while in a modern state the armory in the hands of private individuals is practically insignificant when compared to the weaponry controlled by the public powers, in preindustrial Europe the situation was totally different. Troyes is a

---

69. Felloni, *Gli Investimenti Finanziari*, p. 49.

medium-sized city in France which in October 1474 counted some 2,300 households. An official inspection of all homes showed that at the time the citizens owned 208 jacks, 51 complete suits of armor, 109 breastplates and overshirts, 199 shirts of mail and coats of mail, 73 surcoats, 49 brigandines and underskirts, 785 sallets and armets, 151 barbutes and basinets, 271 crossbows, 547 muskets, with both automatic recoil and manual, 4 cannons, one serpentine, 389 lances, 855 hatchets and hammers, 1047 spears, 201 javelins, double-hooked lances, and pikes, 37 bows, 657 two-headed hammers of lead, copper, and iron. Moreover, in the shops of the town merchants there were for sale: 69 jacks, 6 complete suits of armor, one decorated breastplate, 5 overshirts, 14 brigandines, 6 shirts of mail, 79 lances, 110 sallets, 16 steel crossbows, 8 hammers, 56 swords, 17 pairs of gauntlets.[70] Admittedly that was a turbulent period for France, and in particular the citizens of Troyes feared the consequences of the war between Louis XI and Charles le Temeraire. Still, even for calmer periods and quieter areas, if one combines the armory in the hands of private citizens and the weaponry owned by the public powers, one always finds that that particular form of capital represented quite a sizable amount of wealth.

There are no reliable statistics to evaluate precisely the relative importance of the various kinds of fixed capital in preindustrial Europe. The only data available are the educated guesses of Gregory King for England in 1688 (see Table 2-17), but they seem to confirm the general impression one obtains from the scanty and

Table 2–17

Gregory King's Estimate of English Capital in 1688

		Million Pounds
Fixed Capital	Buildings	54
	Livestock	25
Working Capital	Plants, tools and machinery	33
	Stocks and inventories	
	Total	112

SOURCE: Dean, *Capital Formation*, p. 96.

---

70. Contamine, *Consommation et demande militaires*, p. 8.

casual information provided by the surviving records—namely, that the most important form of fixed reproducible capital was buildings, followed by livestock, with plants, tools, and machinery ranking in third place.

If one were to distinguish among the various uses to which fixed capital was put, one would notice that churches and monasteries abounded. A medium-sized city such as Pavia (Italy) in the fifteenth century, with about 16,000 inhabitants, had over one hundred churches, and this was in no way exceptional. Hospital beds, on the other hand, were so scarce that, until well into the nineteenth century, it was common practice in every part of Europe to place two or three patients in one bed. Bridges were few and roads inadequate, but castles were abundant.

The distribution of capital among various forms and uses is influenced by technological as well as economic factors. The building of magnificent cathedrals at a time when hospital beds were so scarce that the sick had to be piled up two or more to a bed reflects the unequal distribution of wealth. If wonderful private mansions were built while bridges were few and roads inadequate, this imbalance is related to the fact that, all things considered, public agencies were able to draw on only a limited part of available resources. But the explanation does not end there. The same hospitals which lacked beds were adorned with costly works of art. The state which did not build bridges sank considerable resources into military expenditures. The direction of investment was and is determined by the structure of demand—that is, by tastes and standards of value.

Working capital essentially consists of *stocks and inventories*, which can conveniently be subdivided into

    a. stocks of raw materials
    b. stocks of semi-finished goods
    c. stocks of finished goods

There is no doubt that in preindustrial Europe the ratio of working to fixed capital was much higher than it is nowadays. The reason for this difference may be explained as follows: The maximum possible consumption of a given society at a given time is determined by the volume of stocks plus the volume of current production. Therefore, the significance of stocks is a function of both the intensity of fluctuations in current production, and the inelasticity of demand. As the economic life of preindustrial Europe was characterized by violent fluctuations in harvests; insecurity of transportation and, therefore, irregularity of supplies, both of foodstuffs and of raw materials; expensive transportation, which made long-distance transport of low-priced commodities an uneconomical proposition, people usually built up stocks of foodstuffs wherever they could, and businessmen normally built up ample stocks of raw materials and/or finished goods. Stocks of food were particularly important. As the specter of famine and hunger continually loomed over the consciousness of the people, everybody strove to put aside reserves of food whenever possible. It was investment prompted by fear. Pavia, a small city of northern Italy, at the middle of the sixteenth century numbered about 12,000 inhabitants. In one year this community obtained from its surrounding territory about 28,000 bags of wheat (almost 100,000 bushels) for current consumption. In 1555 it was found that people held in their homes about 3,700 bags.[71] It was already May, and one-tenth, at most, of the stock was destined for the year's consumption until the harvest. The remaining 3,330 bags were, therefore, long-term reserves.

The reader will have noted that this discussion of food reserves has been couched in the context of investment. It may seem strange to some that wheat and bread should be treated as capital. In fact, when they are consumed, bread and wheat are consumption goods. But when they are spared from consumption and kept in storage, even goods like bread and wheat become by definition part of the stock of wealth which we call capital. Capital formation is future oriented, and the supply of capital is determined by how much consumption it promises for the future and by how much consumption it takes away in the present.

Creating and maintaining stocks generate costs. There are costs related to warehousing and to the possible deterioration of all or part of the product. If the businessman finances the building up of stocks with borrowed money, costs also include the rate of interest

---

71. Zanetti, *Problemi Alimentari*, pp. 56–71.

paid. If the businessman finances the building up of stocks with his own means, he incurs an opportunity cost.

Because stocks cost money, one tends to keep them at a minimum, and since the industrial world does not operate under as heavy a burden of insecurity and high costs of transportation as preindustrial Europe did, the ratio of working capital to fixed capital is today noticeably reduced. However, even today when fears of international complications and conflicts arise, stocks of strategic materials and basic necessities increase markedly, reflecting conditions reminiscent of those which prevailed in preindustrial Europe.

The storage of foodstuffs. The conditions which existed in preindustrial Europe drove families to keep as large a reserve of foodstuffs as possible. In southern Europe these reserves were kept in cool cellars. In the north the reserves were stored in attics and roofs with special openings for ventilation. This picture shows the roof of such a house in Strasbourg, France. Commission Régionale d'Inventaire d'Alsace, Strasbourg.

So far we have referred only to monetary costs. In preindustrial Europe, however, stocks of foodstuffs implied also a high externality cost, of which the people of the time were not aware. The storing of large quantities of grain was the source of a large and prosperous rat population, which, in turn, was the source of frequent plague and typhus epidemics.

Stocks represent working capital, and in comparison with fixed capital they have a much higher degree of volatility. Fixed capital is *sunk;* it is embodied in a particular form (a building, a machine, a ship) from which it can only gradually, at best, be released. It is hard to disinvest once the investment has been sunk in fixed capital. Working capital, on the contrary, is continually *turned over*; it is continually coming back for reinvestment. When investment is in the form of working capital, disinvestment is easier: One sells existing stocks (if one can) and refrains from replenishing them.

This means that when stocks and inventories make up a large fraction of the existing capital, disinvestment can be more massive and drastic than if a large fraction of investment in sunk in fixed capital. Big recessions are not an exclusive trait of contemporary capitalism. Preindustrial slumps could also be very severe, and one of the reasons was the relative size and the volatility of working capital. The severe recessions of 1619–21 and 1630–32 in northern and central Italy are classical examples of crises which resulted in and were magnified by dramatic reductions in the volume of stocks and inventories.

Natural Resources

The third factor of production consists of *natural resources*. The term is used to mean land as well as other resources. Today it is fashionable to refer to these resources as *nonreproducible capital* in order to emphasize the fact that when, for example, a coal deposit is exhausted, it is beyond human power to reconstitute it. And, if it is true that man can do much with reclaiming-works to increase the available quantity of arable land, it is also true that the amount of land on the earth is finite.

In preindustrial Europe, the natural resource *par excellence* was *land.* In Malthus's and Ricardo's time, land still was the factor which, in the last analysis, "set the limits to population growth and determined the distribution of the population."[72] As has been rightly observed:

It is natural to ascribe a large importance to the *per capita* supply of land in a dominantly agricultural society where levels of technology are low and little capital is employed. Agricultural techniques may improve or nonagricultural pursuits develop, but too slowly to offset the depressive effect of a falling supply of land per head when the population rises. . . . The ratio of cultivable land to population has been the chief determinant of the level of real income of pre-industrial societies. . . . It is tempting to relate the great secular fluctuations [of real wages] of the first five and a half centuries *primarily* to changes in the ratio of population to land.[73]

When one spoke of "land," one meant, above all, arable land. The resources of the subsoil, however, were not ignored. Among the natural resources exploited in Europe prior to the eighteenth century, of particular importance were mineral deposits of silver, mercury, alum, tin, sulfur, copper, and iron. Pit-coal was already in use in the Middle Ages, but medieval people were very suspicious of this type of fuel, vaguely but strongly feeling that its use "poisoned the air." Although with overtones of superstition, medieval people were more conscious of possible pollution damage than people at the time of the Industrial Revolution.

Forests must be dealt with separately. From a theoretical point of view, forests cannot be treated as nonproducible capital because trees can be, and are, planted by man; forests are, therefore, reproducible capital. In fact, during the Middle Ages and the Renaissance, trees were planted and attention was paid to the problem of forest preservation. In mountain districts, the felling of trees in communal woods was regulated, from an early date, by precise rules. In 1281, the English Cistercians established enclosures of five years to protect the seedlings in their forests. In the same period the Statutes of the Commune of Montaguloto dell-'Ardinghesca, in the district of Siena, laid down that every member

---

72. Spengler, *Population Problem*, p. 196.
73. Gould, *Economic Growth*, pp. 39, 81, 82.

of the Commune inheriting a hide had to plant ten trees a year. In France from the end of the thirteenth century public concern about the fate of the forests gave rise to a series of royal as well as local provisions. In 1346 King Philip IV issued an ordinance regulating the cutting of trees and the consumption of timber. In 1669 the great minister Colbert inspired the formulation of an organic law for the protection of the forests. In the Hapsburg territories, Emperor Ferdinand I issued a general ordinance on the matter of forestry in 1557 and instituted the position of *Königlich-Kaiserlich Förstmeister* (Royal and Imperial Master of the Forests) for all hereditary territories of the Crown. One perceives the same kind of concern at the level of the local agricultural units. In the seventeenth-century accounts of the Medicean farm of *Cafaggioli*, it is clearly specified that "the trees are cut in the woods only once every ten years." Ordinances, statutes, decrees, and individual provisions, however, did not prove very efficacious. When population pressure grew and/or the demand for wood increased, the knell of the forest was rung.

Throughout the Middle Ages and the Renaissance, the Europeans behaved toward the trees in an eminently parasitic and extremely wasteful way. Italy exhausted her forest reserves very early, which explains the extensive use of brick and marble in Italian architecture. In Lombardy the area covered with trees was reduced to less than 9 percent of the whole rural territory by 1555.[74] The forested area represented about 33 percent of the French territory around 1500 and only 25 percent around 1650; in the meantime, also, the quality of the forests had noticeably deteriorated.[75] For reasons that we shall analyze below in the sixteenth and seventeenth centuries, England offered the worst example of massive destruction of forests. At the beginning of the nineteenth century, the European forested area was reduced to the levels shown in Table 2-18.

The forests of medieval and Renaissance Europe were a great natural resource. That such a resource was depleted is a sad and regrettable story from the ecological and environmental point of

74. Pugliese, *Condizioni economiche*, Table 2.
75. Devèze, *Histoire des Fôrets*, pp. 52–53.

Table 2–18

Forested Area in Europe about the Middle
of the Nineteenth Century

	Thousand Acres
Russia	429,868
Austro-Hungary	36,546
Germany	34,977
France	21,992
Italy	12,417
Spain	11,737

view, but it was the precondition for the European shift toward the
use of coal and iron.

The main bottleneck of preindustrial economies was the strictly
limited supply of energy. The main sources of energy other than
man's muscular work were plants and animals, and this fact set a
limit to the possible expansion of any given agricultural society.
The limiting factor was again the supply of land on which plants
are grown and animals raised.

Since the earliest antiquity the sailing ship had enabled man to
master the energy of the wind on water, and this fact accounts for
the fortunes of peoples who, like the Greeks and the Phoenicians,
had open access to easily navigable seas. As we shall see below, the
people of medieval and Renaissance Europe learned to harness the
energy of water and wind to a remarkable extent for land-based
activities. The mills of European design could do the work for
which other societies needed gangs of slaves, and the medieval and
Renaissance men feverishly built mills wherever and whenever they
could. Availability of steady winds and the presence of waterfalls
and streams must thus be counted among the relevant natural
resources in preindustrial Europe. They were to the people of the
time what coal, oil, and uranium are to an industrialized society.
The difference is that while the energy potentially embodied in
coal, oil, and uranium can be transported over distance, the energy
of the wind and of the water has to be used on the spot. This fact
dictated the location of most manufactures of preindustrial Europe:
they were normally located where mills could be built.

Organization

In order to result in any production, labor, capital, and natural resources must be combined in organizational forms which vary according to the levels of technology, the size of the markets, and the types of production.

Today, in the manufacturing sector, the technical unit of production is the factory, while in preindustrial Europe it was the workshop. The industrial factory is characterized by a high concentration of wage-labor and machines. In the workshop, the concentration of labor and capital was minimal and wage-labor was scarcely represented.

The wage worker of the modern factory operates with capital not his own, is subject to a strict work discipline, and carries on his activities in a series of highly specialized and routine operations which contribute to a limited part of the final product. The craftsman of the preindustrial workshop often, if not always, owned the capital or at least part of it, worked for more hours than the industrial worker, but was not subject to the hard discipline of the factory, and in some manufacturing sectors had the pleasure and pride of seeing the final good turn out from his own hands. These are the human aspects. But in order to understand the preindustrial workshop, it is necessary to delve also into more technical aspects, in particular into the relation between craftsmen and merchant-entrepreneurs.

In the more highly developed trades, the artisan did not normally produce for the market. With his limited financial resources, he could not undertake the risks connected with such production. He normally worked on commission. The man who gave him the orders was the "merchant," who often advanced to the craftsman the necessary working capital (raw materials) and sometimes also lent him the fixed capital (looms, for example). The economic dimension of the craftsman's business was thus determined by the economic dimension of the business of the merchant, who gave the work order, provided the raw materials, undertook the distribution of the products, developed the markets, determined the type of product, and exercised quality control over the activities of the worker.

The merchant produced for the market and, as one can still see in Florence and Venice, the mansions of the merchants included in their structure large rooms intended solely for the storage of the raw materials and the finished goods.

The organization of production thus revolved around these two poles, the craftsman's workshop and the warehouse of the merchant. In the first, work was done on order. In the second, production was for the market and the merchants concerned themselves with both the supply of raw materials and the marketing of finished goods.

These are the broad lines of the picture but there were countless gradations and exceptions. In the mining sector, some enterprises assumed modern characteristics in relation to size and organization early in Renaissance time. In the shipbuilding sector, the arsenal of Venice was more the prototype of a modern factory than a survival of ancient artisan yards.

In seventeenth-century Amsterdam the size of the workshops was usually very small, but in 1619 a manufacturer of crystal and fine glass possibly employed eighty workmen.[76] In seventeenth-century England "in all dockyard centers and especially at Portsmouth and in the Medway towns there is a clear picture of substantial concentration of workers laboring under conditions very different from those surrounding the domestic system."[77] At Chatham in 1665, eight hundred workers were assembled in the local dockyard.

These were exceptionally large units of production. Between them and the traditional workshops there was a wide spectrum of intermediate forms such as that represented by the glass and earthenware business of Giovan Pietro *Moyollario* in the small town of Pavia (Italy). We have an inventory of it dated 1546. At the head of the enterprise was Giovan Pietro. One part of the business included the workers (*magistri*), a furnace, and the utensils (*fornax et instrumenta*). Another part included the sales shop and special salesman (*venditores*) who shared their time between attending to customers in the shop and wandering around in the city with special baskets (*cavagnolle longhe a venditoribus*) to sell

---

76. Barbour, *Capitalism in Amsterdam*, p. 68.
77. Coleman, *Naval Dockyards*, p. 160.

the product. The house of the master included the furnace and the shop, but also an office (*studieto*), a room for the workers (*camera magistrorum*) with three beds and two tables, and a room for the salesmen (*camera venditorum*) with one bed. That is, the workers and salesman lived and slept in the factory, which was, at the same time, the house of the master.[78]

History is seldom made of schematic typology: instead, hybrid, transitional forms prevail, such as the productive unit of Giovan Pietro, which was no longer a workshop but not yet a factory.

---

78. Cipolla, *Storia del Lavoro*, pp. 12–13.

CHAPTER THREE

Productivity and Production

Choice and Productivity

The level and structure of effective demand are the outcome of a dual order of choices—a choice between how much to spend and how much not to spend, and a choice of how to spend among an infinite number of possible types of spending. These choices have the value of a vote because in acquiring product A and not acquiring product B, one pushes up the price of product A while depressing the price of product B.

On the supply side, in a market economy economic operators decide what and how much to produce on the basis of price indications. Once they have decided what to produce, they must choose the best possible combination of the factors of production.

The whole economic process is therefore a problem of choices —on the part of the consumers and on the part of the producers. In the last analysis, choices are necessary because resources are limited in respect to wants. Production is the outcome of all the choices made at an individual and at a social level, both on the side of demand and on that of supply.

The Determinants of Production

Most simply, one can say that production is a function of capital, labor, and natural resources. Some twenty-five years ago, economists practically stopped at this point in macroeconomic analysis, but since the 1950s economists have begun to split hairs.

The factors of production—labor, capital, and natural resources —are the *inputs* of a productive system. From their combination emerges *output*—that is, production. Any single mixture of *inputs* can produce different *outputs*—different in quality and/or quantity. Physical productivity is the factor which determines the quantity and quality of the product, given the quantity and quality of the inputs.

Economists have lately discovered that, during the last century, output (as measured by Gross National Product) has consistently grown faster than can be accounted for by the increase of the inputs of labor, capital, and natural resources. This discovery led the economists on a hunt for another factor which would explain the difference between "how much has been effectively produced" and "how much would have been produced if the factors at play had been only labor, capital, and natural resources."

However, "how much would have been produced . . ." represents an arbitrary estimate which depends on a series of hypothetical assumptions made by those who undertake research of this kind. Even if some agreement could be reached about the *size* of the residual (the difference between "how much was produced" and "how much would have been produced . . ."), the *source* of the residual remains in question. The following factors are generally quoted:

    a. increase in division of labor between different economies, through the development of trade
    b. economies of scale
    c. more efficient allocation of factors of production
    d. technological development
    e. better education

Classifications of this type are useful for logical-anatomic analysis, but they are artificial. In reality, there are no separate streams; everything flows together. For example, "technological development" springs from the brains of the people—that is, labor—and is incorporated in the machines and tools that they use—that is, in capital. It seem unlikely in any case, that any list can ever be regarded as complete. In 1947, long before Aukrust, Dennison, Solow, and the other "residualists," Joseph Schumpeter wrote that "only in very rare cases" can economic development be explained in terms of "causal factors such as an increase in population or the supply of capital." An economy or a firm often succeeds in doing "something more," Schumpeter wrote, and this thing, "from the standpoint of the observer who is in full possession of all relevant facts . . . can be understood *ex post* but it can never be understood *ex ante*; that is to say, it cannot be predicted by applying the ordinary rules of inference from the preexisting facts."[1] Schumpeter identified this "something more" as the "creative response of history." Schumpeter had a profound intuition but, wishing to reduce the intangible to the tangible, the very complex to the very simple, made the mistake of reducing the whole to a part—in the specific case, to entrepreneurial activity.

Entrepreneurial activity is a necessary ingredient, but not a sufficient one. It is the human vitality of a whole society which, given the opportunity, comes into play and sets loose the "creative response of history."

When a society shows vitality it does so at all levels, not only the economic, and it succeeds better than other societies which seemingly have the same amounts of resources at their disposal. It is not by chance that, when Italian merchants greatly contributed to European economic development, Dante was writing the *Divine Comedy*, Giotto was introducing innovations in painting, and St. Francis was starting his religious movement. In the seventeenth century, when the Low Countries became the prime movers in international trade while producing great entrepreneurs and merchants such as De Geer or the Tripps, they also produced jurists like Grotius, experimentalists such as Huyghens and Leeuwenhoek, and painters such as Rembrandt. Economists who try to split the product of this human vitality, arbitrarily attributing parts of it to this factor and parts to that, bring to mind a fellow who, confronted with one of Giotto's paintings, would try to measure how much of the beauty of the painting was due to the type of brush used, how much to the chemistry of the colors, and how much to

---

1. Schumpeter, *The Creative Response*, p. 150.

the time taken by the artist. In order to understand what happened in certain societies, it is necessary to understand an atmosphere of collective enthusiasm, of exaltation and of cooperation. When the Cathedral of Chartres was being built "people pulled carts loaded with stones and with wood, and with everything necessary for the construction of the church. . . ."[2] "Silence and humility" dominated, wrote Ugo[3] and another chronicler commented, "He who has not seen these facts will never see the same again." When in 1066 the Abbot Desiderio started the construction of a basilica at the top of Monte Cassino, the first great marble column was borne to the summit on the shoulders of people filled with mystical fervor.[4]

In other cases, political ideology operated; in yet others, enthusiasm for new lands, the spirit of the frontier, the feeling of liberation from restrictions imposed by scarcity of resources or by ossified social and political institutions. When one admires certain exquisite works of art by humble craftsmen of the past, knowing how inadequate the economic incentives were, one cannot but conclude that intangible and nonmeasurable factors, such as the creative urge, love of one's work, pride in one's own ability and self-respect, where they exist, make miracles possible; and that the absence of these factors depresses production both quantitatively and qualitatively. Sociologists, analyzing these facts, have coined numerous and varied terms, such as "motivation," "collective enthusiasm," "cooperation," or, in the opposite sense, "alienation." There is no lack of words; what is lacking is the ability to analyze these things in a functional way, to understand them *ex ante* as causal elements rather than *ex post* as a residual which—whether positive or negative remains largely mysterious.

Medieval and Renaissance Productivity Levels

As we shall see later, in the centuries of the Middle Ages and the Renaissance there was marked technological progress. Undoubtedly, the levels of productivity prevailing in Europe at the end of the sixteenth century were considerably higher than they had been

---

2. *Chronique de Robert de Torigny,* p. 238.
3. *Epistole Hugonis,* pp. 318–19.
4. Leo Di Ostia, *Cronica,* III, p. 26.

six hundred years earlier. But by our standards they were still abysmally low. After all, Europe started her ascent from an extremely primitive stage at the turn of our millennium; and until the seventeenth century, the lack of a systematic criterion of experimentation and research made every innovation dependent upon wearisome and rough empiricism. The productivity of labor was adversely affected by the poverty and scarcity of the equipment and by the low educational levels of the labor force itself. The productivity of capital remained depressed because of the low technological levels and by the limited availability of sources of energy, which were essentially still of animal and vegetable nature.[5] Land was by far the most important available natural resource, and its yield was limited.

All this is interesting but extremely vague. Adjectives such as *low, reduced, limited*, are like mist: they leave too much to the imagination. Let us try to emerge from the fog with a few figures, beginning with agriculture.

A pioneer in the quantitative study of agricultural history is Slicher van Bath. Having gathered data on yield-seed ratios from various European countries, van Bath calculated synthetic averages for wheat, rye, barley, and oats. The results are summarized in Table 3-1.[6]

Figures of this kind must be taken with more than a simple grain of salt.[7] J. Z. Titow, who patiently collected a vast amount of data on agricultural returns in medieval England, has shown that, by

---

5. On the influence of sources of energy upon human history, compare Cipolla, *Economic History of World Population,* chapter 2.
6. For wheat only, in England, yields were:
   1200–49: 2.9
   1250–99: 4.2
   1300–49: 3.9
   1350–99: 5.2
   1400–49: 4.1
   1450–99: 4.9
Slicher van Bath, *Accounts and Diaries*, p. 22. The discrepancy between Slicher van Bath's data in Table 3-2 and those of the same author in Table 3-1 arises from the fact that data in Table 3-1 are averages of the yields of wheat, rye, barley, and oats, while those of Table 3-2 are yields of wheat only.
7. E. LeRoy Ladurie, in a moment of polemical skepticism, has defined such figures above as a *"mirage chiffré* (numerical mirage)." See LeRoy Ladurie, *Paysans de Languedoc,* and Morineau, *Les Faux-semblants.*

Table 3–1

Average Gross Yields per Seed for Wheat, Rye, Barley, and Oats
in Selected European Countries, 1200–1699

Period	England	France	Germany
	(Grains Yielded per Seed Planted)		
1200–1249	3.7		
1250–1499	4.7	4.3	
1500–1699	7.0	6.3	4.2

SOURCE: Slicher van Bath, *Yield Ratios*, p. 15.

extending the sample, one obtains results which differ noticeably
from those of van Bath (Table 3-2). Averages for individual
manors are perhaps more realistic measurements than averages for
whole areas. Table 3-3 shows the highest and lowest yields in terms
of manorial averages on the estates of the Bishopric of Winchester
(England).

Table 3–2

Average Yields per Unit of Seed of Wheat
in England, 1200–1349

	According to Slicher van Bath	According to Titow
1200–49	2.9	3.8
1250–99	4.2	3.8
1300–49	3.9	3.9

SOURCE: Titow, *Winchester Yields*, p. 4.

Table 3–3

Highest and Lowest Yields in Terms of Manorial Averages
on the Estates of the Bishopric of Winchester
(England), 1209–1349

	Yield per unit of seed (grains)		Yield per acre of land (bushels)	
	Max.	Min.	Max.	Min.
Wheat	5.3	2.6	13.8	5.8
Barley	5.6	2.8	27.6	11.0
Oats	3.4	1.8	16.0	7.5

SOURCE: Titow, *Winchester Yields*, p. 14.

Table 3-4 contains analogous data for selected areas of Italy, from the fertile plain of the Po Valley (Imola), to the Tuscan

Table 3–4

Average Yields per Unit of Seed of Wheat in Selected Areas of Italy, 1300–1600

Area	Year	Yield	Area	Year	Yield
Arezzo[1]	1386	5.3		1615–24	5.4
	1387	11		1625–34	5.6
	1390	6.5		1635–44	5.7
Siena[2]	1569–86	6		1645–54	4.9
	1640	5		1655–64	5.5
	1676	5		1665–74	6.6
	1682	5		1675–84	6.0
	1683	4		1685–94	6.6
	1691	5		1695–1704	5.8
	1694	5	Montaldeo[5]	1560	1
				1649	<1
Florence[3]	1611–20	9.4		1650	<1
	1621–30	7.6		1664	3
	1631–40	7.4		1672	2.3
	1641–44	7.5		1673	1.3
	1656–60	6.7		1674	2.9
	1661–70	6.1		1677	1.3
	1671–80	5.9		1678	3.5
	1681–90	6.7		1681	1.8
	1691–1700	6.0		1683	4
				1686	2.5
Imola[4]	1515–24	7.3		1687	3
	1525–34	6.3		1688	3.3
	1535–44	6.7		1692	1.9
	1545–54	6.3		1693	2.5
	1555–64	5.2		1694	2.6
	1565–74	6.0		1695	1
	1585–94	5.6		1697	1
	1595–1604	5.1		1699	2
	1605–14	6.4		1700	1.5

SOURCE: 1. Cherubini, *Proprietà fondiaria*, p. 40. 2. Parenti, *Prezzo e Mercato*, p. 118, and Di Simplicio, *Due Secoli di Produzione*, pp. 789, 813. 3. Conti, *Formazione della Struttura Agraria*, vol. 1, p. 359. 4. Rotelli, *Rendimenti*. 5. Doria, *Uomini e Terre*, p. 29.

farms, to the poor soils of the Ligurian Appennines (Montaldeo).

A superficial glance at the figures in Tables 3-1, 3-2, 3-3, and 3-4 is enough to show that agricultural yields varied greatly from one period to another and from one area to another, owing to differences in soils and climates. But even when one selects the most fertile areas and the most propitious periods one still finds depressingly low yields. In the territory of Bologna (Italy) in the second half of the fifteenth century 2.5 acres of vineyard produced on average fifty gallons of wine per year. Today in the same region the production is seven times greater and of much better quality.[8] The land produced little because seeds were not selected, crop rotation and implements were primitive, pesticides were unknown, and last, but not least, manure, the only known fertilizer, was always in very short supply; on the landed property of the abbey of Staffelsee in the Dark Ages the manure available was barely sufficient for only 0.5 percent of the land, and in the thirteenth century in the regions around Paris, certainly one of the more advanced areas of the time, fields were fertilized with manure only once in every nine years.[9]

The animals, like the land, performed rather poorly, because they were not adequately fed and there was no adequate selective breeding. Cows' milk production was meager. It is estimated that milk production per cow in fourteenth-century England was about 500 liters per year, with a low butterfat content.[10] In the late 1960s in the United States, though state averages varied noticeably, the overall national average was almost 3,000 liters per year, with a high (about 4 percent) butterfat content.

Since the beasts were small, they also produced little meat. Table 3-5 shows data comparing seventeenth-century weights of cattle in the area of Montaldeo (Italy) with weights of cattle of the same age today. The disparity is striking. Data available for northern Europe in the seventeenth century are no more cheerful; even there, where pastures were richer than in Montaldeo, the weight of an ox was only about 400 to 500 pounds, and that of a cow about 220 pounds.[11]

8. Pini, *La Viticultura*, p. 74.
9. Duby, *Guerriers et Paysans*, pp. 37 and 214.
10. Slicher van Bath, *Agrarian History*, pp. 182, 334, 335.
11. Slicher van Bath, pp. 334–35; and Benassar, *L'Alimentation d'une Capitale*, p. 53.

ITALY DURING
THE RENAISSANCE

REP.—Republic
D.—Duchy
M.—Marquisate

H. Faye

Table 3–5

Deadweight of Male Cattle in the District of
Montaldeo (Italy), Seventeenth Century

Year	Age of animal	Weight in Pounds	
		17th Century	20th Century
1684	5 months	72	245
1690	1 year	130	540
1686	2 years	240	880
1675	3 years	320	1100
1675	4 years	480	1310
1675	5 years	560	1550

SOURCE: Doria, *Uomini e Terre*, p. 57.

For the nonagricultural sectors information is much poorer.
However, much of the available data suggests that productivity in
these areas was hardly more encouraging than in the agricultural
sectors. We know, for instance, that at the beginning of the seventeenth century, the situation of the woollen manufacturers in Florence was as follows:[12]

	1604	1627
Number of firms	120	52
Number of looms	1420	782
Number of weavers: males	878	268
females	1457	1315
Total	2335[13]	1583
Number of pieces[14] produced annually	14,000	7998
Value of annual production (in *scudi*)	>900,000	430,000
Percent of wages on value of production	55	

From the above data one derives the following ratios:[15]

---

12. Lastri, *L'Osservatore*, pp. 163–67.
13. According to a document published by Carmona, *Sull'economia Toscana*, p. 43, among the weavers, besides the 878 men and 1457 women, there
were also 358 children.
14. A "piece" was about 35 yards in length.
15. The figures reveal that, during the decline of the industry in the period
1604–1627 (a) the larger firms survived, and (b) among the weavers employment of males diminished far more than employment of females.

	1604	1627
Number of weavers per firm[16]	19	30
Number of looms per firm	12	15
Number of weavers per loom	1.6	2
Number of pieces produced annually per firm	117	154
Number of pieces produced annually per loom	10	10
Number of pieces produced annually per weaver	6	5

Toward the middle of the fifteenth century a weaver normally produced from 12 to 16 inches (23 inches wide) of velvet per day. In Genoa, at the end of the sixteenth century, a weaver produced on average slightly more than 16 inches (28 inches wide) of velvet per day.[17] In Milan at the beginning of the seventeenth century, a weaver produced, on average, little more than half a yard of velvet per work day.[18] In Venice, also at the beginning of the seventeenth century, the average daily production of a silk-loom varied between a minimum of .4 yards for the *gold velvets* to a maximum of 1.5 yards for satin and damask, and with a general average for all the various types of silk materials of about 1.2 yards.[19] In 1621, John Browne claimed that in the foundry at Brenchley (England), he could cast two hundred iron cannon in 200 days; in all likelihood, 200 was the number of working days in a year at the furnace. At about the same time, in Sweden, a foundry produced between 100 and 150 tons a year of cast-iron cannons.[20] In Italy, again in the seventeenth century, most of the paper mills possessed only one or two vats and the average daily production of one vat did not exceed a maximum of 4,500 sheets—in this instance, approximately 110 pounds of paper.[21]

Of course, in a number of sectors noticeable improvements were

---

16. Weavers were not necessarily concentrated in the workshops, that is, in the firms. They usually worked at home, on commission from the "merchants." See above pp. 112–13.
17. Massa, *Un'impresa serica genovese,* pp. 109–10.
18. Archivio di Stato di Milano. Commercio P.A., b. 228.
19. Sella, *Commerci e Industrie a Venezia,* p. 127.
20. Cipolla, *Guns and Sails,* p. 154.
21. Scavia, *Industria della Carta,* p. 10.

achieved in the course of the Middle Ages and the Renaissance. In iron production in England, for instance, between 1350 and 1550, productivity allegedly increased seven or eightfold.[22] Although, in regard to book production, it would be absurd from an esthetic point of view to compare a handwritten book with a printed one, it is not absurd from the point of view of the diffusion of ideas, to compare the number of manuscripts a copyist could prepare in one year with the number of volumes a printer could print within the same period. After Gutenberg's invention, a continuous series of technical improvements progressively increased printers' productivity. The first printers succeeded in printing (in the language of the trade, "pulling") about 300 pages a day. At the end of the century, the average had risen to over a thousand. At the beginning of the eighteenth century, two printers could pull about 250 pages an hour, that is, given the high number of working hours per day in those times, about 3,000 pages a day. In the shipping sector, the ratio of crew to cargo improved even if defense requirements sensibly slowed down this progress. About the year 1400 the crew-to-cargo ratio averaged one sailor for every 5 or 6 tons. By the middle of the sixteenth century, the ratio was one man per 7 or 8 tons. When peace and the decrease of piracy reduced the needs for defense, the ratio dropped to one man per 10 tons. Of course these gains in the crew-to-cargo ratio must also be considered in the light of the notable gains in the speed and safety of ships and in the rate of their utilization.

The main reason for productivity gains was technological progress, and we shall discuss this in chapter 6. The gains which were achieved in western Europe in the course of the Middle Ages and the Renaissance were conspicuous when compared to the productivity levels typical of the traditional agricultural societies. But the highest productivity levels reached by preindustrial Europe still look abysmally low when compared with the productivity levels of the least efficient industrial society.

Once the foregoing facts about preindustrial European productivity have been established, one important qualification remains to be

---

22. Schubert, *British Iron Industry*, p. 345.

made. The data which allow us to measure productivity in the past refer exclusively to quantity and leave aside quality. Now, it is simply not true that all the products of the preindustrial era were of better quality than those of the industrial era. Our maps, even if less artistic, are qualitatively better than those of the preindustrial era, and so are our telescopes, our microscopes, and perhaps also our fruits and vegetables. But if one states simply that the average production of a weaver consisted of so many yards of cloth a day, that the average production of a cabinetmaker consisted of so many pieces of furniture a year, or that of the locksmith so many locks a month, one ignores the fact that some of those pieces of cloth, many of those pieces of furniture and many of those locks were exquisite works of art, infinitely more beautiful and better than analogous, contemporary products. If one could adequately take into consideration the qualitative element, then the productivity of the craftsmen of the preindustrial age would appear astonishingly high.

Positive Production

The combination of the available factors of production results in production. Production as a whole is made up of the most extraordinary variety of goods and services. It includes the apple and the ship, the needle and the plough, the services of a chambermaid and those of a surgeon. To analyze such a complex of different things one must have recourse to broad categories. Oversimplifying an otherwise very complex matter, one may say that in response to the structure of demand as defined above in chapter 1, the greatest part of production in preindustrial Europe took the form of foodstuff, textiles, buildings, and domestic services. By the end of the seventeenth century England was no more a typical preindustrial country. The extraordinary development of her foreign trade had given her economy characteristics of an altogether peculiar nature. Yet about 1688 in England and Wales agriculture still accounted for some 50 percent or more of the national product, the textile manufactures for some 8 percent, building for more than 5 percent, and domestic services for some 10 percent.

Negative Production

When textbooks refer to production they generally mean *positive production*, but human societies, by combining labor, capital, and natural resources, also give rise to *negative production*. There are essentially two types of *negative production*:

    a. voluntary destruction of men and wealth
    b. pollution and the destruction of the environment.

Let us analyze these two types of negative production separately. In all human societies there are perverse people who destroy human lives and wealth, for one reason or another. Some of these persons place their acts in the framework of political ideology or religious doctrine, but in essence they are nevertheless agents of destruction. The assassin is "labor" which by the use of "capital" (say, a gun) brings about a negative production by destroying human capital. The arsonist is "labor" which, in combination with "capital" (often, a match and a gasoline can) destroys physical capital. The bomb-thrower is "labor" which, making use of "capital" (dynamite) destroys human and physical capital at the same time. The mass of those who, with one excuse or another, or without any excuse whatever, destroy instead of build varies from society to society and from period to period. Their potential number is, however, always higher than their actual number because society defends itself, devoting resources—labor and capital—in an effort to control the phenomenon.

At a macroscopic level, the negative production of major significance is war. The first victim of every war is truth. There is no war that has not been cloaked in lies and specious arguments designed to convince people of its timeliness or necessity, in the same way as there is no bomb thrower who does not try to convince himself and others of the need or worth of his criminal action. In the course of human history, men have been massacred and riches have been destroyed continually, and the most absurd and cruel crimes have been committed, always in the name of some remote ideal, at times religious, at times political, at times social and economic. Whatever the ultimate motivation, war remains essentially the organization of "labor" (the military) and "capital" (weaponry) with the avowed intention of destroying the maximum quantity and quality of the labor and capital of the so-called enemy. In the animal world, only man and the ant have developed mass organization for the destruction of their own kind.

We have seen that man's productive capacity is a function of the quality and quantity of labor and capital, of the state of the arts, and of a certain collective psychological climate. The same can be said of man's destructive capacity. Capital, technology, and the organizational skills which assist him in his productive activities also help him in his destructive activities. Consequently, a criminal in an industrial society has a destructive potential infinitely superior to that of his counterpart in a preindustrial society. In the same way, an industrial-era army has a destructive power infinitely greater than that of an army in preindustrial times. A battalion of any contemporary Central American republic would destroy the armies of imperial Rome in the course of a few hours.

These considerations must be borne in mind when one speaks of wars of the past. It has been written that "some thousand fighters, some hundred dead" was the balance sheet of most conflicts of the preindustrial era. Nevertheless, if the wars of bygone days were hardly murderous in a direct sense, they could cause serious destruction of physical capital and could cause high mortality via famine and disease. Passing armies killed or confiscated livestock, burned or confiscated food reserves, and destroyed houses, mills, barns, and other agricultural buildings. Since the armies of the past inflicted the worst damages on rural areas, the societies in question predominantly agricultural were struck at the very foundation of their economic structure. From a purely economic point of view, war was a much greater evil than the plague, and all the more evil as the societies in question suffered from a relative scarcity of capital in relation to existing population. The plague destroyed men, but not capital, and those who survived the onslaught of the disease usually found themselves in more favorable economic conditions. War, instead, hit capital above all, and those who survived found themselves in conditions of the most abject misery. In the chronicles and documents of the time, descriptions abound of countrysides and towns reduced to flaming wastes and of children who, crying and begging for bread, died of hunger in the streets. Phrases such as "the whole area was turned into a desert" or "where men

lived there are now only savage animals" recur frequently in the
documents of those times.[23] They were not rhetorical exaggera-
tions. The historian often can replace the prose with figures and
confirm the dismal, anguished accounts of the time with factual
data. In Cheshire (England) out of a total of 264 villages, 52 were
wholly or partly devastated in the Norman invasion in 1066. By
1070, as a result of William's campaign of 1069–70, this figure had
increased to 162.[24] About the middle of the fourteenth century,
the armies engaged in the Hundred Years' War ravaged, among
innumerable others, the possessions of the Abbey du Lys (near
Melun, France). In 1384, fifteen years after the most recent pil-
lage, the estate was in the following condition:

> forest: 460 *arpents* of which 300 were burned
> vineyards: 32 *arpents* of which 22 were destroyed
> arable land: 190 *arpents* of which 90 were waste.[25]

In Haute-Provence (France) at la Bastide des Jourdans, on the
possessions of the Order of Saint John of Jerusalem, early in the
fifteenth century, of 346 acres of good arable land, 336 had been
laid waste, and a vineyard of 178 acres had been completely
destroyed. Near Grambois, a vineyard of 74 acres was destroyed,
and most of the 618 acres of arable land were abandoned. At Mon-
tegut, "where there used to be a beautiful farm there is now neither
a man, nor a woman, nor a chicken."[26] The effects of the various
campaigns of the Hundred Years' War (1337–1453) on the
volume of trade in northern France are reflected in the dramatic
fluctuations of the revenues from the toll at the *Port de Neuilly,* in
the valley of Paris:[27]

> 1301: 250 livres
> 1340: 200
> 1376: 248
> 1409: 320
> 1425:   36
> 1428:   80
> 1444:   26

---

23. See for instance Sclafert, *Culture en Haute-Provence,* p. 9.
24. Darby, *A New Historical Geography,* p. 61.
25. Fourquin, *Histoire économique,* p. 335.
26. Sclafert, *Culture en Haute-Provence,* p. 88.
27. Forquin, *Histoire économique,* p. 348.

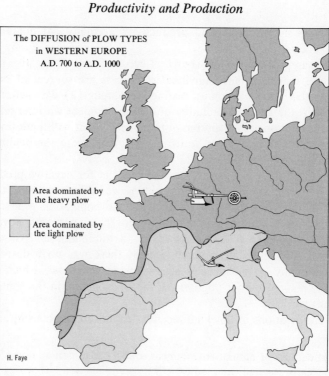

In the territory of Saarburg (Germany) during the Thirty Years' War, (1618–48) the livestock was drastically reduced as shown in Table 3-6. Such destructions were particularly disastrous because

Table 3–6

Livestock Losses in Saarburg Territory (Germany)
During the Thirty Years' War

	Number of Head	
Livestock	Before the War	After the War
Horses	2,651	116
Oxen	5,077	36
Hogs	5,927	10
Sheep	18,267	
Goats	2,749	

SOURCE: Franz, *Dreissigjahrige Krieg*, p. 45.

the available resources and productivity normally did not allow rapid recovery.

Human perversity is the source of certain forms of negative production. Ignorance and individual selfishness are sources of other ills. In this respect one must distinguish among (a) destruction of natural resources, (b) pollution of the environment with the refuse of consumption, (c) pollution of the environment with undesirable by-products of productive activities, (d) damage to the health of those engaged in production.

From all these points of view, the capacity for negative production of European preindustrial societies was infinitely lower than that of industrial societies. First of all, the population was small and per-capita production limited. Moreover, the pervasive poverty compelled people to reduce waste to a minimum, and durable goods were continually re-used. Lastly, there was no widespread use of many products such as petroleum and coal, which are mainly responsible for pollution of the environment in the contemporary world.

Considerations of this kind recently led an economic historian to assert:

Pollution, loss of natural environment, traffic congestion and accidents have clearly resulted from industrialization and modern technology and have no obviously important analogues in preindustrial societies. Moreover, the more work that is done on traditional peasant societies the clearer does it become that these societies have often achieved an almost miraculous accommodation with nature, balancing present use and preservation for the future with a degree of success which the modern economic machine has rarely approached.[28]

Unfortunately, however, things were not so rosy in preindustrial Europe. Undoubtedly the capacity of preindustrial societies for disturbing ecological equilibria was infinitely smaller than that of industrial societies. But, this limitation aside, even preindustrial societies managed to mismanage. The destruction of forests, the frequency of epidemics in overcrowded, unsanitary agglomerations are significant indices of abnormal and deleterious situations created by shortsighted behavior.

---

28. Gould, *Economic Growth*, p. 9.

With regard to the destruction of forests in various districts of Europe, one example that might be mentioned is Central Italy, where the negative production in mountainous and hilly areas meant not only the direct destruction of rich capital, but also the deterioration of the environment in the plains below, facilitating floods and the accumulation of stagnant waters, which became the breeding grounds of malaria.

Within the city walls, one ought not to be dazzled by the presence of magnificent structures, such as the cathedrals, the large *palazzi* of the rich, or the palace of the Commune. As Robert Dallington wrote about Tuscany at the beginning of the seventeenth century:

All is not gold in Italy, though many travellers gazing onelly at the beautie of their cities and the painted surface of their houses, thinke it the only Paradise of Europe.[29]

In order to remain within the shelter of the walls, people crowded into relatively small areas, creating dangerous population densities. Water wells were unsafe. The almost complete lack of hygienic facilities created serious problems in relation to the disposal of human wastes. People used streets and squares as public latrines and threw everything out of the window without care for passersby.

At the middle of the seventeenth century, the mother of the Regent of France wrote:

Paris is a horrible place and ill smelling. The streets are so mephitic that one cannot linger there because of the stench of rotting meat and fish and because of a crowd of people who urinate in the streets.

At the end of the eighteenth century, the English diplomat John Barrow remarked that Peking "enjoys one important advantage, which is rarely found in capitals out of England: no kind of filth or nastiness, creating offensive smells, is thrown out into the streets."[30]

To the refuse of men was added the refuse of animals. Automobile-exhaust fumes are nefarious. The refuse of numerous horses in

---

29. Dallington, *Survey of Tuscany,* pp. 15–16.
30. Barrow, *Travels in China,* p. 67.

the narrow and airless streets of preindustrial towns was, perhaps, not as harmful to health, but no more pleasant.

From the thirteenth century onward, town administrations made numerous provisions to take care of such inconveniences. How effective these measures were is hard to say, but the fact that prohibitions and threats were continually repeated makes one suspect that people took little notice of the ordinances and that penalties were not applied with adequate severity. On occasion the municipal authorities took positive measures. In Siena, toward the end of the thirteenth century, the town administration was concerned with the garbage and filth which accumulated daily in the Piazza del Campo. So it entrusted the cleaning of the square to Giovannino di Ventura, who kept a sow and four piglets in the Piazza to eat the abundant supply of refuse.[31]

Even traffic congestion is not an altogether new problem. By the early sixteenth century, traffic had become so congested in Florence that the town administration issued an ordinance prohibiting the circulation of animals and carts on certain days of the week.

With the sixteenth century, the growing use of coal in England, first for domestic and then for industrial purposes, opened the doors to the Industrial Revolution but also to our pollution problems. By the seventeenth century, that eminent physician, Thomas Sydenham (1624–89), advised living in the country because "the town air is full of vapors." In 1661 John Evelyn wrote his famous pamphlet *Fumifugium* in which, among other things, one reads:

in London we see people walk and converse pursued and haunted by that infernal smoake. The inhabitants breathe nothing but an impure and thick mist, accompanied by a fuliginous and filthy vapour, which renders them obnoxious to a thousand inconveniences, corrupting the lungs and disordering the entire habit of their bodies, so that catharrs, phtisicks, coughs and consumption rage more in that one City than in the whole Earth besides.

Many activities damaged not only the environment, but also the health of the men who participated in them. The founder of industrial medicine was Bernardino Ramazzini of Bologna, profes-

---

31. Garosi, *Siena*, p. 11.

sor of practical medicine at the University of Modena from 1682 to 1700 and at the University of Padua from 1700 to 1714. It is sufficient to open at random his masterpiece *De Morbis Artificum Diatriba* to find innumerable examples of the fatal consequences of many activities:[32]

. . . *miners:* Whatever the nature of the material mined, they always end up with complaints of very serious illnesses, rebellious to all remedies. . . .

gilders: No one ignores the terrible diseases which afflict the gliders, who are engaged in gilding with gold or with copper. Since this operation can be accomplished only by amalgamating gold and mercury, and then by evaporating the mercury with fire, no matter what precautions these workers take, turning their faces away, they cannot avoid inhaling the poisonous vapors, which soon make them prey to dizziness and paralysis and give them a cadaverous aspect. Few grow old in the trade, and if they do not rapidly succumb, they are reduced to such a miserable state as to wish for death. . . .

potters: To varnish the potteries they need burnt and pulverized lead. . . . and after a short while they incur very serious diseases; they begin having a trembling of the hands, then they have attacks of paralysis suffer afflictions of the spleen, are affected by dropsy, become cachetic, lose their teeth, so that it is difficult to see a potter who does not have a leaden and cadaverous countenance. In the Copenhagen medical journal is recalled the case of a potter whose autopsy revealed the right lung, shifted toward the rib cage, almost dried up and consumptive. . . .

glass-makers: More serious are the ills of those who produce colored glass for making bracelets and ornaments and for other uses. To color the crystal they must use calcined borax and antimony, mixed with a certan quantity of gold. . . . It often happens, that some fall to the ground unconscious, or suffocate or with the passing of time, have the mouth, the oesophagus, the trachea covered in sores and end up with ulcerated lungs, to form part of the family of consumptives, as is clear from their autopsies. . . .

More than two centuries were to pass before Dr. Ramazzini's concern for the working conditions of labor became public concern and found expression in preventive legislation.

---

32. Ramazzini, *Le malattie*, pp. 6, 11, 20.

PART 2

TOWARD A DYNAMIC

DESCRIPTION

CHAPTER FOUR

The Urban Revolution: The Communes

The rise of the cities in Europe in the tenth and twelfth centuries marked a turning point in the history of the West—and, for that matter, of the whole world.

Towns had prospered and proliferated in the Greco-Roman world, but the decline of the Empire brought with it their ruin. In a letter dated A.D., 381 Ambrose, bishop of Milan, described the towns of central Italy as *"semirutarum urbium cadavera"*—remains of half-ruined cities. If some urban centers survived, their role was simply that of headquarters of religious and/or military administrations. In the primitive world of the Dark Ages, the city was an anachronism.

The areas of Europe which had been part of the Roman Empire most certainly experienced a drastic process of economic decadence from the beginning of the fifth century of our era onward. Outside the Empire, in the northern part of Europe, there had been nothing in the way of towns and little in the way of industry and commerce; after the fall of the Empire, the north slowly but definitely improved its relative position, partly because of more active contacts with the south. Consequently, the startling contrast which had sharply divided the north and the south in Roman times diminished. On the other hand, the Muslim invasion loosened the ties which had linked southern Europe with North Africa and the Near East. In Roman times, there had been two separate worlds: the

Mediterranean world and the northern world. In the seventh century, the Mediterranean world was split in two, and the impoverished European half tied itself more closely to the northern part of the subcontinent. Under the aegis of a common religious creed, Europe emerged in embryo.

It was a poor and primitive Europe, a Europe made up of numberless rural microcosms—the manors, largely self-sufficient, whose autarchy was in part the consequence of the decline of trade and to a large extent its cause as well. Society was dominated by a spirit of resignation, suspicion, and fear toward the outside world. People withdrew into the economic isolation of the manors as they sought spiritual isolation in the monasteries and social and political isolation in the feudal arrangement.

The arts, education, trade, production, and the division of labor were reduced to a minimal level. The use of money almost completely disappeared. The population was small, production meager, and poverty extreme. The social structures were primitive. There were those who prayed, those who fought, and those who labored. The prevailing values reflected a brutal and superstitious society —fighting and praying were the only respectable activities, and those who fought did it mostly for robbing, and those who prayed did it superstitiously. Those who labored were regarded as despicable serfs. The forests encroached, inhabited by wild animals and also, according to the popular imagination, by gnomes, fairies, witches, and goblins. In this depressed and depressing world, the rise of cities between the tenth and thirteenth centuries represented a new element which changed the course of history.

Years ago, the Belgian historian Henri Pirenne formulated a general theory to explain the rise of cities in the various parts of Europe.[1] Pirenne attempted to reduce extremely different experiences to a single model, and no one can deny that the model is both ingenious and thought provoking. Yet Pirenne failed, and he did so essentially because he stressed the morphology of the phenomenon instead of aiming at its intimate nature. The theory of the *portus*, which spread out, absorbed the original fortified feudal nucleus, and eventually gave birth to the new urban unit is valid for

---

1. Pirenne, *Medieval Cities.*

the Low Countries, northern France, and parts of England, but finds no correspondence in the factual reality of other parts of western Europe.

According to Edith Ennen, three areas must be distinguished in western Europe: (a) Italy, Spain, and southern France, in which the towns, however impoverished, continued to exist through the Dark Ages so that there was an essential continuity in the existence of towns; (b) England, Northern France, the Low Countries, Switzerland, the Rhinelands, Southern Germany, and Austria, all regions in which Roman urban life substantially disappeared with the fall of the Empire but in which, nevertheless, medieval towns show the imprint of Roman activity; and (c) Northern Germany and Scandinavia, in which the Roman urban tradition had no significance whatsoever.[2]

The disadvantage of subdivisions of this kind is that they can be endlessly multiplied. In southern Europe, which Ennen considered a unit, distinctions could be made between northern and southern Italy, and northern and southern France. Significant differences can easily be identified between northern Italy and Spain: in northern Italy, the lesser nobility played an essential part in the urban movement;[3] in Spain, the urban movement cannot be understood if separated from the movement of *Reconquista* and the Arab tradition.

All these differences cannot, however, obliterate the essential unity of a sociocultural and economic movement which had common roots, whether it took the form of a return to life of an ancient Roman town or of the formation of a new town around a fort, a monastery, or an imperial palace. Unity cannot be sought in forms which are bound to vary from place to place. Unity must be sought in the essence of the evolution.

At the root of urban growth was a massive migratory movement. Towns grew because their populations grew. But the urban population did not grow naturally. Fertility in urban centers was never appreciably higher than mortality: urban population grew because of an influx of people from the rural areas.

---

2. Ennen, *Different Types,* pp. 399–411.
3. Sestan, *Città comunale italiana,* pp. 75–95.

People migrate for two sets of reasons, not necessarily alternative: reasons of repulsion and reasons of attraction (the *push* and *pull* of Anglo-Saxon demographers). Between the tenth and thirteenth centuries, the economic trend was upward in rural Europe, partly because of technological innovations, partly because of investments, and partly because of reorganization of property. But although economic conditions were generally improving, life remained essentially unpleasant for the mass of the people. The serfs saw no means of escaping serfdom, and the lesser nobility could hardly see a way of breaking the predominance of the establishment. It was at this point that the town came into play as an element of innovation, as a place to seek one's fortune. The town was to the people of Europe from the eleventh to the thirteenth centuries what America was to Europeans in the nineteenth century. The town was the "frontier," a new and dynamic world where people felt they could break their ties with an unpleasant past, where people hoped they would find opportunities for economic and social success, where sclerotic traditional institutions and discriminations no longer counted, and where there would be ample reward for initiative, daring, and industriousness. "*Stadtluft machts frei,*" ("The air of the city makes one free") it was said in German towns. What counted was not only the legal fact that the serf, having escaped from the countryside, found himself free in the towns, but that the whole social atmosphere in the towns was open to ambition and talent, whether the town-dweller was a member of the lesser feudal nobility, or a merchant, or a craftsman.

Towns were filled with people who had left behind the rural and feudal world without regret, for a new, different world. The urban society grew and developed in sharp contrast to the surrounding countryside. The walls of the town had a practical purpose but also a symbolic significance; they represented the boundary between two cultures in conflict. It was this conflict which gave to the medieval city its unmistakable character and made of the urban movement of the eleventh to thirteenth centuries the turning point of world history.

Towns had existed in ancient Egypt, as in the classical world of Greece and Rome. In the Middle Ages, towns existed in China as well as in the Byzantine Empire. But the cities of Medieval and Renaissance Europe had something essentially different from the towns of other areas and other times. In the towns of the classical world, as in the towns of China and the Byzantine Empire, the merchants, the professionals, and the craftsmen never acquired a socially prominent position. Even when they acquired wealth, they acquiesced in an inferior social position. The rural ideals of the upper classes permeated the whole society; and as the landed gentry dominated both the countryside and the towns, socially as well as politically and culturally, powerful elements of cohesion obliterated the differences between the urban and the rural worlds. The town was not an organism in itself but rather an organ within the broader context of an urban-rural continuum.

In medieval Europe, by contrast the town came to represent a specialized entity. The medieval city was not an organ of a larger organism, but an organism in itself, proudly autonomous and clearly separated from the surrounding countryside. In a physical sense, the city was separated from the countryside by the walls, the moat, and the gates. Juridically, it was another world. When a person passed through the gates of a city, he was subject to different laws, as when we today cross the border from one country to another. Culturally the contrast was no less violent than economically. The merchants, the professionals, the craftsmen who lived in the towns did not recognize the control of the rural world or its cultural values; on the contrary, they evolved their own culture and their own values. The emergence of the European towns in the eleventh to thirteenth centuries was not the appendage of a regional evolution. It was rather the expression of a cultural and social revolution which found its base of operations in the towns. The champions of the rural-feudal establishment were well aware of this, and they did not hide their indignation. *"Communio-novum ac pessimum nomen,"* commented Guibert of Nogent. And Otto of Frisingen, uncle of Frederic Barbarossa, wrote:[4]

In the Italian communes they do not disdain to grant the girdle of knighthood or honorable positions to young people of inferior station, and even to workers of the vile mechanical arts, whom other peoples bar like the plague from the more respectable and honorable circles.

---

4. *Gesta Federici*, 2, 12, RRGGSS 54.

The political and social triumph of the urban middle class, and of its peculiar sets of values, had revolutionary consequences in economics. The new set of values determined new kinds of wants, and the economic success of the new classes gave these wants the support of considerable purchasing power. The fact that the history of the medieval city proved so different in its ultimate effects from the history of the Greek *polis*, the Roman *urbs*, or the Chinese city, depended in large part on the structure of effective demand.

Surrounded by a hostile world, the people of the town intuitively developed feelings for union and cooperation. The men of the frontier have to unite. In the feudal world, a typically vertical arrangement had prevailed, where relations between men were dictated by the concepts of fief and service; investiture and homage; lord, vassal, and serf. In the cities, a horizontal arrangement emerged, characterized by cooperation among equals. The *gild*; the *confraternity*; the *university*; and above all of them, that gild of gilds, that university of the citizens, the *Commune* were the institutions created by the new outlook and which reflected the new ideals.

Thus, the city, whether developing from a *portus* beside a feudal castle or resurging over the foundations of a Roman town, was essentially a new phenomenon: It was the core of a new society which evolved new social structures, rediscovered the state, developed a new culture and a new economy. Where the sourrounding feudal world was too powerful for the town's forces, as in Germany the city remained on the defensive, sheltered behind the protection afforded by its walls, its wealth, and its pride in what it was able to express artistically as well as economically. Where the town developed to the point of being able to alter the existing equilibrium with the surrounding feudal world, as in Italy, the town moved to the conquest of the surrounding area. The events that followed bore the mark of the urban-versus-rural cultural dichotomy. The town did not create or intend to create a regional body, but asserted instead the right of conquest. The relationship between towns and their conquered territories in the thirteenth and fourteenth centuries reminds one more of the relationship between the European states and their colonies in the nineteenth century than of the relationship between a provincial capital and its province in our contemporary society.

With the appearance of the medieval city and the emergence of the urban bourgeoisie, a new Europe was born. Every sector of social and economic life was transformed. Sets of values, personal conditions and relations, types of administration, education, production, and exchange, all underwent drastic transformation.

The urban revolution of the eleventh and twelfth centuries was the prelude to, and created the prerequisites for, the Industrial Revolution of the nineteenth century.

CHAPTER FIVE

Population:
Trends and Plagues

Broadly speaking one can say that at the beginning of the new millennium Europe's population was thinly scattered across the continent: around the year A.D. 1000 there were probably no more than 30 to 35 million people in the whole of Europe (Russia and the Balkans included). From the tenth century until the beginning of the fourteenth century the population grew slowly but continuously.[1] During that period the populations of France, Germany, and the British Isles possibly tripled, while the population of Italy possibly doubled. By the 1330s and 1340s the total population of Europe must have been at least 80 million. Then in 1348 came the Black Death, which wiped out some 25 million in a matter of about two years. Wars, famines, and above all dreadful epidemics kept striking unremittingly during the following 150 years or so, and the population recovery was painfully slowed down. At the end of the fifteenth century the total population of Europe was still around the 80 million mark. The sixteenth century witnessed a substantial growth, and by the beginning of the 17th century Europe must have counted about 105 million people. The wars and epidemics of the seventeenth century practically stabilized the population at that level, and around 1700 Europe must have

---

1. The evidence for this growth is discussed in Genicot, *On the Evidence of Growth of Population*, pp. 14–23.

numbered around 115 million inhabitants. This is the very sketchy outline of the story of population totals in preindustrial Europe (see Tables 1-1 above).

Some of the major characteristics of the population in question have already been discussed, but it may be useful to recall at least two points. First, through its ups and downs the population of preindustrial Europe was always young—in other words, the age structure constantly showed a marked prevalence of the younger age groups. Secondly, notwithstanding the growth of the tenth to thirteenth centuries and of the sixteenth century, the population of Europe remained relatively small. At the limit of their demographic expansion the largest countries ranged from ten to eighteen million people (see Table 1-1) and very few metropolises ever reached the 100,000 mark. (See Table A-1 in the Appendix). If one were to give an extremely concise and sweeping explanation for these characteristics, one could say that fundamentally the European population remained young because of high fertility and small because of high mortality. Both points deserve further comment.

It is fashionable nowadays in scholarly circles to point to several cultural factors which favored, in one way or the other, the limitation of fertility in preindustrial Europe. It is commonly agreed, for instance, that western Europe was characterized by a marriage pattern unique or almost unique in the world. The distinctive marks of the European patterns were (a) a high proportion of people never married and (b) an advanced age at marriage.[2] In regard to point (a) one has to keep in mind the misogynist tradition of the Church. In preindustrial Europe, celibacy, far from being condemned as it was in the oriental societies,[3] was generally praised. For priests, monks, and nuns, celibacy actually became a rule of life. Until modern times in Europe intellectualism was inconceiv-

---

2. Hajnal, *European Marriage Patterns,* pp. 101–140.
3. The Italian missionary, Father Matteo Ricci, reported from China in the sixteenth century that "celibacy is not approved of and poligamy is permitted" (Gallagher, *The Journals,* p. 97). At the end of the eighteenth century, the Englishman John Barrow reported from China, "Public opinion considers celibacy as disgraceful and a sort of infamy is attached to a man who continues unmarried beyond a certain time of life." (Barrow, *Travels,* pp. 398–99).

able except in a state of celibacy. The tragedy of Abélard was rooted in this social convention. Until the end of the Middle Ages, the school of medicine at Paris did not allow married men to graduate. At Oxford and Cambridge until the end of the nineteenth century, married men were not admitted among the fellows of the colleges.

Marriage was also avoided for economic reasons—to preserve a family estate from too many subdivisions or to avoid the cost of a household. Fynes Moryson, the keen and witty English traveler who visited the continent between the end of the sixteenth century and the beginning of the seventeenth, observed that:[4]

In Italy marryage is indeed a yoke, and that not easy one but so grevious as brethren nowhere better agreeing yet contend among themselves to be free from marryage and he that of free will or by persuasion will take a wife to continue their posterity, shall be sure to have his wife and her honour as much respected by the rest, besyde their liberall contribution to mantayne her, so as themselves may be free to take the pleasure of women at large. By which liberty they live more happily than other nations. For in those frugall commonwealths the unmarryed live at a small rate of expenses and they make small conscience of fornication, esteemed a small sinne and easily remitted by Confessors. . . .

Still, even in Italy the majority of people got married. When people married, however, they tended to marry at a relatively advanced age. Custom in this regard varied from class to class and from country to country. Moryson reported that in Germany "women are seldom marryed till they be twenty-fyve years old."[5] The tone of his remark would make one believe that in England girls married at a younger age. In the village of Colyton (England), however, over the period 1560–1646, the age at first marriage for women was twenty-seven.[6] In any case, in medieval and Renaissance Europe girls never married as early as girls in ancient Rome or in Asian societies, and obviously the higher the age of a woman at marriage, the lower are her probabilities of legitimate fertility over time. Table 5-1 shows data on the percentage of people who never married and the age at first marriage of those who did among

---

4. Moryson, *Itinerary*, pp. 156 and 409.
5. Moryson, *Itinerary*, p. 296.
6. Wrigley, *Population and History*, pp. 86–7.

Table 5–1
Marriage Patterns in Selected Social
Groups in Preindustrial Europe

English Nobility

Born in the Period	Percentage Unmarried at 45	
	M	F
1330–1479	9	7
1480–1679	19	6
1680–1729	30	17

Geneva Bourgeoisie

Born in the Period	Percentage Unmarried among the Deceased of Over 50		Average Age at First Marriage	
	M	F	M	F
1550–99	9	2	27.2	21.4
1600–49	15	7	29.1	24.6
1650–99	15	26	32.6	25.7

Milanese Nobility

Born in the Period	Percentage Unmarried among the Deceased of Over 50		Average Age at First Marriage	
	M	F	M	F
1600–49	49	75	30.8	19.6
1650–99	56	49	30.9	19.7
1700–49	51	35	33.4	21.2

SOURCES: Hollingsworth, *British Ducal Families*, p. 364; Henry, *Familles Genevoises,* pp. 52–55; Zanetti, *Patriziato Milanese,* pp. 84–88.

the upper classes in England, Geneva, and Milan in the fourteenth to eighteenth centuries.

As has been said, there is no doubt that "in preindustrial Europe the chief means of social control over fertility was by prescribing the circumstances in which marriage was to be permitted." On the other hand, it would be a mistake to suppose that once marriage had taken place fertility was governed solely by physiological and nutritional factors.[7] Certain customary practices had some effect on fertility after marriage had taken place. For parts of France in the seventeenth century, it has been suggested that a long suckling period was a practice followed to cause prolonged amenor-

---

7. Wrigley, *Population and History*, p. 119.

rhea among married women and thus increase the interval between births. E. A. Wrigley maintains that "there is strong statistical evidence pointing to the existence of family limitation in (the little village of) Colyton (England) during the late 17th century and *coitus interruptus* appears more likely to have been used than any other method."[8]

All this is interesting and undoubtedly correct but it appears possible that in reaction to the previous belief in unrestrained fertility, researchers now tend to exaggerate the ultimate results of the facts and circumstances mentioned above. It is true that a number of Europeans did not marry, but those who did so made up for the others. Average age at marriage might have been delayed, but the number of children born to any married woman was still generally very high. Long periods of suckling might have been resorted to, but the frequency of infant mortality reduced the efficacy of this method. The fact of the matter is that whenever we are able to calculate some rough figures we often find crude birth rates above 35 per thousand and almost never find rates below 30 per thousand. (see Tables A-2 and A-4 in Appendix). Fertility could have been higher—but this fact does not mean that it was low. The high fertility largely explains the youthful age structure of the population. It also accounts for the survival of the European population in the presence of a very high mortality.

As we have seen, one must distinguish between normal and catastrophic mortality. The major components of *normal* mortality were infant and adolescent mortalities.[9] Although our information is fragmentary, there is reason to believe that in every part of Europe before the Industrial Revolution, for every 1,000 births, from 150 to 350 died before reaching one year of age, and another 100 to 200 died before reaching ten (see Table A-3 in Appendix).

---

8. Wrigley, *Population and History*, p. 124.
9. Infant mortality relates infant deaths (number of children dying at less than one year of age) to live births in the same year. The infant mortality rate is thus obtained by dividing the number of deaths of infants during a calendar year by the number of live births in the same period and by multiplying the result by 1000. Adolescent mortality relates the number of deaths of children one to nine years old during a calendar year to the population of the same age group.

The high mortality of the young was essentially an index of the poverty of the population and of the difficult conditions in which people lived. It was also a selective element which left alive only the strongest. However, even those who survived the hard apprenticeship of the first ten years did not have an easy life for the rest of their days.

The fundamental characteristic of preindustrial societies was their extreme vulnerability to calamities of all sorts. The most common invocation in preindustrial Europe was *"a bello, fame, et peste libera nos Domine,"* (God deliver us from war, famine, and plague). War, famine and epidemics incessantly caused dramatic peaks of *catastrophic* mortality.

Of the three calamities, war was perhaps the least murderous directly. People spoke of it with terror because the atrocities and infamies of the soldier caught the imagination of all. But war was disastrous largely because of its indirect consequences; that is, to the extent that it provoked greater frequency or intensity of the other two evils, namely, famines and epidemics. Famine could easily result from the destruction and the pillaging of the harvests, herds, and agricultural implements which the passing armies indulged in. Epidemics were another common by-product of wars. The sanitary and hygenic conditions of medieval and Renaissance armies were absolutely appalling. As late as the early eighteenth century Ramazzini wrote that "in the summer there is a stench so strong from the camps that no cavern of hell could be more fetid."[10] Armies were more efficient in disseminating epidemics than in waging wars and, as Hans Zinsser observed, "Epidemics often determined victory or defeat before the generals knew where to place the headquarters' mess."

It is difficult for those living in the industrialized countries of the 20th century to imagine hunger and famine. People literally died of hunger, and it was not unusual to find men dead at the roadside, their mouths full of grass and their teeth sunk in the earth.

Apart from contributing directly to the increase in mortality,

10. Ramazzini, *Malattie dei Lavoratori,* Chapter XL, p. 109.

famines also contributed indirectly by encouraging the outbreak of epidemics. The abbot Segni noted at the beginning of the seventeenth century that in a time of famine "most of the poor people" were attacked by illnesses "born from grasses and from poor foods," and the good abbot explained that thus, "since the stomach cannot cook such food, nor can the liver reduce it to blood, the natural order of the body is ruined and wind, or indeed, water develops in the belly and in the legs, the skin takes on a yellow color, and people die."[11]

An anonymous chronicler of Busto Arsizio (Lombardy) noted that during the famine of 1629 the people were reduced to eating things from which "there followed most atrocious and incurable diseases, which neither physicians nor surgeons were able to identify and which lasted for 6, 8, 10, or 12 months, and a great multitude of people died of them and the population of our community was reduced from eight thousand to three thousand."[12]

Epidemics were the element which contributed most to the frequency and the intensity of catastrophic mortality.[13] Historians always mention the Black Death but generally leave the readers with the impression that no serious epidemics hit Europe before 1348 or afterwards. The fact of the matter is that to the end of the seventeenth century not a year passed without various cities or entire regions of Europe suffering badly from some epidemic. The most frequent epidemics were those of typhoid fever, typhus, dysentery, plague, and influenza with its lethal bronchial-pulmonary complications. Of all the infectious diseases, plague was by far the most tragic and lethal.

Though wars, famines, and epidemics were not absent in the 11th, 12th and 13th centuries, low population densities limited the devastating effects of epidemics. However, as the population grew and concentrated in the towns, the terms of the problem were significantly modified.

---

11. Segni, *Trattato*, p. 55.
12. Johnsson, *Storia della peste di Busto Arsizio,* p. 15.
13. As has been said, "War and famine have probably always taken their toll of human life more through the intermediary of the microbe than by starvation and the sword" (Burnett White, *Natural History of Infectious Disease*, p. 12).

The population growth that took place between 1000 and 1348 did not have the intensity of the demographic developments of the nineteenth and twentieth centuries, but even relatively low growth rates, if protracted over centuries, clearly result in explosive situations. At the beginning of the fourteenth century, several areas of Europe were overpopulated in relation to the prevailing technological and productive levels. By 1339 the barren mountains of Oisans (France) achieved a population density comparable to that reached again in 1911.[14] In Tuscany, the population of the territory of San Gimignano reached, in 1332, a density higher than in 1951. The population density of the territory of Volterra in the 1330s was as high as it was in 1931.[15] To make things worse, people crowded into towns where water-wells were unsafe; sanitary arrangements were nonexistent; rats, fleas, and lice were overabundant. The garbage and the wastes of men and animals piled up in heaps in the roads and the yards, soap was a scarce commodity, personal hygiene was seldom practiced, although it was preached by the physicians. The imbalance between demographic development on the one hand and the lack of medical and public-health development on the other reached a critical point at the beginning of the fourteenth century. One may, in fact, say that at that point a state of ecological disequilibrium existed in the form of an imbalance between population densities, especially in the towns, and public-health conditions. What happened next in Europe is a good example of how, once human action has created dangerous imbalances, equilibrium is eventually restored and demonstrates that famines are not the only equilibrating device in the hands of nature.

Between 1348 and 1351, a frightening epidemic of plague killed about 25 million people out of a total European population of about 80 million. But the tragedy did not end there. With the epidemic of 1348–51, the plague established itself in Europe in a more or less endemic form, and from then onward, for about three centuries, horrible epidemics flared up from time to time on a local or regional or national scale.

---

14. Allix, *L'Oisans*, p. 32.
15. Fiumi, *La Popolazione del Territorio Volterrano-Sangimignanese*, p. 283.

In England between 1351 and 1485, plague epidemics prevailed in thirty different years. In eight of these years—1382, 1426, 1433, 1437, 1445, 1449, 1454 and 1467—the plague seems to have been limited to London. Years of epidemics on a national scale were 1361–1362, 1369, 1375, 1390, 1400, 1407, 1413, 1434, 1439, 1464, 1471 and 1479.[16] Between 1543 and 1593 England suffered from plague in twenty-six years. In Venice between 1348 and 1630 plague broke out in epidemic form in twenty-one years. Between 1348 and 1596 Paris was hit by plague epidemics in twenty-two years. Between 1457 and 1590 Barcelona suffered from plague epidemics in seventeen years.[17]

To estimate accurately the number of casualties of plague epidemics is a difficult proposition. In his famous *Natural and Political Observations upon the Bills of Mortality*, first published in 1662, John Graunt remarked "that the knowledge even of the numbers which dye of the plague is not sufficiently deduced from the mere report of the searchers" and that it was necessary to make "corrections upon the perhaps ignorant and careless searchers reports."[18] Sir William Petty, who liked to indulge in all kinds of exercises of "political arithmetic," wrote in 1667 that

London within ye bills* hath 696 thousand people in 108 thousand houses. In pestilential yeares, which are one in twenty, there dye one sixth of ye people of ye plague and one fifth of all diseases. The people which ye next plague of London will sweep away will be probably 120 thousand, which at £7 per head is a losse of 8,400 thousand.[19]

More accurate estimates are available for Italian towns, and Table 5-2 shows the ravages caused by the epidemic of 1630.

One can hardly overestimate the importance of epidemics as a regulatory device in the long term movements of preindustrial populations. Fertility was generally higher than normal mortality. Under those conditions population grew. Soon, however, a peak of

---

16. Bean, *Plague*, pp. 423–27. Compare also Shrewsbury, *Bubonic Plague*, Chapter 5.
17. For England see Shrewsbury, *Bubonic Plague*, p. 231; for Venice see Carbone, *Provveditori*, p. 8; for Paris see Franklin, *Vie privée*, vol. 14, pp. 18–75; for Barcelona see Nadal, *Poblacion española*, p. 596.
18. Hull, *The Economic Writings*, vol. 2, p. 347.
19. Hull, *The Economic Writings*, vol. 1, p. 109.

Table 5–2

Mortality in Selected Italian Cities During
the Plague Epidemic of 1630–31

City	Population before Epidemic	No. of Deaths
Bergamo	25,000	10,000
Bologna	62,000	15,000
Brescia	24,000	11,000
Como	12,000	5,000
Cremona	37,000	17,000
Mantua	32,000	25,000
Milan	130,000	65,000
Padua	32,000	18,000
Parma	30,000	15,000
Verona	54,000	31,000
Venice	140,000	46,000

catastrophic mortality would cancel out the previous demographic
gains and the cycle would start all over again. In this way the frequency and severity of the peaks of catastrophic mortality determined the population trend. Turbulent political and social conditions naturally favor the destructive action of microbes and this
explains why the period of the Hundred Years' War (1337–1453)
and that of the Thirty Years' War (1618–48) were also periods of
demographic stagnation and decline.

Clearly, there was a link between the frequency of epidemics on
the one hand and density of population and degree of urbanization
on the other. The people living in the countryside neither were
cleaner nor enjoyed better conditions than the town-dwellers. But
population densities in the villages were not as high as in the cities.
Moreover, because of commercial intercourse, cities were much
more exposed to contagion from without. The result was that epidemics hit the cities more frequently than the countryside. On the
other hand, fertility was probably lower in the cities than in the
country.

The general impression is that the cities of preindustrial Europe
had a negative demographic balance and that they survived only
because of a continual inflow of people from the countryside. One

of the first, if not the first scholar to make this point on the basis of statistical observation was John Graunt, who wrote in 1662:

In the said Bills of London there are far more burials than christenings. This is plain, depending only upon arithmetical computation for in forty years, from the year 1603 to the year 1644, exclusive of both years, there have been set down 363,935 burials and but 330,747 christenings within the 97, 16 and 10 out parishes; those of Westminster, Lambeth, Newington, Redriff, Stepney, Hackney and Islington not being included. From this single observation it will follow that London should have decreased in its people; the contrary whereof we see by its daily increase of buildings upon new foundations, and by the turning of great palacious houses into small tenements. It is therefore certain that London is supplied with people from out the country, whereby not only to supply the overplus differences of burials above-mentioned, but likewise to increase its inhabitants according to the said increase of housing.[20]

In spite of their vitality in the economic, political, artistic, and cultural spheres, from a purely biological point of view the cities of preindustrial Europe were large graveyards.

This fact set a limit to the process of urbanization. If more people died than were born in the cities, obviously the more the percentage of urban population grew, the stronger was the brake on the growth of the total population.[21] According to Father Mols, eighteenth century Holland, for instance, was "too much urbanized" and "the natural reserve" of the country with its positive demographic balance was not enough to fill the gaps in the negative balance of the urban population.

The history of the population of preindustrial Europe must end on a mysterious note. As M. Goubert wrote of the eighteenth century, "un monde démographique semble défunt" (certain demographic patterns died out). The great peaks of mortality due to epidemics progressively subsided. Not that epidemics had become a thing of the past: for instance, there were epidemics of influenza in London in 1685 and in 1782 and an epidemic of measles in 1670. The late 1730s and 1740s saw pandemics of influenza and typhus

---

20. Hull, *The Economic Writings,* vol. 2, pp. 369–70.
21. Mols, *Introduction*, vol. 2, p. 334.

striking at most countries in Europe. However, while death rates greatly increased in such periods, momentarily exceeding birth rates, mortality no longer assumed catastrophic proportions. Even death rates of 69 and 112 per thousand, such as were recorded in Norway and the Swedish province of Värmland respectively in 1742, are still a far cry from those experienced by some regions of Europe in previous centuries.[22] The most dramatic aspect of the phenomenon was the disappearance of plague. The great killer vanished as mysteriously as it had appeared in pandemic form three centuries earlier. There were no more plague epidemics in Italy after 1657, in England and France after the 1660s, or in Austria and Germany after the 1670s. All kinds of ingenious hypotheses have been constructed to explain this mysterous disappearance— from the alleged improvements in building, to better ways of burying corpses, to the story of the invasion of the gray rat and the disappearance of the black rat. But all hypotheses have proven untenable.

Medieval and Renaissance Europe did not follow the destiny of Asia. European development was not halted by a suffocating population pressure. The praise for this restraint, however, does not go so much to the rationality of the Europeans (i.e., to low fertility) as to the blind action of microbes (i.e., to high mortality). With the end of the seventeenth century the deadliest among the microbes stopped its nefarious activities; and this event again was not man's achievement, but the result of an obscure ecological revolution. Europe then entered the initial stage of the so-called demographic revolution. The fact, however, that the ensuing demographic growth was not arrested soon by the inexorable operation of Malthusian forces was attributable to the technological and economic achievements of western Europe.

---

22. Helleiner, *The Vital Revolution,* p. 85.

CHAPTER SIX

Technology

Technological Developments: 1000–1700

In the history of technology, it is often stated that, after a series of startling innovations, a phase of long secular stagnation took place in the Western world during classical times:

Around 2500 B.C. technological advance ground almost to a stop and during the next three thousand years rather little progress took place. ... When compared with the revolution that preceded them, these three-millennia constitute a technological stagnation.[23]

The Greco-Roman world, and especially the Roman world, while highly creative in other fields of human activity, remained, according to this point of view, strangely inert in the technological field.[24] Of Rome, the classic example of the water mill and the anecdote about Vespasian are always quoted. The Romans were aware of the water mill, but they built relatively few of them and continued to make far wider use of mills employing animal or human power.[25] Of Vespasian, it is said that when offered the plans of machines which would have saved on human labor, the emperor, though awarding a prize to the inventor, prohibited the

---

23. Lilley, *Technological Progress*, p. 188. See also Gould, *Economic Growth*, pp. 327 ff.
24. Compare Finley, *Technical Innovation*, pp. 29–45; Kiechle, *Probleme der Stagnation;* and Pleket, *Technology and Society*, pp. 1–24.
25. On the windmills of antiquity, compare Moritz, *Grain-mills*.

construction of the machines "to allow the populace to make their living."[26]

Starting from observations of this kind, historians have undertaken research into the possible reasons for the "failure" of the classical world, some pointing out the overabundance of slave labor, others the type of culture and the prevailing sets of values. Possibly, the Greek and Roman technological "failure" has been exaggerated. All too often we tend to identify technology with mechanics, because our civilization is essentially mechanical. Political and administrative organization, military organization, architecture and road construction, even artistic products such as frescoes, bear the marks of technology, and in all these fields the Greeks and Romans were not failures.

It remains true, however, that with the Dark Ages began a period in which technological innovations succeeded each other at an accelerated rate, and with an increasing emphasis on the mechanical aspects. As Samuel Lilley wrote, "It was early in the Middle Ages that men began to find a way out of the [technological] impasse."[27] Lynn White put it this way:

The millennial span of the Middle Ages has the interest of being the period during which Europe built up the self-confidence and the technical competence which, after 1500, enabled it to invade the rest of the world, conquering, looting, trading and colonizing.[28]

Undeniably "modern technology is the extrapolation of that of the Western Middle Ages, not merely in detail but also in the spirit that infuses it."[29]

A schematic inventory of the main technological developments of the West from the sixth to the eleventh century should include:

    a. from the sixth century: diffusion of the water mill
    b. from the seventh century: diffusion, in northern Europe, of the heavy plough

---

26. The episode is recounted by Suetonius in Chapter 18 of his *Life of Vespasian.*
27. Lilley, *Technological Progress*, p. 188.
28. White, *The Expansion of Technology*, p. 143.
29. White, *Cultural Climates*, p. 172.

   c. from the eighth century: diffusion of the three-field system
   d. from the ninth century: diffusion of the horseshoe; diffusion of
      a new method of harnessing draught animals

In relation to these developments three points should be made: First, the innovations just listed were not, properly speaking, inventions. The water mill, as previously noted, was known to the Romans. The heavy plough had a Slavic origin.[30] The horseshoe seems to have been known to the Celts before the Roman conquests.[31] The new methods for harnessing horses originated in distant China.[32] What the Europeans showed from the sixth to the eleventh centuries was not so much inventive ingenuity as a remarkable capacity for assimilation. They knew how to take good ideas where they found them and how to apply them on a large scale to productive activity. Perhaps this attitude was influenced by the fresh outlook of the German invaders: The pride which drove the Romans and the Chinese to describe as barbarians all those who did not belong to their empires had made them unreceptive to foreign ideas. Secondly, the innovations mentioned above were linked to agricultural activity and, in combination, strengthened each other. As Lynn White noted,

The heavy plough, the open fields, the new integration of agriculture and herding, three field rotation, modern horse harness, nailed horseshoes and the whipple tree had combined into a total system of agrarian exploitation by the year 1100 to provide a zone of peasant prosperity stretching across Northern Europe from the Atlantic to the Dnieper.[33]

Finally, some of these innovations allowed a more effective use of horsepower. The horseshoe increased the effectiveness and therefore the value of the horse. At the end of the eleventh century, a toll's tariff of the Angers region (France) taxed a horse without horseshoes at one penny and a horse with horseshoes at two pennies. At the same time, in all of Europe the breeding of horses increased markedly, and efforts were made to improve the breeds by importing horses from the Muslim countries. The horse was

---

30. White, *Expansion of Technology,* p. 147.
31. Leighton, *Transport and Communication,* p. 105.
32. Needham, *Science and Civilization,* vol. 4, pp. 303–27.
33. White, *Expansion of Technology,* p. 153.

increasingly substituted for the ox, so that more animal power was available for productive activity. In Picardy (France) after 1160 the *corvées* with oxen progressively diminished in number. Between 1125 and 1160, on one of the manors of the abbey of Ramsey (England), the number of oxen diminished by 50 percent while those of horses increased by 400 percent. The horse is stronger and faster than the ox and it can do more work than an ox before tiring, and in less time.

Some of these innovations implied big social adjustments. The novel shaping of fields connected with the adoption of the heavy plough and the three-field system involved radically new patterns of peasant cooperation and the development of a strong system of self-government among the peasants for their own affairs.[34]

Until the tenth century mills were used in the West for grinding grains. In contrast, the early information on water mills in China suggests they were used not for turning simple millstones, but for the more complicated job of blowing bellows in metal work. The difference should not be surprising: the West in the Dark Ages was essentially agrarian and, in comparison with China, was poorer and underdeveloped. But as cities, trade, and manufacturing grew in Europe from the tenth century onward, motive power derived from hydraulic energy was applied to an increasing variety of productive processes. Water mills became more complicated and powerful. Perhaps as early as 822, and certainly by 861, in Picardy, water mills were used to prepare the malt necessary for the manufacture of beer. The adaptation of the mill to this type of operation involved the introduction of new mechanisms, in particular a series of vertical hammers set in motion by cams inserted on one of the axes of the mill.

Between 990 and 1040 at Grenoble and Lérin, water mills were used for the fulling of cloth. In the course of the eleventh century, the use of the water mill for fulling cloth reached Normandy and soon spread to the rest of France and to Germany and England. The adoption of the new process revolutionized the textile industry of the time to such an extent that Professor Carus-Wilson, describ-

---

34. White, *Expansion of Technology*, p. 148.

ing these developments in England, labeled them "An Industrial Revolution of the Thirteenth Century."[35] The English textile industry, which until then had been concentrated mainly in the southeastern areas of the country, moved into the northwestern areas, where the existence of adequate flows of water made possible the construction of mills.

There is evidence of the use of water mills in the production of iron in Styria in 1135, in Normandy in 1204, in Southern Sweden in 1224, and in Moravia in 1269. In Normandy, in 1204, a mill operated saws for wood. Mills were used in the manufacture of paper at Fabriano in 1276, at Troyes in 1338, and at Nuremberg in 1390. By the late fifteenth century any large western European city could be pictured much as a middle-sixteenth-century traveler described Bologna (Italy). He told of sluice from the river Reno that provided water power

> to turn various machines to grind grain, to make copper pots and weapons of war, to pound herbs as well as oakgalls [for dying], to spin silk, polish arms, sharpen various instruments, saw planks.[36]

By the thirteenth century water mills in the West had wheels 1 to 3.5 meters in diameter with a corresponding power of 1 to 3.5 horsepower. By the seventeenth century it was possible to make wheels 10 meters in diameter. The Italian water mills for the production of silk thread were not only extremely complicated but also monstrously large pieces of machinery. However, the majority of the mills were still built with wheels 2 to 4 meters in diameter. Builders preferred to increase the number of wheels rather than deal with all the complicated technological problems involved in the concentration of energy on one single wheel.

The story of the water mill is paralleled by the story of the windmill. When the windmill first appeared in Persia, possibly in the seventh century A.D., it was mounted on a vertical axle and appears to have been used mostly for irrigation purposes. The Chinese became acquainted with the Persian mill in the course of the thirteenth century A.D. and soon adopted it. As far as we know, the

---

35. Carus-Wilson, *An Industrial Revolution.*
36. White, *The Expansion of Technology*, p. 157.

windmill first appeared in Europe at the end of the twelfth century in Normandy. The tradition persists that the windmill was brought back to Europe by the Crusaders. The European windmill, however, shows elements of originality. While the oriental mill had the sails mounted on a vertical axis, the European mill had the sails mounted on a horizontal one. It appears that someone brought back from the Middle East not a description of the local windmills,

The Winged Mill. An engraving by Johannes Stradanus (1523–1605). The caption reads "The winged mill which now wants to be driven by the winds is said to have been unknown to the Romans." In this Flemish setting are shown both types of windmills, those set to operate by the prevailing winds and those that are pivoted to face into chance winds. New York Public Library.

but the idea of exploiting the energy of the winds, and the European craftsmen made up a totally new contraption. Originally the Western windmill was mounted on a heavy post and the mill had to be turned to face into the wind. This constraint limited the size of the mills. By the fourteenth century, however, the tower mill had been developed; in this type of mill the building and the machinery remain stationary; only the top rotates to face the sails into the wind. This innovation allowed the erection of much larger and more powerful units. The sails had to be turned into the wind manually, but this task was later eased by the introduction of cranks and gears. Finally, in 1745, Edmund Lee invented the fantail, a device which held the sails into the wind automatically, probably the earliest example of automatic control in machinery.

Many tower mills could produce as much as 20 or 30 horsepower. Thus the windmill was a more powerful motor than the water mill. But its diffusion was severely restricted by geography and climate. This fact explains why, although windmills became characteristic landmarks in some areas, they never became as numerous or as widespread as water mills. But like the water mills, the windmills, originally built for grinding grains, were later employed in an increasing variety of productive processes. In Amsterdam in 1578, there were windmills used in throwing silk, printing ribbons, fulling and calendering cloth, dressing leather, extracting oil, making gunpowder, and rolling copper plates.[37]

The proliferation and increasing power of water mills and windmills, like the increased use of horses, meant more energy for productive uses. Unlike horses, however, the mills supplied inanimate energy. Their widespread use marked the beginning of the breakdown of the traditional world in which man had to depend for power on animal or vegetable sources of energy.[38] It was the distant announcement of the Industrial Revolution.

The use of the mill in the manufacturing sector was indicative of a new trend: thus far innovations had occurred only in the agricultural sector; now they increasingly began to occur in the manufacturing and service sectors. This trend was both a consequence and an evidence of the expansion of these two sectors.

About the middle of the eleventh century in Flanders, and possibly in Champagne, the vertical loom was introduced. In comparison with the traditional horizontal loom, the new tool allegedly increased the productivity of the workers from three to five times

---

37. Honig, *De Molens,* p. 79.
38. Compare Cipolla, *The Economic History of World Population,* Chapter 2.

and also made possible substantial qualitative improvement of production.

The twelfth century saw the adoption of the compass, the perfecting of the gyroscopic compass, the adoption of the waterclock for measuring the movement of the ship, the drawing up of naval charts with related instructions, the compilation of trigonometric tables for navigation, and the adoption of the stern rudder on the central line of the ship. These innovations made possible instrumental or mathematical navigation, which in turn made possible a greater utilization of the ship as capital. Frederic C. Lane has shown that during the thirteenth century the idle period of ships in winter was gradually shortened and that, by the last quarter of the century, a ship could complete two round trips a year throughout the Mediterranean, traveling even in winter.[39]

The contemporaries of Dante (1265–1321) had the sensation of living in a period of great technological change. In 1267 Theodoric, Bishop of Bitonto, wrote that "*quotidie instrumentum novum et modus novus solertia et ingenio medici invenitur*" ("owing to the laboriousness and ingenuity of the physicians, every day a new instrument and a new technology are invented"). In a sermon delivered in Florence in 1306, father Giordano da Pisa declared "Every day new arts are discovered." Among the inventions of the period one should mention the spinning wheel and the spectacles. About the latter, in the sermon mentioned above, Father Giordano had the following to say:

It is not twenty years since there was discovered the art of making spectacles which help you to see well, and which is one of the best and most necessary in the world. I myself saw the man who discovered and practiced it, and I talked with him.[40]

At the beginning of the fourteenth century came the first clocks and the first firearms. The fourteenth century also saw the invention of locks for canals.

In the course of the fifteenth century the full-rigged ship was

---

39. Compare Lane, *The Economic Meaning of the Invention of the Compass.* Compare also Taylor, *Mathematics and the Navigator.*
40. Narducci, *Tre prediche,* pp. 125–26, and Rosen, *The Invention of the Eyeglasses,* pp. 13–46 and 183–218.

developed. This type of ship combined the best of both the northern and the southern European traditions. The hull was carvel-built, but the greatest innovation was in the rigging. A full-rigged ship carried three masts, the fore- and mainmasts with square sails and the mizzenmast with a lateen (triangular) sail. With this combination, the square sails could be made large, while the lateen sail made sailing close to the wind possible. As time went on, more sails were added, and the big, bulging mainsail which was characteristic of the early caracks was divided into several smaller square sails hung on as many yards on the same mast—a change that made the canvas stand flatter and the ship better able to beat to windward. To understand fully the importance of these developments, one must place them against the background of that hopelessly chronic shortage of energy which thwarted the activity of preindustrial people. The full-rigged ship enabled the Europeans to harness the energy of the wind over the seas to an extent inconceivable in previous times.

The economic consequences were immediately felt. Full-rigged ships no longer had to wait for only the most favorable breeze, and consequently the elapsed time of voyages diminished. Since the sail area could be increased and more energy exploited, the size of vessels grew and their carrying capacity rose until the middle of the sixteenth century,[41] and costs were correspondingly reduced. Eventually the development of the Dutch *fluyt* (see p. 254) brought

41. We know, for example, that at the beginning of the fourteenth century the normal size of a Hanseatic ship was about 75 tons. Around 1400, the traditional "Kogge" was replaced by larger vessels of the "Holk" type. Around 1440 the average size of the Hanseatic vessels was about 150 tons. Thirty years later, when the carvel-type vessels were introduced in the Hanseatic fleet, the average tonnage was about 300 tons. For the French-English wine trade it has been observed that early in the fifteenth century few ships can have carried more than 100 tuns of wine. But by the middle of the century ships from Bordeaux brought an average of 150 tuns, and there were a few ships which could carry as many as 500 tuns of wine. For Portuguese ships, it has been suggested that between 1450 and 1550 the average tonnage at least doubled. In Venice about 1450, anything over 200 tons was considered big. Later, 400 tons became a normal size for most cogs, and by the mid-sixteenth century there were numerous Venetian carracks of 600 to 700 tons.

to a stop the growth in size of cargo ships, well below the tech- nically feasible maximum that was 2,000 tons and more. The *fluyt* showed that the optimum tonnage for intra-European and for many extra-European trades in the seventeenth and eighteenth centuries was in the range of 300 to 500 tons. Ships in Europe did not grow much above that maximum until after 1800.

While naval construction was progressing, more sophisticated techniques of open-seas navigation were being developed. By 1434, the Portuguese, who had succeeded in rounding the formidable and feared Cape Bojador on the west coast of Africa, had developed systematic knowledge of the winds in the Atlantic. Before 1480 they learned to calculate latitude by converting, with the help of declination tables, the heights of the sun or the North Star over the horizon. The quadrant for measuring latitude must have come into use in about 1450, and in 1480 the astrolabe was in use.

Navigation was hardly a peaceful occupation in those days, and ships carried ordnance for both defensive and offensive purposes. Traditionally, naval guns were made of bronze, and in the course of the sixteenth and seventeenth centuries noticeable progress was made in the casting of bronze. Beginning in the middle of the six- teenth century, however, England first, and then Holland and Sweden, developed the techinique of casting iron guns, which were much less expensive than bronze cannon. Thus it became possible to put more guns aboard ships at lower expense.

The combination of innovations and progress in the techniques of naval construction, navigation, and armament production was at the origin of the overseas expansion of Europe. And that changed the course of world history.

Another revolutionary technological innovation of the fifteenth century was heralded by Gutenberg's printing of the Bible with mov- able characters. Before that event books were so expensive that only a few wealthy people could afford to own them. In Spain, around 800, a book cost roughly as much as two cows. In Lom- bardy between the end of the fourteenth and the end of the fif- teenth century the average price of a medical book equaled the living costs of an average person for about three months, and a law book cost as much as such a person's maintenance for one year and four months.[42] One understands why in 1392 tht Countess of Blois, wife of the Baron of Castellane, willing to her daughter a parchment manuscript of the *Corpus Juris,* made the specification that the daughter should marry a jurist so that the valuable treasure would come into the right hands. As long as books were so outrageously expensive it was most unlikely that literacy would become widespread. The introduction of movable type opened a new era. As the full-rigged ship opened vast new geographical horizons to the Europeans, so the press with movable characters opened to them vast new horizons and possibilities in the fields of knowledge and education.

These are but a few of the innovations that emerged in the Middle Ages and the Renaissance. They were only part of a broader process of innovation. More often than not the innovative process was carried out in small steps with numerous minor experiments, by the gradual cumulation of small improvements rather than by distinct bursts of invention. The approach was always empirical and unsystematic. It was only after the Industrial Revolution, with the emergence of modern science and the controlled experiment that the essential character of this process changed. Anyhow many innovations were interrelated. For instance, the success of Gutenberg's invention can be understood only in the context of the presence and diffusion of the optical glass, the water-powered mills for pulping rags for paper, and a system of schooling. Similarly, the development of the techniques of ocean navigation can be understood only in the context of the improved techniques of shipbuilding, the advances in the production of naval ordnance, and the spread of literacy among sea captains.

As noted above, many of the innovations which occurred in Europe after the eleventh century were adaptations of ideas developed elsewhere. In all likelihood the windmill was a Persian invention; the spinning wheel, was known in China in the eleventh century, more than one hundred years before it first appeared in Europe; the compass, the Europeans learned to use from the Arabs, who also

---

42. Cipolla, *Money, Prices and Civilization*, p. 61.

taught them the distilling of alcohol; gunpowder, in all probability was a Chinese invention.

Europe always proved extraordinarily receptive, and the enthusiastic curiosity of a Marco Polo is evidence of this open-minded attitude. But this is not the whole story. From the twelfth century western Europe developed an original inventiveness which manifested itself in a rapid crescendo of new ideas. Spectacles, the mechanical clock, artillery, new types of sailing ships and new navigational techniques, together with a thousand other innovations big and small, were the original product of European experimental curiosity and imagination. It must also be noted that when Europe absorbed new ideas from outside, it did not do so in a purely passive and imitative manner, but often adapted them to local conditions or to new uses with distinct elements of originality. The Persian windmill was built with a vertical axis. The windmill that spread throughout Europe, the type we know today, with great sails and a horizontal axis, was a much more efficient machine than the original conceived by the Persians. Though the Chinese invented gunpowder, they used it mostly for fireworks. The adoption of gunpowder by Europeans was accompanied by the manufacture of firearms, the construction of which rapidly improved, so much so that, at the beginning of the sixteenth century, when the Europeans arrived in China aboard their galleons, the Chinese were astounded and terrified by Western guns. Paper was invented in China, and its manufacture spread to the Muslim Empire during the eighth century. The Byzantines, typically conservative, never learned how to manufacture paper. The Europeans learned the technique during the thirteenth century. The appearance of the first paper factories at Xátiva and at Fabriano represented the trasplanting into Europe of an idea born elsewhere. But while the production of paper outside of Europe remained at the level of manual production, it is typical that, in the West, the pulp was processed by machines driven by water mills. Printing was invented by the Chinese, but the Europeans turned it into an extremely efficient mass-production process by the end of the fifteenth century.

One of the original features of Western technological development after the twelfth century was the increasing stress placed on the mechanical aspects of technology. There was a real passion for the mechanization of all productive processes. In the Forez by 1251, there was a mill to grind mustard, and by the end of the Middle Ages mechanical clockwork was successfully applied to the roasting of meats on fire. The basic reason for this attitude is not easy to grasp. One may argue that the shortage of labor brought about by repeated epidemics favored the adoption of labor-saving devices, but a phenomenon by its nature so complex can scarcely be reduced to a naive and simplistic determinism.

Necessity explains nothing; the crucial question is why some groups respond in a particular way to needs or wants which in other groups remain unformulated and unfilled. The case of the mechanical clock is particularly instructive.

From the earliest antiquity man had created various devices to solve the problem of measuring time. The sundial was the first solution, followed by the *clepsydra*, or water clock. Occasional use was also made of sticks of combustible material (incense or wax), properly graded, which marked the passage of time while burning. The Europe of the Dark Ages inherited these techniques without adding new ones. But at least from the thirteenth century onward, there were people in Europe who sought a mechnical solution to the problem. In 1271, Robertus Anglicus reported efforts but acknowledged that the solution had not yet been found. A few decades later, however, mechanical clocks rang the hours on the bell towers of St. Eustorgio and St. Gottardo in Milan, and of the Cathedral of Beauvais. About the middle of the fourteenth century Giovanni De' Dondi produced a mechanical masterpiece which marked not only the hours, but also the days, the months, the years, and the revolutions of the planets.

In all probability the mechanical solution of the problem of the measurement of time was found in northern Italy. It has been argued that the invention of the mechanical clock came in response to the European climate because during the winters the water in the clepsydras froze and the clouds all too often rendered the sundials useless. Such an explanation exemplifies the kind of simplistic determinism criticized above. The first mechanical clocks kept time so imperfectly that they had to be continually adjusted, the corrections being made by "clock governors" who turned the hour hand (the minute hand appeared only a good deal later) backward or forward precisely on the basis of sundials and water clocks. Thus the first mechanical clocks cannot be regarded as substitutes for sundials and water clocks.

"Why" Europeans produced the mechanical clock is much more subtle. Some years ago P. G. Walker wrote:

> Because we see the machine reshaping society and changing man's habits and ways of life, we are apt to conclude that the machine is, so to speak, an autonomous force that determines the social superstructure. In fact, things happened the other way around. . . . The reason why the machine originated in Europe is to be found in human terms. Before men could evolve and apply the machine as a social phenomenon they had to become mechanics.[43]

The men of the thirteenth century thought of measuring time in mechanical terms because they had developed a mechanical outlook of which the mills and the bell ringing mechanisms were significant evidence. Clocks rapidly spread throughout Europe, but production was not limited to clock faces, hands, and motors. On public buildings, as in Basel and Bologna, or inside churches, as in Strasbourg and Lund, extremely complicated clocks were built, in which the showing of time was almost accidental, accompanied as it was by revolution of stars, by movements and pirouettes of angels, saints, and Madonnas. These contraptions were both the result and the evidence of an irrepressible taste for mechanical achievements. This taste assumed extreme forms during the Renaissance and it had practical application. Efforts were directed at replacing the scarcer factor of production while at the same time increasing specific productivity. In 1402 the managers of the *Fabbrica del Duomo* in Milan studied the proposals for a stone cutting machine which, with the help of a horse (costing three shillings a day), would do work for which four men (at a wage of 13⅓ shillings per man per day) would otherwise be needed. A few years later, the same managers studied the plans for another machine—this one for the transport of marble—which would reduce the labor force normally required.[44]

The constant and generalized preoccupation with machines and

43. Walker, *The Origins of the Machine Age*, pp. 591–92.
44. *Annali*, vol. 1, p. 248.

mechanical solutions had a double order of consequences. On the one hand, undeniable productivity gains were achieved in a number of productive sectors. On the other hand, a cumulative process was set into motion by which the more the machine was studied the more it reinforced the mechanical outlook of the people. Books on mechanics proliferated in the course of the sixteenth and seventeenth centuries. More significant than that, the mechanical outlook began to pervade such improbable fields as art and philosophy. While the artist of the Far East delighted in painting flowers, fish, and horses, Leonardo da Vinci and Francesco di Giorgio Martini were obsessed with machinery. Philosophers came to regard the universe as a great piece of clockwork, the human body as a piece of machinery, and God as an outstanding "clockmaker."

If, at the time of the Scientific Revolution, the leading branch of learning was mechanics, if the very characteristic of the Scientific Revolution was, as has been said, the "mechanization of the world view," all this was not a new development unrelated to previous events; on the contrary, it was the logical consequence of a mental outlook which had matured in the preceding centuries. And we, with our obsession for computers, mechanical gadgetry and mathematical models, represent the final outcome of a centuries-long development.

The dominant theme of the Greco-Roman and the oriental conceptions of the world was that of harmony between man and nature —a relationship that presupposed the existence of irresistible forces in nature to which man was compelled inevitably to submit. The myths of Daedalus, Prometheus, and the Tower of Babel indicated the fate of those who attempted to reverse the man-nature relationship, presuming to assert the dominance of man. When the inhabitants of Cnidus asked the oracle of Delphi its opinion on the timeliness of digging a canal bisecting the isthmus of their peninsula, the oracle replied: "Jove would have created an island instead of a peninsula if that had been his wish."

The medieval world somehow managed to break this tradition. Still too backward technically to dominate nature to any appreciable degree, the Europeans of the Middle Ages found refuge in the world of dreams. The "animism" of the ancients and of the orientals was replaced by the cult of the Saints. The Saints were not devils or demons; they were men—men in the grace of God, but still men whose features everyone could see on the portals of, or inside, the churches. Their features were like those of all other men. The saints did not take their ease in the hieratic immobility of the oriental holymen, nor did they amuse themselves like the Greek gods by punishing men for their audacity. On the contrary, they were always at work to overcome the adverse forces of nature: they defeated diseases, calmed stormy seas, saved the harvests from storms and locusts, softened the fall for whoever leapt into a ravine, stopped fires, made the drowning float, and guided ships in danger. The saints practiced what the commoners dreamed: they harnessed nature and, far from being condemned for doing so, they lived pleasantly in Paradise in the company of God. Harnessing nature was not regarded as a sin; it was a miracle. A belief in miracles is the first step toward making them possible. Inadvertently, medieval man moved in the direction of making miracles less the result of the action of saints and more the result of his own actions.

Easy explanations of complex historic phenomena fascinate people, precisely because they are easy and, therefore, comfortable. The explanation pleases, the problem irritates. And yet the explanation is often unattainable, while the problem remains the only valid thing.

It is tempting to say that the Greco-Roman world failed to develop technologically because it had an abundance of slaves, and that medieval and Rennaissance Europe produced notable technological developments in reaction to the scarcity of labor caused by epidemics. But the factors at play were much more numerous and complex. What has been mentioned, albeit briefly, in the preceding paragraphs about mental attitudes and aspirations can serve to warn against easy explanations, though it does not pretend to offer alternative solutions. Europe's receptive attitude, the substitution of the cult of the saints and the faith in miracles for animism, the rise and spread of a mechanical outlook—these and similar things are not explanations but only problems in a wider and more intricate context. Why *was* Western Europe so receptive and favorable to change? Why did medieval Europe obsessively dream of mastering nature? Why was it looking for mechanical solutions? We do not know.

The Diffusion of Techniques

Up to this point we have referred to western Europe as a single entity, but at various periods some areas were more innovative than others. From the twelfth to the fifteenth century the Italians were in the forefront not only of economic development but also of technological progress. In the sixteenth and seventeenth centuries this primacy passed to the English and the Dutch. A key point in the analysis, then, is the diffusion of technological innovations from their area of origin to other areas, and the migrations of the technicians.[45]

In 1607 Vittorio Zonca published in Padua his *Nuovo Teatro di Machine et Edificii*, which included, among numerous engravings of various contraptions, the description of an intricate machine for throwing silk by water power in a large factory. Zonca's book went into a second edition in 1621 and a third in 1656, and still the details of the mill were considered a state secret. In Piedmont (Italy), where silk production played a major economic role, law regarded "the disclosing or attempting to discover" anything relating to the making of the engines a crime punishable by death. G. N. Clark has shown that a copy of the first edition of Zonca's book had been on the open-access shelves of the Bodleian Library from at least as early as 1620. Yet it was nearly one hundred years later that the English succeeded in building a mill for the throwing of silk, and then only after John Lombe, during two years of industrial espionage in Italy, "found means to see this engine so often that he made himself master of the whole invention and of all the different parts and motions."[46] Critics of this story have

---

45. The pages which follow are partially derived from an article of the author's which appeared under the title "The Diffusion of Innovations in Early Modern Europe," *Comparative Studies in Society and History,* 14 1972. I should like to express my thanks to the journal and to the Cambridge University Press for kindly giving me permission to reproduce here some pages of the article in question.
46. On the whole story, consult W. H. Chaloner, *Sir Thomas Lombe.*

pointed out that John Lombe's journey was really unnecessary because the silk-throwing machines could have been constructed

A water-powered throwing mill. Engraving from Vittorio Zonca's *Nuovo Teatro di Machine et Edificii* published in 1607. The machine was used to twist filaments of raw silk into long threads that were strong enough to weave. Master throwers owned the machine, employed eight to ten journeymen, and worked for silk merchants on a piece basis.

with the help of Zonca's book. They are perfectly right when they point out that Zonca's engravings are in fact more revealing than Lombe's own patent specification. But they miss the point. The point is, as Oakeshott wrote:[47]

It might be supposed that an ignorant man, some edible materials and a cookery book compose together the necessities of a self-moved activity called cooking. But nothing is further from the truth. The cookery book is not an independently generated beginning from which cooking can spring; it is nothing more than an abstract of somebody's knowledge of how to cook: it is the stepchild, not the parent of the activity The book, in its turn, may help to set a man on to dressing a dinner, but if it were his sole guide he could never, in fact, begin: the book speaks only to those who know already the kind of thing to expect from it and consequently how to interpret it.

Even today, blueprints are considered inadequate to transmit full information, and when a firm buys new and elaborate machinery it sends some of its workers to acquire, directly from the manufacturers, the knowledge of how to operate it. Through the ages, the main channel for the diffusion of innovations has been the migration of people. The diffusion of technology has been mostly the product of the migrations of human capital.

Cases of individuals who migrated temporarily in order to acquire information about innovations and to bring it back to their own countries were not unheard of before the Industrial Revolution. Nicholaes Witsen, in a passage quoted below, mentions people who went to Holland to study "economical building in the dockyards." In 1657, John Fromanteel of London went to Holland to learn the art of making pendulum clocks as recently invented by Huygens and made by Coster: on Fromanteel's return his family firm was the first to make pendulum clocks in England.[48] In the second half of the seventeenth century, Dionigi Comollo, from Como, according to his own words, "spent many a year in Amsterdam and other main towns of Holland where, at his expense and with great care, he learned how to make woollens in the way the Dutch had newly developed."[49] In 1684 the Republic of

47. Oakeshott, *Education*, p. 15.
48. Britten, *Old Clocks and Their Makers*, p. 272.
49. Archivio di Stato, Milano, *Commercio* P.A.b 264/fasc.2.

Venice sent Sigismondo Alberghetti, Jr., gunsmith, to England in order to acquire the new English technique of casting ordnance.[50] However, there were obstacles to this type of transmission of skills. Especially in fields where economic interests were at stake, communities and guilds were intractably jealous of their technologies and usually opposed the dissemination of their secrets.

The propagating of innovations took place mostly through the migration of skilled craftsmen who decided to settle in foreign countries. For the sixteenth and seventeenth centuries there is abundant literature about the French Huguenots and the Flemish Protestants who brought advanced technologies to England, Sweden, and other parts of Europe and started new trades. The dramatic story of the religious refugee has such an appeal that one is often inclined to forget that not all migrations of skilled workers and innovations in the sixteenth and seventeenth centuries can be ascribed to religious intolerance. A number of the Walloons who brought to Sweden the new techniques of casting iron cannon in the first part of the seventh century were Catholic, and they were for a time allowed to retain their faith as well as priests in their communities.[51] Although most of the French clockmakers who moved to London in the course of the seventeenth century were Huguenots, John Goddard, in Portsoken Ward, was known as a "papist."[52] The Swedish and Flemish craftsmen who moved to Russia in the seventeenth century and introduced the technique of casting iron guns were certainly not motivated by religious preoccupations.[53] Paul Roumieu, who reintroduced the art of watchmaking into Scotland, was traditionally supposed to have been one of the refugees driven out of France in consequence of the Edict of Nantes. It has now been established that he had moved to Edinburgh at least eight years before the persecution of 1685.[54]

This brings us to the question of the forces behind the mobility of skilled labor in preindustrial Europe. As is customary in such

---

50. Casoni, *Note Sull'artiglieria Veneta*, pp. 177–180.
51. Cipolla, *Guns and Sails*, p. 54, n. 1.
52. Ullyett, *British Clocks and Clockmakers*, p. 18.
53. Amburger, *Die Familie Marselis*.
54. Smith, *Old Scottish Clockmakers*, p. 323.

cases, one can distinguish between the forces that act on the side of the "push" and the forces that act on the side of the "pull." On the side of the "push" there is the long, grim list of misfortunes that made life unbearable for the preindustrial craftsman: famines, plagues, wars, taxations, shortages of demand for labor, and political and religious intolerance. For the average worker life was pretty miserable at best. A small extra dose of misfortune was more than enough to make it unendurable. The attachment of preindustrial workers to a given place was directly proportionate to their living conditions.

Governments and administrators were perfectly aware of the situation and knew that the loss of able craftsmen had ominous consequences for the economy. Decrees forbidding the emigration of skilled workers were not uncommon in the late Middle Ages as well as in the sixteenth and seventeenth centuries. Special attention was given to certain categories of workers whose activity was considered either essential for the safety of the state or particularly important for the economy. The Venetian government, for instance, strictly prohibited the emigration of caulkers, and from a document of 1460 we learn that a caulker who left Venice risked six years in prison and a two-hundred-lire fine if apprehended.[55] In those days, however, the effectiveness of governmental control was, of necessity, rather tenuous. The repetitious insistence with which the governments issued decrees threatening penalties for workers who fled the country and refused to return offers conspicuous evidence of the inefficacy of control over emigration. Typically enough, impotence bred ferocity. In 1545 and 1559 the Grand Duke of Florence decreed that workers in the brocade trade who had left the town should return to it. Special favors were announced for those who would comply with the order, and penalties were threatened for those who did not. But in all likelihood the results were not satisfactory: in 1575 the Grand Duke authorized "any person to kill with impunity any of the above-mentioned expatriates" and posted a reward of two hundred scudi for each expatriate craftsman who could be brought back "dead or alive."[56]

---

55. Luzzatto, *Studi di Storia Economica,* pp. 42–43.
56. Fanfani, *Storia del Lavoro in Italia,* pp. 147–48.

The circumstances which "pulled" craftsmen into a given area ranged from employment opportunities to political peace to religious tolerance. Quite often there was also a conscious policy on the part of governments. Administrators busied themselves not only with menacing emigrants but also with devising ways to attract foreign craftsmen, especially those who could bring them new industries or new techniques. In the twelth and thirteenth centuries the champions of the *Drang nach Osten* attracted Dutch peasants into eastern Europe with generous grants of good virgin land. As mentioned above,[57] in 1230–31 the Commune of Bologna (Italy) attracted 150 artisans with their families and assistants, granting them all kinds of privileges and aid in order to develop the woollens and silk industries. In 1442 the Duke Filippo Maria Visconti brought a Florentine craftsman to Milan (Italy) who was supposed to start "some special work of silk"; for this effort the Duke offered a monthly subsidy, tax exemption for the craftsman and all his employees, and freedom from import duties for all the raw materials necessary for the enterprise.[58] Colbert was generous in granting privileges, land, and titles to Abraham and Hubert (Jr.) De Beche, when he invited them to France to set up an iron industry on the model of that of Sweden.[59] On occasion, recourse to force was considered a legitimate solution, and craftsmen were literally kidnaped. An inquiry made by the Bergskollegium in the 1660s on the emigration of Swedish iron masters, revealed that a number of workers sailed from Nyköping believing that they were being brought to some other part of Sweden. Instead they were brought to Lübeck, from there to Hamburg, and finally to France, where Colbert was determined to start an iron industry on the Swedish model. A few workers escaped; one of them, Anders Sigfersson, returned to Sweden in 1675.[60]

Of course, it is one thing to lead a horse to water; it is quite another to make it drink. The fact that a person or group of persons with knowledge about an innovation moves into a geographic area

---

57. pp. 89–90 of this volume.
58. Cipolla, *L'Economia Milanese*, p. 353.
59. Cipolla, *Guns and Sails*, p. 69, n. 2.
60. *Svenskt Biografiskt Lexicon* ad vocem *De Besche*.

does not assure that the innovation will actually take root in the new environment. Whether it does depends on a number of circumstances. The personality of the migrants has to be taken into account as well as their number in relation to the size of the recipient society. No less important is the nature of the recipient environment. Many Italian technicians moved to Turkey in the course of the fifteenth, sixteenth, and seventeenth centuries, bringing techniques and ideas with them. Yet no appreciable innovations occurred in Turkey. The refugees who moved to England on the other hand, found an extremely fertile ground. The Huguenot clockmakers who taught the English the art of clock and watchmaking, the refugees from the Low Countries who brought the techniques of the "new drapery" to Norwich, the French glassmakers who established the manufacture of window glass in England[61] soon found ingenious local imitators who, by pursuing their ideas along original lines, further developed the foreign techniques and opened the way to more innovations. What makes an environment responsive or not is difficult to determine. At first sight the problem of transplanting an innovation into an alien environment might appear to be merely one of introducing new methods of production and the instruments, tools, or machines appropriate to them. But what is really involved is a particular and more profound condition which can be understood and must be assessed only in human and social terms.[62] This notion was perceived centuries ago by the Dutchman Nicolaes Witsen, who wrote in his great treatise on shipping, published in Amsterdam in 1671:

It is surprising that foreigners, though they may have studied economical building in the dockyards of this country, can never practice it in their own land. . . . And this in my opinion proceeds from the fact that they are then working in an alien environment and with alien artisans. From which it follows that even if a foreigner had all the building rules in his head, they would not serve him, unless he had learned everything here in this country by experience, and still that would not help him,

61. Cipolla, *Clocks and Culture*, pp. 65 ff.; Kenyon, *The Glass Industry of the Weald*; Cunningham, *Alien Immigrants*; Bodmer, *Der Einfluss der Refugianten*.
62. Frankel, *The Economic Impact on Underdeveloped Societies*, pp. 22–24.

unless he should find a way to inculcate in his workmen the thrifty and neat disposition of the Hollander, which is impossible.[63]

As good old Nicholaes Witsen observed, it all depends on *disposition*. And this allows one to end this chapter for a change, on a cheerful note. Throughout the centuries the countries in which intolerance and fanaticism prevailed lost to more tolerant countries the most precious of all possible forms of wealth: good human minds. The qualities that make people tolerant also make them receptive to new ideas. The inflow of good minds, and a receptiveness to new ideas were among the main sources of the success stories of England, Holland, Sweden, and Switzerland in the sixteenth and seventeenth centuries.

---

63. Quoted and translated by Barbour, *Dutch and English Merchant Shipping*, p. 234.

CHAPTER SEVEN

Enterprise,
Credit, and Money

Enterprise and Credit

We saw that in regard to the Greco-Roman world, scholars seem to have restricted their attention to the mechanical aspect of technology, ignoring the other aspects, and particularly organization. One must avoid making the same mistake for medieval and Renaissance Europe.

From the eleventh century onward there was a remarkable development of business techniques. The list of innovations is long: one need only consider the organization of the fairs, the development of the bill of exchange, the appearance and spread of the manuals of commerce, the evolution of new techniques of accounting, the check, the endorsement, insurance, and so on.[1] From the eleventh to the sixteenth century Italy was the birthplace of most of these innovations. Even the monks interested themselves in business:

---

1. It is possible that double-entry bookkeeping developed in Tuscany in the thirteenth century. In the fourteenth and fifteenth centuries this type of accounting spread to other Italian cities. On the subject, see De Roover, *Aux Origines d'une Technique*, and Melis, *Storia della Ragioneria*. Prototypes of marine insurance may have emerged in the thirteenth century, but the extant documents which undoubtedly refer to insurance contracts go back to the fourteenth century. Genoa long remained the major center for this type of business. See De Roover, *Marine Insurance*. From the seventeenth century, the major center of insurance in Europe was London.

Father Luca Pacioli sent to press in 1494 a famous treatise on accounting, and Father Bernardino da Feltre thought up and organized the *Monti di Pietà*, destined to become important institutions in the credit structure. After the middle of the sixteenth century, the Dutch and the English took over and further developed business techniques with the establishment of the great trading companies, the first joint stock companies, the stock exchange, and the Central Bank.

I shall not discuss these innovations in detail, not because they are unimportant, but to avoid boring the reader. I will examine instead the importance of some of them, especially in regard to the activation of saving.

In Europe from the fifth to the eleventh century there were practically no financial mechanisms to facilitate the transformation of saving into investment. Those who saved either invested directly or hoarded, and loans were made mostly for consumption purposes. The economy thus suffered from the deflationary effects of hoarding and from an inadequate amount of productive investments. With the growth of the cities, credit developed very rapidly in the shape of deferred payments for goods sold—sale credit—which to a great extent favored the expansion of consumption as well as investment (especially the formation of stocks of raw materials and inventories by the merchants).[2] However, a whole series of more sophisticated innovations were introduced to make the collection and activation of savings for productive purposes easier. A typical example is the appearance in the tenth century and the subsequent spread of the so-called *contratto di commenda.*

In the *commenda,* also called the *collegantia* in Venice, Tom gave to Dick a sum which Dick used in business, usually in foreign trade. When Dick came back from his business trip he gave an account of the results to Tom. If there were losses, these were charged against Tom. If there was profit, three-quarters went to Tom and one-quarter to Dick. If Dick also brought part of the capital, the profits were divided according to the proportions of capital put up. While Dick was traveling and doing business, Tom stayed at home and did not concern himself with the affair until Dick's return. Moreover, Tom was not responsible for what Dick did. For

---

2. Postan, *Credit in Medieval Trade,* pp. 65–71.

every business trip Dick could also collect liquid funds from other investors, entering with each of them into relationships analogous to that which he had with Tom. The more partners he found the more he could increase the volume of his business and, therefore, the greater the possibilities of profit, which was reaped not only by him but also by his partners.

The jurists have discussed at length whether the real nature of the *commenda* was that of a partnership or that of a loan. These quibbles are not of interest here. Of interest, rather, are the consequences of the spread of these contracts, consequences which will be better understood after an examination of the environment in which such contracts were drawn up.

Picture a maritime city of the twelfth, thirteenth, or fourteenth century. When the season is propitious the merchants prepare for a voyage. They need financial means to buy the goods which they will try to sell on far-off markets, and they need other financial means which they may eventually be able to use abroad, together with the revenue from their sales, to buy goods to bring back home. There is, therefore, a strong demand for liquid funds. Generally the merchants have their own funds available, but if they manage to increase their liquid assets they can increase the volume of their business, with obvious advantages; moreover, if they manage to involve other individuals in the enterprise, they can share the risks. At this point the merchants advertise this business trip. In the square, or near the harbor, there are notaries. Anyone who holds savings and does not want to leave them lying under the bed can contact the merchants and draw up a *contratto di commenda*.

The important aspect of the arrangement is that with this system not only institutional operators but all the members of society with liquid funds could take part in the productive process. In many respects the diffusion of the *commenda* had the same effects as the establishment of a stock exchange. Small as well as large savings could be put to use—the few shillings of the widow and the craftsman as well as the bags of gold and silver coins of the rich man. The following contract was drawn up in Genoa (Italy) on December 22, 1198 between two merchants and a number of humble people who were prepared to invest their savings in a trading expedition:

We, Embrone of Sozziglia and Master Alberto, acknowledge that we carry in *accomandatio* for the purpose of trading £ 142 Genoese to the port of Bonifacio and through or in Corsica and Sardinia; and from there we are to come [back]. And of this [sum], £ 25 Genoese belong to you, Giordano Clerico; and £ 10 to you, Oberto Croce. And to you, Vassallo Rapallino, [belong] £ 10; and to you, Bonsignore Torre, £ 10. And £ 5 [belong] to Pietro Bonfante; and to you, Michele, tanner, [belong] £ 5; and to you, Giovanni del Pero, £ 5; and to Ara Dolce, £ 6; and to Ansaldo Mirto, £ 5; and to Martino, hemp-seller, £ 5; and to Ansaldo Fanti, £ 8; and to you, Lanfranco of Crosa, £ 20; and to Josbert, nephew of Charles of Besançon, £ 10. And £ 6 belong to me, Embrone; and £ 2 to me, Alberto. And all the pounds mentioned above are to be profitably employed and invested, and they are to draw by the pound. And we promise to send [back] the capital and the profit which God shall have granted from this *accomandatio*, [to be placed] in the power of the aforesaid persons to whom they belong. And after deduction of the capital we are to have one fourth of the profit; but the [entire] profit which comes to our [own] pounds is to be ours. . . .[3]

The case of the *commenda* is typical but not unique. In overland trade—in which the figure of the businessman more rapidly lost its itinerant character—analogous partnerships developed which were gradually perfected over time and which made possible the participation of capital in the productive process under differing headings and in differing forms.[4]

A form of partnership in maritime trade which qualified more as a credit mechanism than a business partnership was the *sea loan*. Its main peculiarity was that the borrower pledged the return of the loan only on condition that the ship carrying the borrowed

---

3. The original document, in Latin, is preserved in the Archive of Genoa. The English translation is by Lopez and Raymond, *Medieval Trade*, pp. 182–83.

4. Among the many who have written on this subject, compare Sapori, *Le Campagnie Mercantili Toscane,* pp. 803–5. The author observes that initially the "company" was formed from the union of blood relations. However, the *corpo di compagnia,* or capital of the society, soon came to be formed from quotas drawn from more family estates and "finally became independent of each of them. This independence in its turn facilitated entrance into the company of less close relations and years later came to be the pre-condition for the entrance of strangers into the companies. . . . In time the shares constituing the *corpi di compagnia* became insufficient. It was necessary to call on the inflow of other forms and this was done through *participation* and the *deposit*."

money or goods bought with it safely completed its voyage.[5] Sea loans lost their popularity around 1250 to be replaced by the *cambium maritimum* (sea exchange). In this new form interest on the loan could be hidden by making repayment in another currency at a given rate of exchange.

Partnerships in the Hanseatic zone[6] had certain similarities with the Italian forms, although they were usually on a smaller scale. A common form was the *Sendeve,* which was limited to one venture, with one party contributing the labor and the other the capital. All decisions were made by the party contributing the capital. A contrasting form of agreement was the *Wenderlegginge,* in which the traveling partner was also the managing partner making the decisions. The most common form was the *Gegenseitige Ferngesellschaft,* or mutual-agency partnership, under which partners in different towns represented each other, but without publicizing the partnership.

Unlike the *cambium maritimum* mentioned above, the contract of exchange was not limited to maritime trade. On the contrary, it developed widely in the business community at large, and although theoretically it was a technique for transferring capital from one monetary area to another, in practice it became a choice form of credit and speculation.[7]

With the appearance and dissemination of these innovations, from the eleventh century onward savings were activated for productive purposes to a degree inconceivable in previous centuries. In a society suffering from a chronic shortage of capital, the availability of even marginal amounts of savings was a fact of utmost importance.

All this had an ethical aspect also. The development and spread of the *contratto di commenda,* as of other partnership contracts, would not have been possible without the precondition of a spirit of mutual trust and a sense of honesty in business. The merchant to whom others entrusted their savings could easily have disappeared with the capital or cheated in business conducted in far-off markets where none of his associates had any control. But if the trader

---

5. For examples see Lopez and Raymond, *Medieval Trade,* pp. 168 ff.
6. On the history of the Hansa and the Hanseatic towns, see Dollinger, *The Hansa.*
7. De Roover, *Lettres de Change,* passim.

showed himself to be dishonest, after a while no one would have entrusted savings to him. It was the widespread sense of honesty, strengthened by the sense of belonging to an integrated community, quite apart from definite legal provisions, which made possible the participation of all kinds of people with their savings in the productive process. The evolution of civil and criminal legislation on commercial activities should also be considered from this point of view and should be included among the institutional factors which encouraged development.

Monetary Trends

The development of new forms of credit and partnership and the new social and economic climate of the cities progressively reduced the deflationary pressure of hoarding. But hoarding was not the only source of deflationary pressures.

In the last quarter of the eighth century Charlemagne adopted a monetary reform which was soon extended to all parts of Christian Europe. This reform based the monetary system on a new coin, named denarius (penny) which was made of pure silver and weighed approximately 1.7 grams. The new coin corresponded to twelve solidi (shillings) of the old currency and 240 of the new pennies weighed one pound. Thus the following relationship emerged

1 pound = 20 shillings = 240 pennies

which prevailed on continental Europe until the French Revolution and on the British Isles until the 1960s.

The monetary system that emerged from the Carolingian reform was a most rudimentary one. The pound was a weight, shilling was the name of an old coin, and the silver penny was the only piece in circulation. It was as if we had in circulation only one-dollar pieces and neither multiples nor fractions. The inherent difficulties were not much felt because exchanges were few and most transactions took the form of barter.

From the tenth century onward, however, the population grew and the economy developed and the need was soon felt for a more elaborate monetary system. With the end of the twelfth century and even more during the thirteenth century one state after another began to issue denominations larger than the penny. Genoa around

1172 issued a silver coin worth four pennies of the standard then current. Pisa, Florence, and Venice soon followed the example of Genoa and began to strike their groats. Then Genoa and Florence in 1252 and Venice in 1284 issued gold pieces which became known respectively as genovini, florins, and ducats. The example of the Italian city-states was soon followed by all the other states in Europe.[8]

As population and income grew and people had more recourse to money in their exchanges, the demand for money increased. Currency, however, was exclusively metallic, and until the end of the fifteenth century the production of gold and silver did not grow as rapidly as the demand for money. Thus in terms of commodities and services the value of gold and silver grew in the long run, which meant that the price of commodities and services in terms of gold and silver fell with obvious deflationary effects. The possible ways out of a prolonged shortage of money and falling prices were development of credit, use of means of exchange other than metallic currency, and debasement of the currency in relation to its gold or silver content. Between the tenth and the fifteenth centuries all three solutions were resorted to, but the one most frequently adopted was the debasement of the currency.

Tables 7-1 and 7-2 provide some data on the debasement of the currency in selected European states from about A.D. 900 to about A.D. 1700. It is apparent from the tables that during the Middle Ages the countries which experienced the greatest economic development were also those which experienced the greatest debasement.

Table 7–1

Equivalent of the Local Monetary Unit (Pound)
in Grams of Pure Silver in Selected European States, 900–1700

Approx. Year	England	France	Milan	Venice	Florence
800	330	390	390	390	
1250	324	80	70	20	35
1500	172	22	8.6	6.2	5.7
1600	112	11	4.9	3.5	4.5
1700	112	6	3.9	3.0	3.9

8. Cipolla, *Money, Prices and Civilization*, pp. 42 and ff.

Table 7–2

Equivalent of the Local Monetary Unit (Pound)
in Grams of Pure Silver in Selected Italian States 1252–1700

Year	Milan	Genoa	Venice	Florence
1252	70.0	70.0	20.0	35.0
1315–1325	31.5	39.4	14.8	15.2
1390–1400	20.6	29.2	7.6	9.2
1490–1500	8.6	12.8	6.2	5.7
1545–1555	5.9	9.7	5.0	4.5
1615–1625	4.9	7.1	3.5	4.5
1690–1700	3.9	4.9	3.0	3.9

As noted above, one of the "causes" of the progressive deterioration in the metallic content of the currencies before 1500 was a long-term increase in the demand for money resulting from growth of population, income, and degree of monetarization of the economy, or any combination of these phenomena in the presence of an inadequately elastic supply of gold and silver. However, this was not the only root of monetary debasement. Other main "causes" were the increase of government expenditure, the pressure of social groups interested in inflation, and deficits in the balances of payments.

All the above-mentioned points, however, can be regarded as "causes" only *ex post*. *Ex ante* they merely represented problems, to each of which there could have been various alternative solutions. Devaluation was not the unavoidable effect of certain causes but the solution more frequently adopted among various alternatives because it was the easiest way out to a whole series of problems.[9]

To the extent that the devaluation of the metallic value of money and the relative increase in the volume in circulation were proportional to the increase in the demand for money, the depreciation itself was not inflationary; in other words, it did not necessarily result in higher prices. But when the debasement was practiced to finance budgetary deficits, its effects were definitely inflationary.

---

9. On all this see Cipolla, *Currency Depreciation*, pp. 413–21.

CHAPTER EIGHT

Production, Incomes, and Consumption: 1000-1500

The Great Expansion: 1000–1300

The development of towns, and with it, of a new sociocultural environment, the development of new technologies, the mobilization of saving, the monetarization of the economy all acted in favor of economic expansion. What happened from the tenth through the thirteenth century, however, can hardly be understood if we do not take into account another important factor.

As already mentioned, until the nineteenth century the development of Europe, like that of any other preindustrial society, was ultimately constrained by the availability of land, because the energy which fed every biological and economic process was at least nine-tenths animal or vegetable in origin.

In the tenth century, when European development began to take shape, there was great abundance of land in relation to scarce population. Until the middle of the thirteenth century land was amply available and as development took place the frontier continually expanded. Economists are accustomed to considering situations in which, as new lands are gradually brought into cultivation, diminishing returns inevitably follow. The rationale for this phenomenon is that the first areas brought into cultivation supposedly are the best and that as expansion progresses, people proceed to till progressively less fertile, marginal lands. Conditions of this kind prevailed in Europe at the middle of the thirteenth century, but not before. In fact, paradoxically enough, the expansion of the tenth through twelfth centuries, at least in some parts of Europe, was possibly characterized by increasing marginal returns. In the anarchy of the previous centuries, people had often entrenched themselves not where land was best, but where the position was most easily defensible—on the crest of a hill or at the end of a gorge. As population grew and more stable conditions prevailed, some of the new areas taken into cultivation were in fact better than those already cultivated.

Internal colonization was accompanied by external expansion. Most dramatic was the German eastward movement (*Drang nach Osten*). This movement was already under way early in the tenth century when the Germans conquered the Sorbenland, between the Elbe and the Saale Rivers. But it gained momentum only with the middle of the twelfth century. Conquests were then made from the Slavs in Holstein, Mecklenburg, and Brandenburg. Lubeck was founded in 1143 and planned villages were created in Holstein a few years later; moreover, the conquest of Mecklenburg set in motion a forward movement all along the line of the Elbe. By the end of the twelfth century the settlement frontier had advanced by fifty to seventy miles. The movement reached its maximum activity in the first half of the thirteenth century. On the Baltic, starting in 1186 a German expedition conquered Livonia and Courland; in 1201 Riga was founded; from 1231 on the Order of the Teutonic Knights proceeded to conquer East Prussia. South of the Baltic, Germans reached the Oder River by 1240 and in the next fifty years advanced their settlements along the Pomeranian coast. Farther south, with the overrunning of the crestlines of the Erzgebirge and the Sudeten Mountains, German settlement reached its maximum extent in the Oder Valley. By 1300 the movement had slowed down considerably, new expansion on a large scale being limited to eastern Pomerania and the territories of the Teutonic Knights. The ravages of the Black Death (1348) further reduced the thrust, and the eastward expansion ceased long before the German defeat at Tannenberg (1401) put an end to German aspirations in Poland for the time being.[1]

---

1. For all that precedes, consult Smith, *An Historical Geography*, pp. 175 ff.

The economic importance of the *Drang nach Osten* must be seen in the light of the following circumstances. In most of the conquered territories, the Slav economy was largely based on fishing, fowling, hunting and stock-rearing. Agriculture was poorly developed. The various groups of Slavs who lived in the area (known to Germans as *Wends*) used a crude form of the light plough and practiced temporary cultivation by which fields were cleared by burning and then abandoned when fertility had declined. The German immigrants, however, who possessed more advanced agricultural technology as well as more abundant and better capital, moved into the new territories with the heavy, wheeled plough and with the heavy falling axes which enabled them to clear the thicker forest and cultivate the heavier soils. In this way the German eastward movement expanded the European farming frontier. Moreover, not only German peasants but also large numbers of German miners moved eastward, and with this process of rural colonization went the founding of new towns and groups of villages.

The effect of the German movement was felt beyond the boundaries reached by German conquest or even by German migrants. German techniques in mining, agriculture, and trade were progressively adopted in eastern Slavic territories. All these developments created the preconditions for the formation of agricultural surplus in eastern Europe, the development of the Baltic trade (Brandenburg was beginning to export grain to England and Flanders around 1250), the growth of the Hanseatic League, and the development of mining and metallurgy in central Europe.

The combination of favorable circumstances made possible a general economic expansion from which everybody in Europe appears to have benefited, though in different degrees. Available information is scarce and imprecise, but in the mist which envelops those distant centuries, one glimpses a situation in which all categories of income grew in real terms; profits, wages, and rents increased. Interest rates may have been the only thing that did not rise, partly, perhaps, because the growth of income made possible greater saving but also because, a series of innovations in business techniques made saving more easily available for both consumption and production.

Until the Industrial Revolution the European economy remained fundamentally based on agriculture. However, the leading sectors in development after the eleventh century were (a) international trade, (b) textile manufactures, and (c) building construction. The bulk of international trade, in turn, remained centered upon foodstuffs and spices, and textiles. Basically one finds in this list a reflection of the basic structure of demand which, as we saw in Chapter 1, centered on food, clothing, and buildings.

As there were leading sectors, so there were leading areas. The regions of Europe in the vanguard of medieval economic development were northern Italy (i.e., Italy north of Rome) and the southern Low Countries. Italy capitalized on the Roman tradition of urban life which had been humbled but not totally destroyed in the Dark Ages, and from the nearness of two empires—the Byzantine and the Arab—which, until the twelfth century, were far more highly developed than any area in Europe. The southern Low Countries capitalized on the economic development which the region had experienced during the Carolingian Renaissance. Italy and the Low Countries derived additional advantages from their respective geographical positions: Italy as a bridge between Europe, North Africa, and the Near East; the southern Low Countries as a crossroads of land and sea routes between the North Sea and the Atlantic coastlines of France and Spain, between England and Italy.

We do not have adequate data for measuring in quantitative terms the long-run increase in production and consumption. Only a few figures are available. It has been estimated that the value of wares imported and exported by sea and subject to duties in Genoa (Italy) increased more than four fold from 1274 to 1293. Between 1280 and 1300 loanable funds became so abundant in Lubeck (Germany) that the rate of interest for money invested in stocks dropped from 10 to 5 percent. The number of lead seals which Ypres (Flanders) had attached to the cloths manufactured by its weavers as checking marks rose from 10,500 in 1306 to 92,500 in 1313. While it would be unwise to generalize solely from these figures, which not only refer to limited areas but also reflect short-term movement, the unanimous voices of the time confirm beyond doubt that the first three centuries of our millennium witnessed a remarkable expansion of all the relevant economic variables.

At the beginning of the fourteenth century Giovanni Villani, a merchant and a chronicler, wrote in glowing terms of "the greatness and magnificence" attained by Florence:[2]

We find after careful investigation that in this period (1336–38) there were in Florence about 25,000 men from the age of fifteen to seventy, fit to bear arms, all citizens. . . . From the amount of bread constantly needed for the city, it was estimated that in Florence there were some 90,000 mouths divided among men, women and children and it was reckoned that in the city there were always about 1,500 foreigners, transients and soldiers, not including in the total the citizens who were clerics and cloistered monks and nuns. . . . We find that the boys and girls learning to read numbered from 8,000 to 10,000, the children learning the abacus and algorism from 1,000 to 1,200 and those learning grammar and logic in four large schools from 550 to 600.

We find that the churches then in Florence and in the suburbs, including the abbeys and the churches of friars, were 110. . . .

The workshops of the *Arte della Lana* (the gild of wool merchants) were 200 or more, and they made from 70,000 to 80,000 pieces of cloth, which were worth more than 1,200,000 gold florins. And a good third of this sum remained in the land as wages to labour, without counting the profits of the enterpreneurs. And more than 30,000 persons lived by it. To be sure, we find that some thirty years earlier there were 300 workshops or thereabouts, and they made more than 100,000 pieces of cloth yearly; but these cloths were coarser and one half less valuable, because at that time English wool was not imported and they did not know, as they did later, how to work it.

The storehouses of the *Arte di Calimala* (the gild of importers, refinishers and sellers of Transalpine cloth) were some 20 and they imported yearly more than 10,000 pieces of cloth, worth 300,000 gold florins. And all these were sold in Florence, without counting those which were re-exported from Florence.

The banks of money-changers were about 80. The gold coins which were struck amounted to some 350,000 gold florins and at times 400,-000 yearly. And as for deniers of four pennies each, about 20,000 *liras* of them were struck yearly.

The association of the judges was composed of some 80 members; the notaries public were some 600; physicians and surgeons some 60; shops of apothecaries and dealers in spices, some 100.

---

2. Giovanni Villani, *Cronica*, book 11, Chapter 94. The English translation is by Lopez and Raymond, *Medieval Trade*, pp. 71–74.

Merchants and mercers were a large number; the shops of shoe-makers, slipper makers and wooden-shoe makers were so numerous that they could not be counted. There were some 300 persons and more who went to do business out of Florence and so did many other masters in many crafts and stone and carpentry masters.

There were then in Florence 146 bakeries, and from the amount of the tax on grinding and through information furnished by the bakers we find that the city within the walls needed 140 *moggia*[3] of grain every day. . . . Through the amount of tax at the gates we find that some 55,000 *cogna* of wine entered Florence yearly, and in times of plenty about 10,000 *cogna* more.

Every year the city consumed about 4,000 oxen and calves, 60,000 mutton and sheep, 20,000 she-goats and he-goats, 30,000 pigs.

During the month of July 4,000 loads of melons came through Porta San Friano. . . .

Florence within the walls was well built, with many beautiful houses and at that time people kept building with improved techniques to obtain comfort and every kind of improvement was imported. . . .

A few decades earlier, another chronicler, Bonvesin della Riva, had written similar things about Milan (Italy), pointing to "the abundance of all goods," "the almost innumerable merchants with their variety of wares," and the ample opportunities for employment ("here any man, if he is healthy and not a good-for-nothing, may earn his living expenses and esteem according to his station").[4]

The moralists were dismayed. In his *Paradiso*, Dante countered with this ideal vision, in which[5]

> Florence within the ancient cincture sate
>   wherefrom she still hears daily tierce and nones,
>   dwelling in peace, modest and temperate.
>
> She wore no chain or crownet set with stones,
>   no gaudy skirt nor broidered belt, to gather
>   all eyes with more charm than the wearer owns.

---

3. The *moggio* was a dry measure equal to 16.59 bushels.
4. Bonvesin della Riva. *De Magnalibus Urbis Mediolani,* pp. 67–114. For an English translation of the relevant passages see Lopez and Raymond, *Medieval Trade,* pp. 61–69.
5. Dante, *Comedy,* Paradise 15, translation by L. Binyon.

Nor yet did daughter's birth dismay the father;
    for dowry and nuptial-age did not exceed
    the measure, upon one side or the other.

There was no house too vast for household need;
    Sardanapalus was not come to show
    what wanton feats could in the chamber speed.

Nor yet could ever Montemalo crow
    your Uccellatoio, which, as it hath been
    passed in its rise, shall in its fall be so.

Bellincion Berti girdled I have seen
    with leather and bone; and from her looking glass
    his lady come with cheeks of raddle clean.

I have seen a Nerli and a Vecchio pass
    in jerkin of bare hide, and hour by hour
    their wives the flax upon the spindle mass.

Around the end of the thirteenth century and the beginning of
the fourteenth, Ricobaldo da Ferrara, canon of the Cathedral of
Ravenna, wrote of the dramatic improvements in living conditions
in northern Italy.[6] In Milan he was echoed by Galvano Flamma,
who, paraphrasing him, wrote:[7]

Life and customs were hard in Lombardy at the time of Frederic II
[died in 1250]. Men covered their heads with infule made of
scales of iron. Their clothes were cloaks of leather without any adorn-
ments, or clothes of rough wool with no lining. With a few pence,
people felt rich. Men longed to have arms and horses. If one was noble
and rich, one's ambition was to own high towers from which to admire
the city and the mountains and the rivers. The women covered their

---

6. Ricobaldus, *Historia Universalis,* in R.R. II S.S., vol. 9, col. 128. On the
relation between Ricolbaldo's text and the successive texts of Flamma and of
De Mussis, as well as on ideas of economic progress of the time, cfr. Rubinstein, *Some Ideas on Municipal Progress,* pp. 165–83, and Herlihy, *Pistoia,*
pp. 1–5.
7. Flamma, *Opusculum* in R.R. II S.S., vol. 12, col. 1033–4.

chins and their temples with bands. The virgins wore tunics of "pigno-
lato" and petticoats of linen, and on their heads they wore no ornaments at all. A normal dowry was about ten lire and at the utmost
reached one hundred, because the clothes of the woman were ever so
simple. There were no fireplaces in the houses.[8] Expenses were cut down
to a minimum because in summer people drank little wine and wine-
cellars were not kept. At the table, knives were not used; husband and
wife ate off the same plate, and there was one cup or two at most for
the whole family. Candles were not used, and at night one dined by
light of glowing torches. One ate cooked turnips, and ate meat only
three times a week. Clothing was frugal. Today, instead, everything is
sumptuous. Dress has become precious and rich with superfluity. Men
and women bedeck themselves with gold, silver, and pearls. Foreign
wines and from distant countries are drunk, luxurious dinners are
eaten, and cooks are highly valued.

In the second half of the fourteenth century, in Piacenza (Italy),
Giovanni de Mussis wrote:[9]

The people of Piacenza actually live in a clean and luxurious way, and
in the houses are found utensils and crockery far superior to those of
seventy years ago, that is, of about 1320. The houses are more beautiful than they were then, because they have beautiful rooms with fire
places, arches, courtyards, wells, gardens, and sun-parlors. In a house
one finds more fireplaces nowadays, while at one time, there was no
fireplace at all. Fires were then made in the middle room, under the
tiles, and all the inhabitants of the house gathered around the fire on
which the food was cooked. I myself have seen this in many houses. . . .
In general, the people of Piacenze drink better wines nowadays than
did their elders.

These chroniclers referred particularly to the higher classes,
although Giovanni de Mussis, in the heat of his presentation, felt
the need to assert that his description:

applies not only to the nobles and the merchants but also to those who
practice manual trades, who make reckless purchases, especially on
clothes for themselves and their wives; employment seems to provide
them with enough to support all this with honor.

---

8. In Piacenza, the first fireplaces appeared after 1320. In Rome they were
still rare in 1368.
9. De Mussis, *Chronicon Placentium*, cols. 582–84.

It is true of course, that what seemed to be great luxury to those austere moralists would still be, for us, a very primitive way of life. People were beginning to make use of the knife at the table, but forks were still unknown; they normally made use of their fingers to carry food to their mouths, just as they used their fingers to blow their noses; handkerchiefs were a "luxury" of the seventeenth and eighteenth centuries.[10] Even in the richest palaces the "toilettes" were narrow passages with holes in the floor which discharged onto the street. However, with all these limitations, there is no doubt that between the eleventh and the fourteeneth centuries the standard of living rose appreciably—in certain areas more than others, among certain social groups more than others, but improvement there was, and this improvement was general.

And though preachers and moralists found reasons for concern in the improvement in the standard of living, the greater part of the population rejoiced in it. The fourteenth century opened with the flag of optimism flying high. In the course of the thirteenth century, Siena (Italy) had erected a magnificant Duomo, a most refined and elegant testimony of greatly increased wealth. At the beginning of the fourteenth century, the Sienese were convinced that wealth and population would continue to increase, and in 1339, L. Maitani was charged with the preparation of plans for an enormous church, of which the existing cathedral would be only the transept. The plan was made and work begun. But it was never finished. The empty arches, the unfinished walls which break away from the old cathedral are woeful testimony to the fragility of men's dreams.

Economic Trends: 1300–1500

At the beginning of the fourteenth century, the only cause for opti-

---

10. The Emperor Charles V had a dozen forks among his possessions, but the courtiers of Henry III of France were still laughed at for the amount of food they lost on the way to their mouths. As to handkerchiefs, one must keep in mind that the height of good manners in the Middle Ages was to use only the left hand to blow one's nose at the table. In the sixteenth century the middle class had begun to use the sleeve, rather than the fingers. Then the handkerchief slowly came to be adopted. Henry IV of France allegedly possessed five handkerchiefs and this was thought worthy of note.

mism lay in the belief that, in the future, things would go on as they had in the past. During the thirteenth century, certain bottlenecks had begun to manifest themselves. As demographic pressure steadily increased, there eventually came into play the economic law according to which lands with diminishing marginal returns are taken into cultivation. It is by no means improbable that in the second half of the thirteenth century the frontier went beyond the optimum allowable by contemporary agricultural techniques. Various factors lead us to believe that, in several areas of Europe after 1250, the average yield-to-seed ratio began to decrease. At the same time, since population continued to increase while fertile land began to be relatively scarce, the laws of supply and demand inevitably pushed rents up and real wages down.

On the basis of these facts, a modern economist transplanted back into the Europe of the time, could have foreseen a sort of apocalypse in the shape of a series of famines. In northern Europe, one disastrous famine did in fact occur in 1317,[11] and another occurred in southern Europe in 1346–47. But when the apocalypse did come, it was not in the shape of a famine.

We have already noted the shocking results of the plague epidemic of 1348–51. Out of about 80 million people who lived in Europe before the plague, roughly 25 million disappeared in little more than two years. And the tragedy did not end there. From then on, epidemics of various sorts, but especially of plague, afflicted Europe in a lengthy chain of devasting attacks. The age of the *Cantico delle Creature* had given way to the age of the *Danse Macabre*. [12]

The action of germs was compounded by the folly of men. Wars and revolutions dealt men in various parts of Europe the same fate offered by microbes. Between the middle of the fourteenth century and the end of the fifteenth, vast areas of France were laid waste in the course of the Hundred Years' War (1337–1453). In Catalonia, the Civil War of 1462–72 accelerated a process of economic decline which had been taking place for about a century. In Eng-

---

11. Lucas, *The Great European Famine*, pp. 49–72.
12. Concerning the effects of the plague on the collective psychology, and on the art forms, consult, among others, Langer, *Next Assignment*, pp. 283–304; Meiss, *Painting;* Brossolet, *L'Influence de la peste*.

land, the Wars of the Roses (1455–85) caused widespread misery and destruction. These are only a few of the horrors which occurred, and only the most famous; the complete list of general and local conflicts would be too long to be presented here—in Europe, war was as endemic as plague.

History teaches—even if man seldom learns—that if Athens cries, Sparta does not smile. A few European areas were spared from wars or revolutions but nevertheless suffered the repercussions of the distress which afflicted the less fortunate areas. In the first half of the fourteenth century, the outbreak of hostilities between France and England led to a series of disastrous bankruptcies in a number of Tuscan trading centers. Piedmont felt strongly the decrease in transalpine traffic, as Duke Amedeo explicitly declared in a letter of 1346. There is no doubt that in most European areas, the situation around 1450 was much worse than it had been at the dawn of the 1300s. Scholars such as M. M. Postan, R. S. Lopez, and H. Miskimin rightly depict the period from 1330 to 1470 in very somber tones. Nevertheless, one ought not to generalize too much, or give certain indexes a significance they do not possess.

The fundamental fact of the period 1350–1500 is that wars but especially plague and other infectious diseases relieved Europe from the population pressure which had made itself increasingly felt since the middle of the thirteenth century. To speak of an "economic depression of the Renaissance" merely because some rather dubious data suggest that in, let us say, 1450, the global volume of some trade or of some production was below pre-1348 levels makes as much sense as to maintain that Luxembourg is depressed by comparison with India because Luxembourg's total income is lower than that of India. What matters is not the total product, but the product *per capita*. The mortality caused by the Black Death and by ensuing epidemics, maintained the European population, for over a century, at considerably lower levels than those reached before 1347. Between 1347 and 1500 European population declined from 80 million, to possibly 60 or 70 million. Historians have found that in England, with a population reduced to about two-thirds its former size, the production of tin was maintained at the previous level—which naturally meant that production per capita increased by 30 percent. The same can be said of English export of wool and woollen cloth.[13] Around 1400 the total European production of iron was about 25,000 to 30,000 tons. At the end of the century, iron production had probably risen to about 40,000 tons.[14] Marginal lands, occupied in times of population pressure, were abandoned when population decreased. (See in Germany the case of the *Wüstungen*.) Those who would like to see every corner of the earth populated at no matter what cost can, if they wish, complain of this "withdrawal," but economically, it can only have had a positive effect on *per capita* production.

The successive onslaughts of epidemics and the ravages of the war naturally affected the returns to factors of production. Between 1350 and 1500 real wages rose (see Figures 8-1 and 8-2) while rents and interest showed a tendency toward stagnation or reduction.[15] The monetary rents of the abbey of Tremblay (France) fell from about 500 *livres* in 1335–43 to about 205 *livres* in 1368–69. The rents of the abbey of St. Denis (France) were reduced by two-thirds between 1342–43 and 1374–75. The rents of the chapter of the cathedral of Schleswig (Germany) amounted to about 7,600 tons of wheat around 1350 and about 2,400 tons around 1437.[16] We do not know the course of profits in the manufacturing and mercantile sectors. The period 1350–1500 can at any rate be clearly distinguished (a) from the period 1100–1250, during which wages, rents, and profits increased; and (b) from the period 1250–1348, when, because of population pressure, real wages stagnated or fell while rents increased.

The contrasting movements in 1350–1500 of real wages on the one hand and rents and interests on the other, accords with the idea of an economy which was not at all depressed, but in which exogenous factors brought about a persistent relative labor scarcity. The differing trend of returns to the various factors of production meant a different distribution of income. The peasant classes

---

13. Bridbury, *Economic Growth,* pp. 25–33 and 104. On the trade of Bristol, see Carus-Wilson, *The Merchant Adventurers,* p. 3.
14. Sprandel, *Das Eisengewerbe.*
15. For rent, consult Bridbury, *Economic Growth,* Chapters IV-VI. For the interest rate, Homer, *A History of Interest Rates,* pp. 141 ff.
16. Fourquin, *Historie économique,* pp. 334–43.

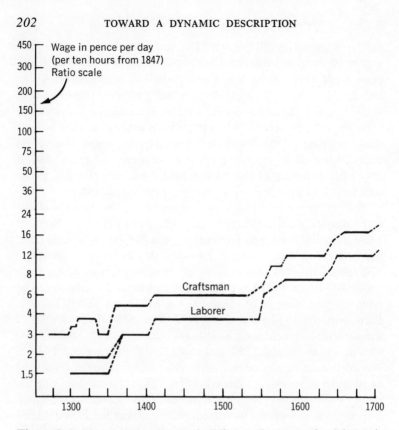

Figure 8–1. Monetary wages of a building craftsman and a laborer in southern England, 1264–1700.

Source: E. H. Phelps Brown and Sheila V. Hopkins, "Wage rates and Prices: Evidence for Population Pressure in the Sixteenth Century."

improved their economic and social position relative to the class of landed proprietors. The weakening of the power of the merchant guild and the formation of numerous craft guilds suggests that craftsmen and workers in the towns were likewise improving their position relative to the groups of the merchant-entrepreneurs. What we know of the history of consumption confirms these views. The above passages from Dante, Galvano Flamma, and Giovanni de Mussis refer above all to the consumption of the wealthy classes. But one has a distinct impression that between 1350 and 1500 a

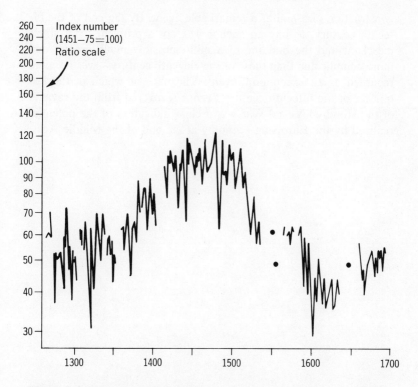

Figure 8–2. Wage-rate of a building craftsman expressed in a composite physical unit of consumable goods in southern England, 1264–1700. Source: See Figure 8–1.

number of those things which to the moralists of the first part of the fourteenth century looked like conspicuous luxuries slowly filtered through to wider sections of the population. At least in the towns, the fireplace, the individual dish, the chair in the place of the bench, and the dowry of some substance became more common even among the lower orders.

By the end of the fifteenth century the progress which had been achieved over the previous five centuries was obvious not only in the levels of consumption but also in those of productive investment. In the eleventh century a number of capitalist Venetian merchants had to join forces to be able to buy an anchor for their merchant ship. The records of the Abbey of St. Bertin pointed to the construction of a mill as a remarkable event. By the end of the fifteenth century, to buy an anchor was not a problem for a single merchant and the building of a mill—possibly much greater and more complicated than those of the eleventh century—was no more regarded as an exceptional event. The pace at which in the last quarter of the fifteenth century France recovered from the ravages of the Hundred Years' War was a clear indication of the potential realized by the European economy at the end of the Middle Ages.

CHAPTER NINE

The Emergence
of the Modern Age

Underdeveloped Europe or Developed Europe?

In the years that immediately followed the Second World War, it became fashionable among economists to discuss economic development and to distinguish between developed and underdeveloped societies. An underdeveloped society is normally defined as a society in which the economy is characterized by underemployment of human and material resources; low real income per capita in comparison with that of the United States, Canada, and western Europe; and prevalence of undernourishment, illiteracy, and disease. If one accepts this definition of underdevelopment, one is inescapably brought to identify development with industrialization and underdevelopment with the preindustrial stage. By this standard, all societies in the world before 1750 were underdeveloped, whether it was a matter of the Tuaregs in Africa or the Florentines at the time of the Medici. Once the limits of one's definitions have been clearly established, one can say anything one likes that does not overstep those limits, but the value of any definition depends upon the assistance it can give in one's inquiries. The statement that the whole world before 1750 was underdeveloped cannot help us in our inquiry. However, the term *underdeveloped* has acquired a certain power of suggestion and it may be retained here provided we redefine it, not as a synonym of "per-capita incomes lower than those of the United States," but to indicate, albeit vaguely, levels of "performance" inferior to those of the advanced societies of the period in question.

If we adopt this criterion, there is no doubt that from the fall of the Roman Empire to the beginning of the thirteenth century Europe was an underdeveloped area in relation to the major centers of civilization at the time, whether the China of the T'ang or Sung Dynasties, the Byzantine Empire under the Macedonian dynasty, or the Arab Empire under the Ommayads or the Abbasids. The situation was an area of so little interest that, while the Arabs' geographic western Europe was clearly a land of barbarians. To the Arabs it was an area of so little interest that, while the Arabs' geographic knowledge continually improved between A.D., 700 and 1000, their "knowledge of Europe did not increase at all." If Arabian geographers did not bother with Europe, it was not because of a hostile attitude, but rather because Europe at the time "had little to offer" of any interest.[1] The accounts by a Liutprando of Cremona of his voyage to Constantinople, or centuries later, those by Marco Polo of his journey to China reflect sentiments of wonder and admiration for societies which were far more refined and developed than their own.

However, from the year 1000, the European economy "took off" and gradually gained ground. One cannot accurately say when the balance first began to redress itself and then to weigh in Europe's favor: among other difficulties, one has to remember that in matters of this kind, not all sectors of a society move at the same pace. One must be satisfied with some indicators to be used as vague points of reference.

In the course of the thirteenth century, Venetian merchants proved they had evolved more advanced business techniques than those used in the Byzantine Empire, and the Byzantine merchants had to give way to their new and aggressive competitors.[2] Until the middle of the thirteenth century the Court of Byzantium used paper imported from the Arab countries; in the second half of the thirteenth century it began to use paper imported from Italy.[3] In the

---

1. Ashtor, *Che cosa sapevano i geografi arabi dell'Europa occidentale?*
2. Andreades, *The Economic Life of the Byzantine Empire.*
3. Irigoin, *Les débuts de l'emploi du papier à Byzance*, p. 314.

summer of 1338 the cargo of a galley which set sail from Venice for the East included a mechanical clock,[4] symbolic beginning of the export of machinery reflecting the incipient technological supremacy of the West. At the end of the fifteenth century, some Byzantine writers, such as Demetrius Cydone, admitted for the first time that the West was not after all the land of primitive barbarians that the Byzantines had always thought it to be.[5] A few decades later the Byzantine Cardinal Bessarion wrote to Constantine Paleologus, urging him to send young Greeks to Italy to learn Western techniques in the field of mechanics, iron metallurgy, and the manufacture of arms.[6] Soon after the arrival of the Portuguese ships in Canton in 1517, the scholar-official Wang Hong wrote that "the westerns are extremely dangerous because of their artillery. No weapon ever made since memorable antiquity is superior to their cannon."[7]

By the beginning of the sixteenth century, the situation which had prevailed five centuries earlier was completely reversed: Western Europe had become the most developed area of the time. As Lynn White wrote, "The Europe which rose to global dominance about 1500 had an industrial capacity and skill vastly greater than that of any of the cultures of Asia—not to mention Africa or America—which it challenged."[8]

European Expansion

The most spectacular consequences of the supremacy acquired by Europe in the technical field were the geographic explorations and the subsequent economic, military, and political expansion of

---

4. Lopez, *Venezia*, pp. 53–59.
5. Sevcenko, *The Decline of Byzantium*, pp. 176 ff., and Geanakoplos, *A Byzantine Look at the Renaissance*, pp. 157–162.
6. Lambros, *Ipomnina tou Kardinaliou Vissarionos*, pp. 15–27, and Keller, *A Byzantine Admirer of Western Progress*, pp. 343–48.
7. Cipolla, *Guns and Sails*, p. 89. For an analysis of the "relative decline" of China compared to Europe on the technological plane from the fourteenth century onward, compare Elvin, *The Patterns of the Chinese Past*, pp. 177–78 and Chapter 14.
8. White, *Expansion of Technology*, p. 157.

Europe. Between the eleventh and the fifteenth centuries Europe was startlingly aggressive in the economic sphere, but on the political and military levels it remained at the mercy of potential invaders. The episode of the Crusades must not deceive us. The success which characterized the first stages of the European attack was largely due to an element of surprise and to the temporary weakness and disorganization of the Arab world. As Grousset said, it was "the victory of the Frankish monarchy over Muslim anarchy." But the forces of Islam reorganized themselves, and the Europeans were compelled to beat a retreat.

The disaster of Wahlstatt (1241) showed dramatically that Europe was militarily incapable of standing up to the Mongol menace. That Europe was not invaded was due to the death of the Mongol chief Ogödäi (December 1241) and to the fact that the Khans were more strongly attracted to the East than to the West. In the following century the Christian defeat at Nicopolis (1396) showed yet again the military weakness of the Europeans in the face of the oriental invaders. Europe was saved once more by fortuitous circumstances. Bayazed, the conqueror, became involved with the Mongols of Timur Lenk (Tamerlane), and one potential danger luckily and unexpectedly eliminated the other.

If, however, exceptional circumstances saved Europe from complete destruction, its chronic weakness was shown by the progressive loss to its enemy of its oriental territories. The Turkish advance continued inexorably, conquering the European outposts one after another. On May 28, 1454, Constantinople fell. "A terrible thing to describe and utterly deplorable for those who still have in them a glimmer of humanity and Christianity," wrote Cardinal Bessarion to the Doge of Venice.

After the fall of Constantinople the European position gradually deteriorated. Northern Serbia was lost in 1459; Bosnia-Herzegovina in 1463–66; the Negroponte and Albania in 1470. "I see nothing good on the horizon," wrote Pope Pius II.

Yet, at the time when the Turks seemed on the point of striking at the very heart of Europe, a sudden and revolutionary change took place. Outflanking the Turkish blockade, some European countries launched successive waves of attacks over the oceans. Their advance was as rapid as it was unexpected. In a little more than a century, first the Portuguese and the Spaniards, then the

Dutch and the English, laid the basis of worldwide European predominance.

The gun-carrying oceangoing sailing ship developed by Atlantic Europe in the course of the fifteenth, sixteenth and seventeenth centuries was the instrument which made possible the European saga. Whenever and wherever the ships of Atlantic Europe appeared, there was no power that could offer any resistance. In 1513 the great Portuguese navigator Albuquerque proudly wrote to his king that "at the rumor of our coming, the native ships all vanished, and even the birds ceased to skim over the water." The prose was rhetorical, but the substance of the statement reflected truth. Within fifteen years after their first arrival in Indian waters, the Portuguese had completely destroyed Arab navigation.[9]

While Atlantic Europe expanded overseas, European Russia launched its expansion to the east across the steppes and to the south against the Turks. The Russian expansion was also the result of European technological superiority. As G. F. Hudson wrote in regard to the Russian attack against the Hordes of the Kasaks,

The collapse of the power of the nomads with so slight a resistance after they had again and again turned the course of history with their military powers, is to be attributed not to any degeneracy of the nomads themselves but to the evolution of the art of war beyond their capacity of adaptation. The Tartars in the seventeenth and eighteenth centuries had lost none of the qualities which had made so terrible the armies of Attila and Baian, of Genghis Khan and Tamerlane. But the increasing use in war of artillery and musketry was fatal to a power which depended on cavalry and had not the economic resources for the new equipment.[10]

The European eastward expansion did not have the dramatic speed of the overseas expansion of Atlantic Europe, essentially because the technological superiority of the Europeans was not as marked on land as it was on the seas. On the open sea, a small band of men exploiting wind and gunpowder in combination stood practically invulnerable. But on land the Asians could counterbalance technological inferiority with weight of numbers. The eastward advance became inexorable only after the middle of the sev-

9. On the preceding, cfr. Cipolla, *Guns and Sails,* pp. 15–18 and 137.
10. Hudson, *Europe and China,* p. 268.

enteenth century, when European technology succeeded in developing more mobile and rapid-firing guns. In the face of a technological gap which constantly widened, numbers counted less and less, and the oriental masses suffered one defeat after another.

The lightning overseas expansion of Europe had immense economic effects. One of the major consequences was the discovery in Mexico and Peru of rich deposits of gold and especially silver. For over a century, the legendary Spanish *Flotas de Indias* brought fabulous treasures to Europe. The figures calculated by E. J. Hamilton are not as reliable as was once thought, but they are sufficient to give an approximate idea of the order of magnitude concerned (see Table 9-1).

A portion of the metals, probably more than 20 percent, was transferred to the mother country as income of the Crown,[11] and with sovereigns such as the Spanish who were obsessed with the idea of a Catholic Crusade, that part of the treasure was immedi-

Table 9–1

Kilograms of Gold and Silver Allegedly
Imported into Spain from the Americas, 1503–1650[1]

Period	Silver	Gold
1503–10		4,965
1511–20		9,153
1521–30	149	4,889
1531–40	86,194	14,466
1541–50	177,573	24,957
1551–60	303,121	42,620
1561–70	942,859	11,531
1571–80	1,118,592	9,429
1581–90	2,103,028	12,102
1591–1600	2,707,627	19,451
1601–10	2,213,631	11,764
1611–20	2,192,256	8,856
1621–30	2,145,339	3,890
1631–40	1,396,760	1,240
1641–50	1,056,431	1,549

SOURCE: Hamilton, *American Treasure*, p. 42.
[1] One Kilogram = 2.2046 pounds.

---

11. Brading and Cross, *Colonial Silver Mining*, pp. 560 ff.

ately transformed into effective demand for military services and for arms and provisions. Some of the remaining 80 percent of the treasure was brought back to Spain by returning *Conquistadores*; most of it, however, came to Europe as effective demand for consumer and capital goods—textiles, wine, weapons, furniture, various implements, jewels, and so forth—and for the commercial and transport services necessary for the transportation of the goods in question to the Americas.

This demand, with its multiplier effects (this being the sequence of spendings set off by the original increase in spending), happened to coincide with a general increase in the population of Europe during the whole of the sixteenth century. To the extent that supply was elastic, the rise in demand resulted in increased production, but to the extent to which certain bottlenecks in the productive apparatus—especially in the agricultural sector—put a brake on the expansion of production, the rise in demand resulted in a rise in prices. The period 1500 to 1620 has been labeled by economic historians —with a bit of exaggeration—the age of the "Price Revolution." It is generally held that between 1500 and 1620, the average level of prices in the various European countries increased by 300 to 400 percent. Statements of this kind look more or less impressive, but they are scarcely significant. The "average general level of prices" is an extremely ambiguous statistical abstraction; the average general index of prices varies according to the prices considered and the weights one adopts. Table 9-2 provides a clear example of the fact that, on the same market, prices of various products moved in different ways. The different behaviors of the different sets of prices can be attributed either to changes in the structure of demand or to the presence (or absence) of bottlenecks in the various productive sectors.

The increase in liquidity brought down the interest rate at least in some major financial centers. At the beginning of the seventeenth century in Genoa, interest rates on safe government securities were down to 1.5 percent, and in Amsterdam in the second half of the seventeenth century it was possible to borrow capital at the rate of 3 percent.[12] Table 9-3 shows this trend for Genoa's major

---

12. Cipolla, *Saggio di Interesse*; Barbour, *Capitalism*, pp. 85 ff.; Homer *Interest Rates*, p. 128.

Table 9–2

Percentage Rise in Prices of Selected Groups of Commodities
at Pavia (Italy), 1548–80

Commodities	(a) Raw Materials and Semi-finished Goods	(b) Finished Goods	Weighted Average of (a) and (b)
Clothing and Textiles	31	58	50
Foodstuffs			86
Metallurgical, Mineral, and Chemical Products	87	57	81
Hides and Leather Goods			18
Spices, Drugs and Dyes			43
Miscellaneous			16
Total	45	58	65

SOURCE: Zanetti, *Rivoluzione dei prezzi*, p. 13.

credit institution of the period. It was perhaps the first time in the history of the world that capital was offered at such low rates.

Gold and silver were accepted all over the world as means of payment for international transactions. The greater supply of precious metals meant greater international liquidity and favored the development of international exchanges. This effect was particularly notable in the trade with the East.

After Europe had established direct relations with the Far East, it faced an economic problem of considerable difficulty in the chronically unfavorable balance of trade. Europeans found products in the East which sold well in Europe,[13] but no European product succeeded in finding similar outlets in the East.

With their powerful galleons, the Europeans destroyed most of the Muslim shipping trade in the Indian Ocean and established themselves as the masters of the high seas. They replaced the tradi-

---

13. For the whole of the sixteenth century and still at the beginning of the seventeenth, nearly 80 percent of European imports from the East consisted of pepper, other spices, and dyes. During the seventeenth century, textiles acquired greater importance and toward the end of the century made up about 60 percent of import into Europe by the English and Dutch East India Companies. Compare Glamann, *Dutch-Asiatic Trade*, pp. 13, 14; and Pach, *The Role of East-Central Europe*, pp. 220–22.

Table 9–3

Rate of Interest (A) and Discount Rate (B) on Bonds of the
Bank of St. George, Genoa (Italy), 1522–1620

Year	A %	B %	Year	A %	B %	Year	A %	B %
1522	4.2	5.0	1555	9.0	3.5	1588	3.3	2.2
1523	3.0	5.1	1556	6.2	3.6	1589	3.4	2.3
1524	4.0	4.4	1557	5.9	3.5	1590	3.3	2.5
1525	2.9	4.1	1558	5.5	3.4	1591	3.3	2.3
1526	5.5	4.1	1559	6.2	3.3	1592	3.4	2.3
1527	6.5	3.7	1560	6.2	3.6	1593	3.3	2.2
1528	5.2	3.7	1561	6.5	3.6	1594	3.8	2.2
1529	4.2	3.8	1562	5.6	3.6	1595	3.7	2.3
1530	4.0	4.0	1563	4.3	4.1	1596	3.5	2.4
1531	4.0	3.8	1564	4.6	3.8	1597	3.1	2.4
1532	5.1	3.5	1565	7.3	3.8	1598	2.5	2.4
1533	4.0	3.7	1566	9.0	3.3	1599	2.9	2.3
1534	5.2	3.5	1567	6.2	3.8	1600	2.9	2.4
1535	4.3	3.7	1568	5.9	4.0	1601	3.0	2.3
1536	4.6	3.7	1569	4.9	4.1	1602	2.9	2.7
1537	4.2	3.7	1570	5.0	4.2	1603	3.6	1.4
1538	4.4	3.6	1571	4.4	3.5	1604	2.4	1.5
1539	4.8	3.7	1572	3.6	3.6	1605	2.1	1.4
1540	4.2	3.8	1573	2.5	4.1	1606	4.4	1.3
1541	4.0	3.8	1574	3.0	3.8	1607	2.4	1.4
1542	3.9	3.6	1575	4.2	3.5	1608	2.6	1.3
1543	4.1	3.8	1576	3.7	2.7	1609	2.6	1.4
1544	4.6	3.7	1577	3.8	2.7	1610	2.4	1.4
1545	5.3	3.1	1578	2.7	3.3	1611	1.9	1.6
1546	3.5	4.2	1579	3.3	3.4	1612	2.0	1.6
1547	3.7	4.1	1580	4.4	2.5	1613	1.6	1.6
1548	4.3	3.9	1581	2.9	2.9	1614	1.7	1.6
1549	4.6	3.8	1582	2.5	2.5	1615	1.6	1.5
1550	4.4	4.3	1583	2.4	2.9	1616	1.6	1.4
1551	4.5	4.1	1584	2.5	2.5	1617	1.4	1.4
1552	4.3	3.8	1585	1.9	2.4	1618	1.4	1.4
1553	4.6	3.9	1586	2.7	2.2	1619	1.1	1.2
1554	7.3	3.5	1587	3.0	2.2	1620	1.2	1.2

SOURCE: Cipolla, *Nota sulla storia del saggio di interesse.*

tional merchants and captured a large share of the intra-Asian trade. By bringing Japanese copper to China and India, Spice Islands cloves to India and China, Indian cotton textiles to Southeast Asia, and Persian carpets to India, the Europeans made good profits and with them paid for some of their imports from Asia. The Dutch, who were allowed to continue to trade in Japan, there obtained silver and, later, gold which they used to pay for their imports from other parts of Asia. Between 1640 and 1699 the Dutch exports of silver and gold from Japan were as follows:[14]

	SILVER (FLORINS)	GOLD (FLORINS)
1640–49	15,188,713	
1650–59	13,151,211	
1660–69	10,488,214	4,060,919
1670–79		11,541,481
1680–89		2,983,830
1690–99		2,289,520

All this, however, was not enough to make up for the deficit in the balance of trade between Europe and the Far East. To settle that deficit Europe used American silver in the form of Mexican dollars, *reales*, or pieces of eight minted in Seville; ducatoons minted in Italy; rixdollars minted in Holland (see Table 9-4). Leaving aside the relatively limited direct traffic between the Spanish Colonies in America and the Philippines, one can say that intercontinental trade in the sixteenth and seventeenth centuries consisted essentially of a large flow of silver which moved eastward from the Americas to Europe and from Europe to the Far East, and a flow of commodities which moved in the opposite direction: Asian products bound for Europe and European products bound for the Americas.

J. H. Van Linschoten, observing the East Indiamen leaving for the East, wrote:

When they go out they are but lightly laden, only with certain pipes of wine and oil, and some small quantity of merchandise; other things they have not in, but balast and victuals for the company, for that the

---

14. Glamann, *Dutch-Asiatic Trade*, p. 58.

Table 9-4

Analysis of Silver and Gold Received in Batavia from the Netherlands 1677/78–1684/85

(thousands of florins)

	1677/78	1678/79	1679/80	1680/81	1681/82	1682/83	1683/84	1684/85
Silver								
Reales of eight	—	—	—	—	—	—	10	—
Mark reales	786	407	503	889	1,182	337	91	316
Ducatoons	101	60	110	36	63	68	—	39
Rixdollars	357	26	44	23	—	—	—	—
Leewendaalders	240	109	254	205	108	331	254	53
Silver in bullion	102	93	500	332	236	1,020	649	532
Payment	472	134	58	339	46	183	45	192
Gold								
Ducats	—	—	20	—	—	—	—	—
Gold in bullion	165	222	89	—	13	209	305	—
Total	2,223	1,051	1,578	1,824	1,648	2,148	1,354	1,132

SOURCE: Glamann, *Dutch-Asiatic Trade*, p. 61.

most and greatest ware that is commonly sent into India are reales of eight.[15]

At the end of the sixteenth century, the Florentine merchant and traveler Francesco Carletti estimated that the Chinese

. . . extracted from these two nations [Portugal and Spain] in silver more than a million and a half écus a year, selling their goods and never buying anything, so that, once the silver gets into their hands it never leaves them.[16]

It is difficult to say what value can be attributed to Carletti's estimate of the Portuguese and Spanish deficit to China, but for England there are the account books of the East India Company, and the figures which emerge from them are significant: the value of the gold and silver exported was never less than two-thirds of total exports (goods plus precious metals) and in the decade 1680–89 it was as much as 87 percent (Table 9-5).

The difficulty caused by a balance of trade chronically deficitary obviously caused much anxiety in mercantilistic Europe. After

Table 9–5
Exports of the English East India Company
to the Far East, 1660–99

Year	Metals	Commodities	Total	Metals as Percentage of Total
	(Thousand of the current £)			
1660–69	879	446	1,325	66
1670–79	2,546	883	3,429	74
1680–89	3,443	505	3,948	87
1690–99	2,100	787	2,887	73

SOURCE: Chaudhuri, *Treasure and Trade Balance*, pp. 497–98.

---

15. Van Linschoten, *The Voyage to the East Indies*, vol. 1, p. 10. Western Europe's trade with the Baltic also showed a deficit. It has been estimated that, at the end of the sixteenth century and the beginning of the seventeenth, of the total value of the goods in transit through the Sound, 70 percent went from the Baltic toward the West as against 30 percent which went in the opposite direction. The deficit was settled with Western exports of silver. Compare Attman, *The Russian and Polish Markets*, pp. 119 ff.
16. Carletti, *Ragionamenti*, p. 189.

unsuccessfully attempting to export all sorts of things from English textiles to religious as well as pornographic paintings Europeans found the solution to their problems after the end of the eighteenth century in Indian opium—which eventually caused a tragic conflict and a definite poisoning of the relations between China and Europe.

Geographic exploration and overseas expansion made available to Europe new and unusual products. Europeans were especially fascinated by the new drugs and medicaments that they encountered. The Spaniards, for instance, did not show any particular interest in or respect for the civilization of the American Indians, but they were remarkable for the interest and respect which they accorded to the pharmacopeia of the Indians of Mexico. In 1570 Philip II of Spain appointed Francisco Hernandes (1517–78) to the position of head physician (proto-physician) of the West Indies and charged him especially with the task of collecting information on the drugs and medicines of the natives. Dr. Hernandes eventually produced his monumental and classic *Treasure of Medical Matters of New Spain*.[17] The subject became very popular. Two Iberian doctors, Garcia d'Orta and Nicolas Monardes, became deservedly famous for writing on *The Simple Aromats and Other Things Pertaining to the Use of Medicine Which are Brought From the East Indies and the West Indies*. From America, they said,

three things [are brought into Europe] which are praised all over the world and which allow the achievement in medicine of results which have never been achieved with any other drug known up to now. These are the wood called guaiacum, the cinchona, and sarsaparillo.[18]

Among the drugs contributed to medicine by the South American Indians were, besides cinchona, curare and ipecac. The Mayas used capsicum, chenopodium, guaiacum, and vanilla. From the Americas the Europeans also learned to use cocoa, tomatoes, maize, and beans. The potato, discovered in 1538 by a Spanish soldier, Pedro de Cieza de Leon, in the Cauca Valley (Colombia) was introduced

---

17. Hernandes, *Rerum Medicarum*.
18. D'Orta and Monardes, *Dell'Historia de i semplici aromati*, part II, p. 19. On Garcia d'Orta and Nicolas Monardes, see Boxer, *Two Pioneers of Tropical Medicine*.

as a curiosity in Europe in 1588. The introduction and later on the diffusion of the culture of maize and the potato in Europe largely contributed, from the eighteenth century onward, to solving the food problem and to reducing the danger of famines when Europe entered a period of accelerated population growth.[19] Tobacco was brought into England by Ralph Lane and popularized by Sir Walter Raleigh. In 1603 James I published a pamphlet pointing out the bad effect of tobacco smoking. In Russia Tsar Michael punished his soldiers with the rack and knout for smoking. The Puritans condemned it. But many people used smoking as a preventive against epidemic disease, and in 1665 the boys at Eton were made to smoke pipes to ward off the plague. As time went on the consumption of tobacco spread among larger strata of the European population. In the early days tobacco was taken either in a pipe or in the form of snuff, while cigars became popular in Regency days; the cigarette was allegedly a South American invention of the 1750s. Imports into London of tobacco from Virginia and Maryland between 1619 and 1701 showed the following trend (in pounds):

    1619: 20,000
    1635: 1,000,000
    1662–63: 7,000,000
    1668–69: 9,000,000
    1689–92: 12,000,000
    1699–1701: 22,000,000

---

19. In the Low Countries, in the period 1557–1710, per-capita consumption of grain was about one liter a day. In the decade 1781–1791, consumption fell to 0.6 liters because, in the interval, the potato had in part replaced grain in daily food consumption. In Ireland, the rate of substitution was very much higher. For what precedes, see Vandenbroeke, *Cultivation and Consumption of the Potato,* pp. 28–29.

With reference to the classic case of Ireland, see Connell, *The Population of Ireland,* Chapter 5, and Davidson, *The History of the Potato and Its Progress in Ireland.* In general, see Salaman, *History and Social Influence of the Potato.* Barrow, *Travels in China,* p. 398n., wrote at the end of the eighteenth century, "The great advantage of a potato crop is the certainty of its success. Were a general failure of this root to take place, as sometimes happens to crops of rice, Ireland, in its present state, would experience all the horrors that attend a famine in some of the provinces of China." In this brief, inconspicuous footnote Barrow was amazingly prophetic. Less than five decades after he wrote these words the potato crops failed in Ireland and the country experienced "all the horrors that attend a famine in some of the provinces of China."

The list of new products which Europe acquired from the East is noticeably shorter than that of the new products from the American continents, the reason being that through various intermediaries, Europe and the East had always been in contact. The great discovery that Europe made through direct contact with China was tea. Tea was first introduced in England in 1664. King Charles II had a passion for exotic birds, and the East India Company was continually requested to contribute new specimens to the king's collection. In 1664 the Company did not succeed in bringing into Europe any bird worthy of the royal collection and, not knowing what else to do, the directors of the Company decided to present the King with a packet of exotic herbs—a packet weighing 2 pounds, 2 ounces, and valued at £4.5.0 of the time. It must have been a success, because the gift was repeated the following year. In 1703, an agent of the Company in Chusan still bemoaned the fact that the Chinese compelled him to buy tea instead of supplying him with the silks he asked for, but in London, it was remarked that "tea is becoming popular with people of all classes" and in the 1720s tea decidedly replaced silk as the principal import of the company.[20]

In fact, tea became popular with people of all classes only in England. On the Continent wine and beer remained the preferred drinks of the masses. The Dutch became great consumers of coffee in the course of the seventeenth century, but on the whole in Continental Europe the consumption of coffee, tea, chocolate, and tobacco remained confined to the upper and upper middle classes until the end of the eighteenth century. In Russia the consumption of tea remained, in fact, a purely aristocratic affair.

Among the aristocracy, the upper bourgeoisie, and the intellectuals the spread of the consumption of tea, as of coffee, chocolate, and tobacco, was facilitated by the fact that considerable medicinal properties were attributed to all these products. Of tea in particular wonders were told, and, noting that in Europe tea did not perform the therapeutic miracles it was claimed to perform in China, the great physician Lionardo di Capua observed:

The tea herb is commonly used by us now, although we do not see

---

20. Morse, *The Chronicles of the East India Company*, vol. 1, pp. 9, 125, and 158.

from it those wonderful effects which it allegedly shows in China—it may be that, during the journey of such long duration, it loses for the most part its volatile alkali and with it, little less than the whole of its virtue—or some other reason.[21]

Other doctors were less critical, and the medical profession as a whole largely favored the consumption of tea, coffee, and chocolate. One may quote as an example the *"Tractaat"* by the Dutch physician Cornelis Bontekoe on the excellence of tea, coffee, and chocolate (The Hague, 1685) and the book by the French Nicolas de Blégny (Paris, 1687) on *"The proper use of tea, coffee and chocolate for the prevention and for the cure of illnesses."* Early in the eighteenth century Dr. Daniel Duncan reversed the trend and wrote a book on the bad effects of the excessive use of these drinks and a number of physicians followed his example,[22] but by then tea, coffee, and chocolate had become objects of current consumption. In regard to tea and coffee, the average annual imports into England reached the following values (in pounds sterling of the time and at official prices):

YEAR	COFFEE	TEA
1700–14	44,000	10,000
1785–89	266,000	1,810,000

Sugar had been known to the Europeans since antiquity but had always been a very scarce commodity. In fact, it was so scarce that in the Middle Ages it was mostly sold in the pharmacies in the form of pills (which is the origin of our candies). To sweeten their daily foods and beverages, Europeans of the time of Chaucer and Leonardo used honey. The colonization of America created the opportunity for the development of sugar plantations. Sugar shipments from the West Indies to London grew from about 15 million pounds per year during the period 1663–69 to about 37 million pounds per year in 1699–1701. Between 1650 and 1700 the price of sugar in London fell by about 50 percent, and sugar progressively became an object of daily and popular consumption.

---

21. Lionardo di Capua, *Parere*, p. 110.
22. Duncan, *Avis Salutaire*. Among his followers see Tissot, *Santé des gens de lettres*, pp. 189 ff.

But not all was sweetness in the sugar business. The growth of the plantations created a heavy demand for black slaves. The slaves were bought by the Europeans on the coast of West Africa in exchange for textiles (about 60 percent of the slaves purchased), guns and gunpowder (about 20 percent), spirits (about 10 percent), and other goods (about 10 percent). Table 9-6 gives some estimates of the approximate number of human beings forcibly taken, wretched, across the Atlantic to the New World.

Table 9–6

Estimated Slave Imports by Importing Region, 1451–1700

Importing Region	*1451–1600*	*1601–1700*
	(thousands of slaves)	
British North America	—	—
Spanish America	75	300
Caribbean	—	450
Brazil	50	550
Europe	50	—
Sao Thomé and Atlantic Isl.	100	25
Total	275	1325
Annual Average	2	13

SOURCE: Curtin: *The Atlantic Slave Trade*, p. 77. Figures have been rounded to indicate a large margin of error.

The influx of precious metals and of exotic products are facts which easily appeal to the imagination, but the overseas expansion of Europe had other effects at least as important, if no more so. For ease of presentation, one can consider separately (a) technology, (b) economics, and (c) demography.

Accordingly, we shall begin with technology. Oceanic navigation was very different from coastal navigation. Its development called forth, and in turn depended upon, the creation and evolution of new instruments and new techniques. Worthy of mention are the invention of the marine chronometer and the new developments in nautical mapmaking, naval artillery, naval construction, and the use of sail. These developments, though primarily technical, of course had economic implications: the invention of the marine chronometer meant new developments in the horological industry; the evolution of naval artillery brought about developments in the metallurgical industry; innovations in naval construction implied developments of the shipbuilding industry. No less important were the innovations in business techniques. The emergence of large companies such as the English East India Company or the Dutch East India Company; the appearance of the "supercargo" or traveling agent, who represented the interests of the company on board the ships and at overseas ports; the development of maritime insurance companies (like Lloyds of London)—all these and other innovations were essentially the result of overseas expansion. Many of the economic effects are implicit in what has already been said with regard to the inflow of precious metals and new products, and to the development of clockmaking, mapmaking, shipbuilding, maritime insurance, and so on. One could add to the list such an item as the rise and rapid diffusion of the coffeehouses, which quickly became numerous in London and spread later over the whole of Europe. Since the catalogue could never be completed, it is more to the point to focus attention on the basic fact that overseas trade carried great risks and great losses but, above all, much greater profits than any other business endeavor. In London as in Amsterdam the trade in imports and re-exports and all the subsidiary activities which this trade set in motion allowed a notable accumulation of capital. There is much talk nowadays of the early accumulation of capital necessary as a precondition for growth. Things are not as simple as certain theorists would have one believe, but it is undeniable that England, for instance, was able to do what she did in the first stages of the Industrial Revolution partly because the previous Commercial Revolution allowed a considerable (for those days) accumulation of capital: the profits of overseas trade overflowed into agriculture, mining, and manufacture.

In marked contrast to the technological and economic effects, the demographic consequences of the transoceanic expansion were altogether negligible until the end of the nineteenth century. About the middle of the seventeenth century in all the Portugese, Spanish, English, and French overseas possessions taken together, there were fewer than one million whites, including those born on the spot of European parents. The fact is that those who left Europe were few, not all reached their destination, and a great many of those who survived the exertions and dangers of the voyage and of life overseas returned to Europe as soon as they could. Until the 1900s European expansion remained essentially a commercial venture.

As far as society was concerned, however, the profound significance of the overseas expansion can be understood only if seen in human terms. Overseas trade was a great practical school of entrepreneurship—not only for those who, like the ships' captains, the supercargo, and the merchants, actually went overseas, but also for the merchants, insurance agents, shipbuilders, re-exporters, victuallers, employees of companies who although remaining in Europe took part in overseas trade in different capacities and degrees. It was also a good school for those savers who learned how to invest their savings in the trading companies or in the insurance ventures. One of the most significant economic consequences of the commercial development of the sixteenth and seventeenth centuries was the unusual cumulation of wealth it made possible in some European countries. But an even more important consequence was the cumulation of a precious and rich "human capital," that is, of people endowed with sturdy standards of business honesty, adventurous attitudes to risk-taking, and a worldwide open mentality. These matters direct one to look more closely at the cultural developments of the period.

The Scientific Revolution

Events such as the discovery of new worlds and new products, the proof of the roundness of the earth, the invention of printing, the perfecting of firearms, the development of shipbuilding and navigation were at the root of a cultural revolution.[23]

In many texts of the seventeenth century one finds the refrain that since the ancients did not know the world in which they lived, they could not be regarded as the source of all knowledge. The blind and absolute faith in the dogmas of antiquity which had prevailed during the centuries of the Middle Ages entered a period of crisis.

---

23. On this point consult in particular the erudite work of Jones, *Ancients and Moderns.*

Instead of continuing to regard the past as a lost golden age, in a mood of nostalgic inadequacy, an increasing number of Europeans began to look optimistically ahead, dreaming of progress and of novelties.

The seventeenth century saw an acrid, violent intellectual battle develop between the "ancients" and the "moderns," between those who upheld the dogma of the authority and omniscience of the classics and those who opposed reason and experiment to the dogma, and subjected the errors and absurdities of the classics to the results of recent discoveries. The age of Galileo, Newton, Huygens, Leeuwenhoek, Harvey, Descartes, Copernicus, and Leibnitz saw the victory of the "moderns," of the experimental method, and of the application of mathematics in the explanation of reality. Physics, and in particular mechanics, in which, by the very nature of the subject, the application of mathematical logic was bound to yield the best results, made spectacular progress, and the fascination with this progress was such that gradually a mechanical conception of the universe came to prevail.[24] It was then that God himself was described as "the perfect clockmaker."

One of the by-products of the revolution in human thought of that period was the growth of the statistical approach. The writers and the experimenters of the seventeenth century endlessly recorded, catalogued, and counted. William Letwin has observed that:

The best minds of England squandered their talents in minutely recording temperature, wind and the look of the skies hour by hour, in various corners of the land. Their efforts produced nothing more than unusable records. This impassioned energy was turned also to the measurement of economic and social dimensions of various sorts.[25]

This judgment is a bit ungenerous. To the educated layman as well as to the government clerk numbers began to take on an aura of reality. The new approach was particularly noticeable in the treatment of the problems of international trade[26] and population.

---

24. Dijksterhuis, *The Mechanization of the World Picture.*
25. Letwin, *The Origins of Scientific Economics,* pp. 99–100.
26. Stone, *Elizabethan Overseas Trade,* p. 30.

It was in this cultural climate that the school of "arithmetic poli-ticians" rose and developed; Graunt, Petty, and Halley put forward their demographic estimates and constructed their first survival tables; and Gregory King calculated the English National Income. Even today in books and articles on the history of population, the historical statistics of world population always begin with 1650 (see Table 9-7). The reason is that precisely just after the middle of the seventeenth century Europeans started making estimates of the population of the world or parts of it (see Table 9-8).

However, the mere use of figures does not mean that the figures are scientifically handled. In 1589, the work of Giovan Maria Bon-ardo, *The Size, Width, and Distance of All Spheres Reduced to*

Table 9–7

Present Mini-Max Estimates of World Population, 1650–1900
(in millions)

Years	Africa	North America	Latin America	Asia (excl. Russia)	Europe and Russia	Oceania	World
1650	100(?)	1	7–12	257–327	103–105	2	470–545
1750	95–106	1–2	10–16	437–498	144–167	2	695–790
1800	90–107	6–7	19–24	595–630	192–208	2	905–980
1850	95–111	26	33–38	656–801	274–285	2	1090–1260
1900	120–141	81–82	63–74	857–925	423–430	6	1570–1650

SOURCES: United Nations, *The Determinants and Consequences of Popu-lation Trends*, p. 11, Table 2; Durand, *The Modern Expansion of World Population*, p. 109.

Table 9–8

Estimates of World Population by Writers
of the Seventeenth and Eighteenth Centuries (in millions)

Year	Author	World	Europe	Asia	Africa	America	Oceania
1661	Riccioli	1000	100	500	100	200	100
1682	Petty	320					
1685	Vossius	500	30	300			
1696	King	700	100	340	95	65	100
1696	Nicholls	960					
1702	Whiston	4000					
1740	Struyck	500	100	250	100	50	
1741	Süssmilch	950	150	500	150	150	

Our Miles, was reprinted in Venice. It maintained, among other things, that "Hell is 3,758¼ miles away from us" and has "a width of 2,505½ miles," while "the Empire of Heaven . . . where the blessed rest in the greatest happiness . . . is 1,799,995,500 miles away from us." The figures compiled in Table 9-8 show that some of the estimates put forward in the second half of the seventeenth century about the world population had no greater merit than those of Giovan Maria Bonardo about the distance of Heaven and Hell from the earth. The two things, however, cannot be put in the same plane. One of the fundamental characteristics of the Scientific Revolution of the seventeenth century was, in fact, that it turned human speculation away from such insoluble and absurd problems, as the distance between hell and earth or the number of angels that can stand on the point of a pin, and directed it instead toward problems which were capable of solution. The estimate of the distance of Hell given by Giovan Maria Bonardo and the estimate of Petty on world population are both improbable, but the first answers an absurd question while the second is merely imperfect measurement of a rationally valid problem. Once a question is correctly formulated, the answer inevitably will follow.

Modern statistics was practically born in those decades, and quantitative information about population, production, trade, and money became increasingly more abundant and more reliable. On the other hand, the new set of problems was the outcome of a new mental attitude which gave greater emphasis to the rational than to the irrational, placed pragmatism before idealism, stressed actuality rather than eschatology. At the level of human relations, the ground was prepared for the tolerance of the Enlightenment. At the technological level, the emphasis on experimentation paved the way to the solution of concrete problems of production.

This whole grandiose movement of ideas had particular importance in another way. In the Middle Ages, according to a tradition inherited from the ancient world, science and technology had remained separate and distinct. As the masterbuilders of the Duomo in Milan emphatically stated in 1392, *"scientia est unum et ars est aliud,"*[27] that is, science is one thing and technology is quite

---

27. *Annali della fabbrica del Duomo*, vol. 1, pp. 209–210.

another. Science was philosophy; technology was the *ars* of the artisan. Official "science" had no interest in, or inclination toward, technological affairs, and technological developments were mostly the results of the toil of unlettered artisans. The Renaissance, with its unquestioning cult for the values of classical antiquity, accentuated this dichotomy, which in Italy from the middle of the fifteenth century onward, was further intensified by the progressive accentuation and hardening of class distinctions. It is in this context that we must see Leonardo's admission of being a "man without letters," Tartaglia's warning that his doctrine was "not taken from Plato nor from Plotino" and the efforts of the physicians who, considering themselves scientists and therefore philosophers,[28] dissociated themselves from the surgeons, who were regarded as technicians and therefore simple artisans.

The "moderns" of the seventeenth century, in their reaction against traditional values and in their effort to impose the experimental method, set themselves doggedly to reappraise the work of craftsmen. Francis Bacon repeatedly emphasized the need for collaboration among scientists and artisans. Galileo, in his famous "Dialogue," made the imaginary Sagredo state that conversation with the artisans of the Venetian Arsenal had helped him considerably in the study of several difficult problems. The Royal Society of London charged some of its members with the compiling of a history of artisan trades and techniques; an idea to be fully adopted later by the editors of the *Encyclopédie*.

While all this was happening in the field of "science," converging developments were taking place in the field of "technology." First, one must take into account the fact that the various sections of society, however divided or distinct, still react to common cultural stimuli. Moroever, Protestantism, with its unconditional worship of books, was a powerful factor in the diffusion of literacy. The spread of literacy signaled the victory of the book over the proverb, of the text over the icon, of reasoned information over slavish reiteration, and all this, in turn, meant the progressive abandonment

---

28. As the Milanese doctor G. B. Silvatico asserted in 1607, paraphrasing a sentence of Galen, *"qui medicus esse vult optimus, is prius philosophus sit necesse est."* See Cipolla, *Public Health.*

of customary and traditional attitudes in favor of more rational and experimental attitudes. Last, but not least, developments in oceanic navigation, of the watch and clock industry, and of experimental science favored the formation of an increasing number of makers of precision instruments. These grew to represent a type of superior technician, capable of conversing with contemporary scientists. It is not by chance that the steam engine was at the root of the Industrial Revolution and that the inventor of the steam engine was one of these makers of precision instruments.

Until the end of the eighteenth century, the contributions of "science" to "technology" remained occasional and of little note. But the cultural development of the seventeenth century brought the two branches closer together and created the conditions for that collaboration which is the basis and the essence of modern industrial development.

An Energy Crisis

In historical description, it is inevitable that the historian should be influenced by the fact that he observes human phenomena *ex post* —that is, with the benefit of hindsight. In the selection of the factors at play, as well as in the interpretation of their role, the historian is inevitably influenced by the fact that he knows how events unfolded. When he describes a failure, in attempting to explain it he will inevitably stress the "negative" circumstances and factors which preceded the disaster. If, instead, the historian describes a success, he will inevitably stress the "positive" circumstances and factors which preceded it. History, however, is never as simple and straightforward as it is told. Disasters are not preceded only by unfavorable situations, and success does not emerge only from paradisiac situations. Moreover, many factors or circumstances can be defined as "positive" or "negative" only after the outcome and after such an outcome has been given a positive or negative sign by us. Another way of expressing the same thing is to say that, in seeing things *ex post,* we give to the events of a period weights and meanings very different from those attributed to the same events by their contemporaries. Atkinson has shown that, of the books printed in

France between 1480 and 1700, more than twice as many dealt with the Turkish Empire than with the Americas.[29]

In the sixteenth and seventeenth centuries, among the circumstances which paved the way to that success known as the Industrial Revolution, there were some that look to us decidedly positive. But mingled with them there were also circumstances of more doubtful character, circumstances which must certainly have appeared to the people of the times to be painted black, even though we tend to color them pink because we know *ex post* that things ended well.

The timber crisis offers an excellent example to illustrate this point. Since the beginning of time, timber had been the fuel *par excellence,* as well as the basic material for construction, shipbuilding, and the manufacture of furniture, tools, and machines. From the twelfth and thirteenth centuries, in the Mediterranean area, timber became scarce and, in building, was increasingly replaced by bricks, stone, and marble, But it remained practically the only fuel in use and continued to be the basic material for the making of furniture, ships, tools, and machines.

During the sixteenth century, the growth of population, the expansion of oceanic navigation and shipbuilding, the development of metallurgy, and the consequent increase in the consumption of charcoal for the smelting of metals caused a considerable increase in the consumption of timber. Toward the middle of the sixteenth century, in the silver mines at Fribourg, approximately 2.1 million cubic feet of wood were used each year. About the same amount was consumed in the Hüttenberg and Joachimstal mines. In the districts of Schlaggenwald and Schönfeld, over 2.6 million cubic feet of wood were used each year. Forests disappeared, and timber became scarce in central and northwestern Europe. From 1470 onward, in all of central Europe, the price of wood was rising, slowly at first, then rapidly. In the district of Hüttenberg, Carinthia, fuel came to represent about 70 percent of the costs for the production of iron; ore about 25 percent, and wages and other costs no more than 5 percent. In England in 1548–49, the government ordered an inquiry into the waste of timber and the destruction

29. Atkinson, *Les nouveaux horizons,* p. 10.

of forests. About 1560, the foundries of State Hory and Harmanec in Slovakia were compelled to reduce drastically their activities or to close altogether because of a shortage of wood. The movements of the prices of timber and charcoal give a measure of the timing and intensity of the crisis. In Genoa the price of oak used in shipbuilding grew from a base price of one hundred in 1463–68 to three hundred in 1546–55, to twelve hundred in 1577–81.[30] With the seventeenth century Italy entered a period of economic decline, the demand for fuel and construction materials stagnated, and the price of timber did not grow any further.[31] But in the north, where economic activity expanded, the price of timber kept growing at an increasing pace, and a timber-energy crisis exploded around 1630. In England, the price index for charcoal rose from sixty to one hundred between 1560 and 1630 and from one hundred to two hundred and fifty between 1630 and 1670 (see Table 10-7).

If one considers the role of timber in the economy of the time as a source of energy and as a raw material, it is obvious that the shortage could have caused a bottleneck with the most disastrous consequences for the further development of Europe. As it happened, the energy crisis served instead to push England on the road to the Industrial Revolution. For that to happen, though, other factors had to enter the play.

---

30. Calegari, *Legname e costruzioni navali*, p. 94.
31. Calegari, *ibid*, and Sella, *Salari e lavoro*, Appendix Table IX.

CHAPTER TEN

The Changing Balance of Economic Power in Europe

Economic Trends: 1500–1700

In current historical and economic literature, the sixteenth and seventeenth centuries are painted in black and white. The sixteenth century is painted as *"el siglo de oro,"* a sort of golden age, not only for Spain, which received substantial quantities of gold and silver from her American colonies, but also for the rest of Europe. In contrast, the seventeenth century is painted gloomily, and it has become fashionable to write of the "crisis of the seventeenth century."[1]

Fashions and descriptions in black and white should always be regarded with suspicion, for while there is some truth in stereotyped narratives, there is also much that is superficial and erroneous. For a considerable section of northern Italy, which was one of the leading areas of the European economy, the first half of the sixteenth century was neither a golden age nor a silver one. It was an age of iron and fire, of destruction and misery. The second half of the century was a golden age for neither France nor the southern Low Countries. On the other land, the seventeenth century was anything but a period of depression for Holland, England, and

---

1. For a salutary reaction to this fashion, see Schöffer, *Holland's Golden Age,* pp. 82–107.

Sweden. The following diagram is also the result of simplification and suffers from the defects inherent in all simplifications, but however superficial and simplistic, it serves at least to indicate how much more so are the descriptions which make of the sixteenth and seventeenth centuries, respectively, "*el siglo de oro*" and "the age of depression."

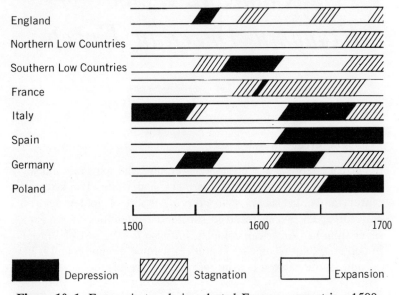

Figure 10–1. Economic trends in selected European countries, 1500–1700.

The most serious drawback to considering the sixteenth century indiscriminately as a period of general prosperity and the seventeenth as a period of general depression or stagnation is that such a view prevents one from understanding the most important aspect of European history at the beginning of the modern era; that is, the upsetting of the traditional balance of economic power within Europe. At the end of the fifteenth century, the most highly developed area in western Europe was the Mediterranean area, and in particular central and northern Italy. During the sixteenth century, because of the influx of American treasure, Spain knew a period of splendor which served to maintain the Mediterranean in a position of economic superiority but by the end of the seventeenth century, the Mediterranean was definitely a backward area. The center of gravity of the European economy had moved to the North Sea. To explain this dramatic overturn with the usual refrain of the "geographical discoveries" and the consequent change in the "trade routes" is superficial and naive. The problem is so complex and intricate that to treat it adequately would require at least a series of volumes. We shall deal here only with certain aspects of it.

The Decline of Spain

The decline of Spain in the seventeenth century is not difficult to understand. The fundamental fact is that Spain never developed to begin with.

At the beginning of the seventeenth century, Francesco Guicciardini, in his *Relazione di Spagna*, wrote:

> . . . poverty is great here, and I believe it is due not so much to the quality of the country as to the nature of the Spaniards, who do not exert themselves; they rather send to other nations the raw materials which grow in their kingdom only to buy them back manufactured by others, as in the case of wool and silk which they sell to others in order to buy them back from them as cloths of silk and wool.[2]

In 1557, the Venetian Ambassador Badoer reiterated, "I do not believe there is another country less well provided with skilled workers than Spain."[3]

The massive inflow of gold and silver from the Americas and the consequent expansion of effective demand could have stimulated the economic development of the country. But the Spain of the sixteenth century can serve as a classic example of the fact that, though demand is a necessary element to stimulate development, it is not a sufficient one.

Spain, as a whole (that is, irrespective of income distribution among regions and social classes), became considerably richer than before during the sixteenth century, and her importance in the

---

2. Guicciardini, *Relazione di Spagna*, p. 131.
3. Cited in Luzzatto, *Storia economica*, vol. 1, p. 139.

European economy increased dramatically because silver and gold were internationally accepted liquid assets. By 1569 the theologian Thomás de Mercado could justifiably write that Seville and the Atlantic provinces of Spain "from being the extreme periphery of the world had become the center of it." The Spanish failure was due to the fact that, because of bottlenecks in the productive system (in particular, lack of skilled labor, standards of value unfavorable to craft and trade activities, the guilds and their restrictive policies), the increase in demand did not succeed in eliciting a corresponding increment of productive capacity. Consequently, prices rose, and a large part of the demand was met by foreign goods and services.

In 1545 it was estimated that the Spanish manufacturers had a six-year backlog of orders from the merchants of Cartagena, Porto Belo, and Vera Cruz.[4] Under these circumstances, the merchants who had to satisfy the demand from the American colonies were soon compelled to turn to foreign producers to whom they lent their name in order to evade the law that forbade the colonies any traffic with non-Spaniards. As Luzzatto put it, "All this gave way to the greatest system of contraband which the history of commerce knew until the Napoleonic blockade."

The prevalent *hidalgo* mentality looked upon imports more as a source of pride than a latent danger for the country's economy. In 1675 Alfonso Nuñez de Castro wrote:

Let London manufacture those fabrics of hers to her heart's content; Holland her chambrays; Florence her cloth; the Indies their beaver and vicuña; Milan her brocades; Italy and Flanders their linens, so long as our capital can enjoy them; the only thing it proves is that all nations train journeymen for Madrid and that Madrid is the queen of Parliaments, for all the world serves her and she serves nobody.

With such ideas prevailing in the country, it is not surprising that, in 1659, in the Peace of the Pyrenées, France obtained the right to introduce into Catalonia all kinds of duty-free products, and that a

---

4. On the importance of the exports to the American colonies see Vilar, *Oro e moneta*, pp. 107 ff. Exports consisted mostly of oil, wine, vinegar, flour, silks, velvets, shoes, hats, textiles, glass, soap, weapons of all kinds, and so on.

few years later, in 1667, the Spanish frontiers were opened to English goods. From then on, there was no longer a need for contraband. "Spain supplies itself from other countries with almost all things which are manufactured for common use and which consist in the industry and toil of man" wrote a well-informed contemporary observer, and the Venetian Ambassador Vendramin commented:

> . . . about this precious metal which comes to Spain from the Indies, the Spaniards say not without reason that it does on Spain as rain does on a roof—it pours on her and it flows away.

At the end of the sixteenth century, Spain was much richer than a century earlier, but she was not more developed—"like an heir endowed by the accident of an eccentric will."[5] The riches of the Americas provided Spain with purchasing power but ultimately they stimulated the development of Holland, England, France, and other European countries. With typical perceptiveness, a Venetian ambassador remarked, "Spain cannot exist unless relieved by others, nor can the rest of the world exist without the money of Spain."

In the course of the seventeenth century, however, the influx of precious metals from America fell drastically, partly because of diminishing production, partly because the colonies were becoming increasingly independent, producing on the spot what they had previously imported from the mother country.[6] Thus, the main source of the Spanish euphoria dried up. In the meanwhile, however, a century of artificial prosperity had induced many to abandon the land; schools had multiplied, but they had served mostly to produce a half-educated intellectual proletariat who scorned productive industry and manual labor and found positions in the bloated state bureaucracy which served above all to disguise unemployment.[7] Spain in the seventeenth century lacked entrepreneurs and

---

5. The simile is by Tawney, *Business and Politics,* p. 28.
6. See Brading and Cross, *Colonial Silver Mining,* pp. 568–79. Among the causes of the phenomenon, one has to take into account Dutch military pressure which encouraged the tendency toward economic independence on the part of the colonies, as it compelled the colonies to produce locally the badly needed weaponry.
7. Trevor Davies, *Spain in Decline,* pp. 92–93.

artisans but had an overabundance of bureaucrats, lawyers, priests, beggars, and bandits. And the country sank into a disheartening decline.

The Decline of Italy

The problem of the Italian economic decline is more complex than that of the Spanish. Starting in the fourteenth century, the decline of communes and the establishment of the *Signorie* had led to a decided deterioration in social life: the masses felt increasingly alienated from the public administration, and social discrimination grew to favor political adherences and family traditions rather than initiative and merit. People began to regard craft and mercantile activities as menial occupations which excluded their practitioners from the upper classes. Yet, however potentially dangerous, these trends had not appreciably affected Italian economic efficiency and wealth.

At the end of the fifteenth century, with good reason and in full knowledge of the facts, Francesco Guicciardini could still write:

Italy had never known such prosperity, nor experienced such a desirable state as that in which she securely rested in the year of Christian grace 1490, and the years linked to that before and after. The reason was that, because she had been brought wholly to peace and tranquillity, tilled no less in the more mountainous and barren places as in the plains and in the most fertile regions, not only did she have an abundance of people and riches, but also, ennobled by the magnificence of many Princes, by the splendor of numerous and very noble cities, by the seat and majesty of the religion, she flowered with eminent men, in the administration of public affairs, in all the sciences, and in every distinguished industry and art.

This was the rosy picture at the end of the fifteenth century. Then suddenly, between 1494 and 1538, the Horsemen of the Apocalypse descended upon Italy. The country became the battlefield for an international conflict which involved Spain, France, and what we would today call Germany. With the war came famines, epidemics, destruction of capital and disruption of trade.

Brescia, which had produced 8,000 pieces of woollen cloth a

year at the beginning of the century, produced no more than 1,000 toward 1540. In Como industry and commerce went from bad to worse. Pavia, which had had about 16,000 inhabitants at the end of the fifteenth century, was reduced to fewer than 7,000 in 1529.[8] In that same year the English ambassadors who were attending the coronation of Charles V in Bologna reported:

It is, Sire, the most pitie to see this contree, as we suppose, that ever was in Christendom; in some places nother horsmet nor mans mete to be found, the goodly towns destroyed and desolate.

Betwexte Verceilles, belongyng to the Duke of Savoye, and Pavye, the space of 50 miles, the moost goodly contree for corne and vynes that maye be seen, is so desolate, in all that weye we sawe oon man or woman laborers in the fylde, nor yett creatour stering, but in great villaiges five or six myserable personnes; sawying in all this waye we saw thre women in oone place, gathering of grapis yett uppon the vynes, for there are nother vynes orderyd and kepte, nor corne sawed in all the weye, nor personnes to gather the grapes that growith upon the vynes, but the vynes growyth wyld, great contreys, and hangyng full of clusters of grapes. In this mydde waye is a towne, the which hath been oone of the goodly townes of Italye, callyd Vegeva; there is a strong hold, the towne is all destroyed and in maner desolate. Pavye is in lyke maner, and great pitie; the chyldryn kreyeng abowt the streates for bred, and ye dying for hungre. They seye that all the hole peuple of that contrey and dyvers other places in Italya, as the Pope also shewyd us, with many other, with warre famine and pestilence are utterly deadde and goone; so that there is no hope many yeres that Italya shalbe any thing well restored, for wante of people; and this distruction hath been as well by Frenche men as the Emperours, for they sey that Monsr de Lautreyght destroyed muche where as he passyd.[9]

A few years later, in 1533, the Venetian ambassador Basadonna reported:

The State of Milan is totally ruined; such poverty and ruin cannot be remedied in a short time because the factories are ruined and the people have died out, which is why industry is lacking.[10]

8. For the above, see Sella, *Venetian Woollen Industry,* pp. 113–15.
9. State Papers, Henry VIII, edition of 1830–52, volume VII (1849), p. 226 (Sir Nicholas Carew and Richard Sampson to Henry VIII from Bologna, 12 December 1529).
10. *Relazione del Ducato di Milano di G. Basadonna,* p. 333.

In Florence things were no better. Between the end of the fifteenth century and 1530–40, the population fell from 72,000 to about 60,000, the number of the woollens workshop fell from about 270 to few more than 60, and the annual production of woollens from about 25,000 pieces to a few hundred.[11]

Peace finally returned about the middle of the century, and the prediction that "poverty and ruin cannot be remedied in a short time" proved wrong. A centuries-old tradition of industriousness and enterprise had created a human capital of remarkable potential. The recovery was amazingly rapid. Bergamo, which had produced some 7,000 to 8,000 pieces of cloth a year about 1540, produced about 26,500 in 1596. In Florence, wool production increased from 14,700 pieces of cloth in 1553 to 30,000 in 1560 as indicated in Table 10-1.

Table 10–1
Woollens Production in Florence, 1537–96

Year	No. Workshops of the Arte della Lana	No. Pieces of Cloth Produced Annually
1537	63	
1553		14,700
1560		30,000
1561		33,000
1571		28,492
1572		33,212
1586	114	
1596	100	

SOURCE: Romano, *A Florence*, pp. 509 and 511; and Sella, *Venetian Woollen Industry*, p. 115.

Wool production in Venice suffered badly from the development of wool production in other centers,[12] but the expansion in the other sectors of the Venetian economy more than offset the losses of the woollens manufactures.[13]

The second half of the sixteenth century was the "Indian

---

11. Sella, *Venetian Woollen Industry*, p. 114.
12. Ibid., p. 116.
13. Pullan, *Crisis and Change,* pp. 8–9.

summer" of the Italian economy. In that Indian summer, however, were sown the seeds of future difficulties. Reconstruction there was, but it was restoration of old structures, and the recovery took place along traditional lines. The guild organization was strengthened, but all the guilds did was prevent competition and innovation.

Italy became progressively less competitive on international markets—unfortunately, at a moment when Italy could ill afford the luxury of becoming less competitive.

Italy had a relatively limited internal market and poor natural endowments. Her economic prosperity was traditionally dependent on her capacity to export a high percentage of the manufactures and services she produced. During the sixteenth century, other countries, particularly the northern Low Countries and England, developed their production on new scales and with new methods, and their products successfully asserted themselves on the international market. As a Milanese official gloomily remarked in 1650, "Of late, man's ingenuity has sharpened everywhere."[14]

Until the end of the sixteenth century demand was booming on the international markets, and this favorable condition kept efficient, less efficient and marginal producers happily alive. Behind a cheerful facade, however, Italy was sliding imperceptibly from a leading position to a marginal one.

Between the second and third decades of the seventeenth century, a series of weighty factors upset the international economic situation. The imports of precious metals from the Americas entered into a long period of sharp decline and Spain started its painful downslide. In central Europe, a disastrous war broke out in 1618 and, for more than thirty years, brought devastation and endless misery to large areas of the German states. From Turkey in 1611 the Venetian ambassador warned of a marked deterioration of the local market as a consequence of turbulent internal conditions which contributed to declines in both population and income. Between 1623 and 1638, the Turko-Persian War further aggravated an already precarious economic situation. The combined collapse of the Spanish, German, and Turkish markets, added to the contraction in international liquidity, had immediate repercussions

---

14. Quoted in Sella, *Industrial Production,* p. 247.

on the international economic scene. There was no longer a place for marginal producers, and Italy, by this time, had become a marginal producer.

The documents of the time give an accurate enough idea of the collapse of Italian exports in the course of the seventeenth century. For Genoa, we know that one of the duties levied on the export of silk cloth, the so-called *additione del 1565*, yielded an average of approximately 24 thousand lire per year when it was first introduced; toward the end of the seventeenth century it yielded only from two to four thousand lire.[15] We know that at the beginning of the seventeenth century Venice exported some 25,000 woollen cloths a year to the Near East. A century later, according to the Venetian ambassador at Constantinople, Venice exported no more than 100 cloths a year, that is, about 50 to Constantinople and the same number to Smyrna. The volume of Venetian business in the two centers had been reduced to an average of 600 thousand ducats a year, while that of the French was about 4 million and that of the English not much less than that of the French.[16] As for Florence, in 1668 Count Priorato Gualdo sadly remarked, "We used to have great success with our woollen cloths, but the Dutch have considerably spoiled our sales with their draperies."[17]

Dutch, English, and French products ousted Italian products not only from foreign markets, but also from the Italian one. The combined loss of foreign and internal markets brought about a drastic collapse of production and a massive disinvestment in the manufacturing and service sectors. Data in Table 10-2 show the collapse in the volume of woollens production in selected major cities. A number of other data relating to other centers or to other sectors confirm the generality of the decline. In Cremona in 1615 there were one hundred eighty-seven firms producing woollens, and they were taxed for the amount of 742 lire. By 1648 the number of firms was down to twenty-three, and the assessment was down to 97 lire. By 1749 only two firms were in business. In Cremona again there were ninety-one firms producing fustian cloth in 1615. By 1648

---

15. Sivori, *Il tramonto dell'industria serica*, p. 935.
16. For all that precedes, compare Cipolla, *The Economic Decline of Italy*, p. 203.
17. Gualdo, *Relatione*, p. 87.

Table 10–2

Production of Woollen Cloth in Selected Italian Cities, 1589–1699

	Average Number of Pieces of Woollen Cloth Produced Per Year			
Decade	Venice	Milan	Como	Florence
1589–1600				13,500
1600–09	22,430	15,000	10,000	14,000
1610–19	18,700			
1620–29	17,270			9,000
1630–39	12,520			6,300
1640–49	11,450	3,000		
1650–59	9,930		400	
1660–69	7,480			
1670–79	5,420			
1680–89	3,050			
1690–99	2,640	100		

SOURCES: Sella, *Venetian Woollen Industry*; Romano, *A Florence*; Cipolla, *The Economic Decline of Italy*.

their number was reduced to forty-one.[18] In Como at the beginning of the seventeenth century there were more than thirty looms in operation in the silk manufactures. By 1650 there were only two, one of which worked for only six months of the year. At the beginning of the eighteenth century there were no longer any looms operating in Como.[19] The silk industry in Genoa numbered about ten thousand looms in 1565, about four thousand in 1630 and about twenty-five hundred in 1675.[20] Venice produced annually about 800,000 yards of silk cloths at the beginning of the seventeenth century. By 1623 it produced about 600,000 yards and by 1695 only about 250,000 (although this decline was partly compensated by an increase in the proportion of more valuable cloth produced).[21] In Florence, the annual average production of tissues (*tele macchiate*) fell from about 13,000 pieces at the beginning of the seventeenth century to about 6,000 pieces around 1650.[22]

18. Meroni, *Cremona fedelissima*, vol. 2, pp. 19–21.
19. Cipolla, *The Economic Decline*, p. 197.
20. Sivori, *Il tramonto dell'industria serica*, p. 896.
21. Sella, *Commercio e industrie*, p. 126.
22. Romano, *A Florence*, pp. 508–11.

The fundamental reason for the replacement of Italian goods and services by foreign ones was always basically the same: English, Dutch, and French commodities and services were offered at lower prices. But why this disparity in prices? Generally Italian products were of a higher quality. Italian manufacturers, partly because of their proud tradition, but mainly because they were conditioned by guild regulations, persisted in producing by traditional methods excellent but outmoded products. In the field of textiles, for example, the English and the Dutch invaded the international market with lighter and less durable products in brighter colors. In qualitative terms the Dutch and English products were inferior to the Italian products, but they cost a good deal less.

Italian products, however, were more expensive not only because they were of better quality, but also because costs of production—other things being equal—were higher in Italy than in Holland, England, and France. This situation was essentially due to three circumstances:

a. Excessive control by the guilds compelled Italian manufacturers to continue to use obsolete methods of production and organization. The guilds had become associations primarily directed at preventing competition among associates, and they constituted a formidable obstacle to technological and organizational innovations.

b. The pressure of taxation in Italian states was too high and badly conceived.

c. Labor costs in Italy were too high in relation to the wage levels in competing countries. During the so-called price revolution of the sixteenth century, nominal wages outside Italy did not keep up with prices. In Italy, because of a stronger guild organization, the workers managed to obtain wage raises proportionate to the rise in prices. While in England the level of real wages at the beginning of the seventeenth century was noticeably lower than one hundred years earlier, in Italy real wages did not show any substantial deterioration in the course of the sixteenth century.[23] Everything points to the fact that, at the beginning of the seventeenth

---

23. Parenti, *Prime Ricerche*, Chapter III, and Pullan, *Wage Earners*, pp. 146–174.

century, Italian wages were out of step in relation to the wages in other countries. If the higher wage levels had been compensated for by higher productivity, Italy would not have suffered, but for the reasons indicated above, the productivity of Italian labor was lower than labor productivity in England, Holland, or France.

As regards shipping, Fynes Moryson wrote of having "observed English Shipps going forth from Venice with Italian Shipps to have sayled into Syria and retorned to Venice twice, before the Italian Shipps made one retorne."[24] This could be an exaggeration, but a century or two earlier, no Englishman would have dreamed of writing such things. People exaggerate easily, but at the root of any exaggeration there is a kernel of truth.

The effects of all these developments on the Italian economy were as follows: (a) a drastic decline in exports which lasted for decades and continually worsened; (b) a prolonged process of disinvestment in manufacturing and shipping.

In 1630 central-northern Italy was devastated by the plague. In less than two years, about 1.1 million people died out of a population of four million. If one concedes that it would have been impossible for Italy to keep her traditional sources of income or to find new ones, then a slow, protracted decline in population might have been a solution for her economic difficulties. But a drastic and rapid fall in population like that caused by the plague of 1630 had the effect of raising wages and putting Italian exports in an even more difficult position. Moreover, in the long run, after the plague, population expanded again. Around 1600 the entire population of the Italian peninsula must have been around 12 million. Around 1700 it was about 13 million.[25] However, about 1700 Italy no longer had her manufactures or her banking or her shipping interests.

By the end of the seventeenth century Italy largely imported manufactures from England, France, and Holland. At this stage she exported mostly agricultural and semi-finished goods, namely, oil, wheat, wine, wool, and especially raw and thrown silk. In the area of maritime services, Italy was reduced to a passive role

---

24. Moryson, *Itinerary*, p. 135.
25. Cipolla, *Four Centuries of Italian Demographic Development,* p. 573.

and the great expansion of the free port of Leghorn in the seventeenth century was the result of the triumph of England and Dutch shipping in the Mediterranean.

What had happened to Italy is a good example of the ambivalence of foreign trade. From the eleventh to the sixteenth centuries foreign trade had been indeed an "engine of growth" for Italy because (a) it provided the country with raw materials and commodities for re-export and (b) it augmented the demand for manufactures, thus stimulating the growth of craft skills and manufacturing production. From the beginning of the seventeeth century, however, as we saw above, the structure of Italian foreign trade changed completely. Foreign manufactures were brought in and drove Italian products and their manufacturers out of the market. At the same time foreign demand favored the production of oil, wine, and raw silk. One may argue that in the short run Italy derived from this new arrangement some comparative advantages of the kind illustrated by the Ricardian theory. In the long run, however, foreign trade acted as an "engine of decline": it contributed to shift both capital and labor from the secondary and tertiary sectors to agriculture. In regard to labor this shift meant, in the long run, a) the reduction in number of both the literate craftsmen and the enterprising merchants, b) the growth in size of the illiterate peasantry, and c) the rise in power of the landed nobility. The nobility asserted its preeminence economically as well as politically, socially and administratively. The cities lost their previous vitality. The great Universities of Padua and Bologna slipped into oblivion. Venice sent her best gun-founder, Alberghetti, to London to learn the most modern techniques for working metals. The few remaining Italian clockmakers copied the style and the mechanisms of the numerous and skillful London clockmakers. Italy had begun her career as an underdeveloped area within Europe.

The Rise of the Northern Low Countries

We found that it is not after all so difficult to explain Spain's economic decline, because Spain basically never developed. One can say exactly the opposite of the northern Low Countries (normally referred to by the name of only one of their provinces—i.e., Holland). It is not so difficult to explain the "Dutch miracle" of 1550–1650, because the northern Low Countries were developed long before the "miracle."[26]

Between the twelfth and the sixteenth centuries, the economic development of the northern Low Countries had been substantial, although overshadowed by the more brilliant successes of the southern Low Countries.[27] Taking the Low Countries (northern and southern) as a whole, one can say that during the Middle Ages their system of agriculture was among the most advanced in Europe and their manufactures both varied and highly developed. Gand, Leyden, Utrecht, and Rotterdam were renowned for their textiles, Dinant for its brass and tinwork, Liège for ironwork, Delft for ceramics. As to foreign trade, its importance in relation to national income was possibly higher in the Low Countries than in any other European country with the exception of Italy. Table 10-3 gives an idea of the value and origin of imports into the Low Countries toward the middle of the sixteenth century.

At this time, the country possibly numbered about 3 million inhabitants. This would mean approximately 7 guilders of imports per capita. The corresponding value for England and for France appears to have been about 1½ guilders.[28]

Of the northern provinces in particular, the Italian Ludovico Guicciardini wrote in the sixteenth century:

This country produces little wheat and not even rye because of the low ground and wateriness, yet enjoys so much plenty that it supplies other countries as much grain is imported, especially from Denmark and

---

26. On the economic history of Holland, consult Baasch, *Hollandische Wirtschaftsgeschichte*, which is methodical and complete. Decidedly more brilliant is Barbour, *Capitalism in Amsterdam;* see also Van Houtte, *Economische en Sociale Geschiedenis;* Boxer, *The Dutch Seaborne Empire;* and Wilson, *The Dutch Republic.*
27. On the development of the Southern Low Countries in the Middle Ages, consult the classic work of Pirenne, *Histoire de Belgique,* and the brief outline of Doehaerd, *L'expansion économique belge au Moyen Age.* On the development of Antwerp and the decline of Bruges, see the brilliant and classic article of Van Houtte, *La genèse du grand marché international d'Anvers à la fin du Moyen Age,* and more recently Van Der Wee, *Antwerp Market.*
28. Brulez, *The Balance of Trade,* p. 48.

Table 10–3

Estimated Value of Yearly Imports into the
Low Countries (Northern and Southern)
about the Middle of the Sixteenth Century

Country or Area of Origin	Value of Imports (Guilders)
England	4,150,000
Baltic	4,500,000
German principalities	2,000,000
France	2,700,000
Spain and Portugal	4,650,000
Italy	4,300,000
Total	22,300,000

SOURCE: Brulez, *The Balance of Trade*, pp. 20–48.

from Ostarlante [countries of the Baltic]. It does not make wine, and there is more wine and more of it is drunk than in any other part where it is made, and it is brought from a number of places, particularly Rhine wine. It has no flax, yet it makes finer textiles than any other region of the world [and it still imports such textiles] from Flanders and from the area of Liège. . . . It has no wool, and it makes countless woollens [and even imports some] from England, Scotland, Spain, and a few from Brabant. It has no wood and makes more furniture and more stacks of wood and other things than does the whole of the rest of Europe.[29]

With these words Guicciardini highlighted both the importance of international trade for the northern Low Countries and the close relationship between international trade and the manufacturing sector. Another activity of major importance to the economy of the northern Low Countries was fishing, particularly for herring and whales. International trade and fishing were made possible by a rich tradition of seamanship. This by itself was a "miraculous" development, because nature had put the Dutch behind sandbars in shallow waters that were frozen three months of the year and with prevailing winds dead against their getting to sea at all. During the Middle Ages, various Dutch cities had become members of the

---

29. Guicciardini, *Descrittione*, p. 176.

Hanseatic League. From the beginning of the fifteenth century, however, when their power grew, they broke away from the League, which had been attempting to exclude them from the Baltic, and after an obstinate struggle (1438–1471) they succeeded in ensuring that the Baltic, so essential to their supply of wheat and timber, would remain open to their shipping. This accomplishment proves that already at that time (a) the Dutch were well aware of the fact that their livelihood and prosperity depended upon freedom of the seas, and (b) the cities of the northern United Provinces were a naval power not to be lightly dismissed.

Until the middle of the sixteenth century, the development in the southern provinces confined the activities of the northern provinces to the North Sea and the Baltic. In the second half of the sixteenth century, however, came the revolt against Spain, and with the revolt came the war and the ruin of the southern provinces. In 1571 the fulling mills of Ninove and Ath were reduced to ashes. In 1584 in all of Flanders the only fulling mills left standing were those of Blendesques. Hondschote, Bailleul, Nieuwkerke, Weert, Zichem, and other centers of textile production were also seriously damaged by the war. In 1585 Antwerp was savagely sacked. The Dutch had remained masters of the seas, and the ruin of the southern provinces gave them a free hand for the commercial penetration of the southern seas and the oceans. Not only did they take advantage of the situation, but they gave events a helping hand. Since the southern Low Countries were now under Spanish domination and the war continued to drag on, the Dutch blockaded the southern ports and did their best to delay the recovery of the southern provinces.

After the peace of 1609, the Northern United Provinces emerged with political independence and religious freedom. An even more startling fact was that the economy of the new state was far more vital than ever—in fact, it was the most dynamic, the best developed, and the most competitive economy in Europe, despite forty years of war against the Spanish giant and despite the fact that the country was poorly endowed with natural resources. (A seventeeth-century Englishman described Holland as "such a spot as if God had reserved it as a place only to dig turf out of.")

Attempting to explain this "miracle," Charles Wilson[30] stressed the importance of the "old Burgundian tradition"—in other words, as already noted, the country which rose against Spain, fought for forty years, and emerged victorious was not an underdeveloped country, but an advanced and civilized country of old tradition. What Charles Wilson wrote with special attention to the political and military aspects of the "miracle" can be repeated about the economic aspects—with an important addition.

The most damaging blow which Spanish fanaticism and intolerance dealt to the southern Low Countries was perhaps not the destruction of wealth and physical capital, however great such destruction was, but the flight of "human capital." Involuntarily, Spain enriched her own enemy with the most precious of all capital. The fugitives from the southern provinces—known throughout northern Europe as Walloons—went here, there, and everywhere: to England, to Germany, to Sweden, but, naturally, mostly to the northern Low Countries. Among them were craftsmen, sailors, merchants, financiers, and professionals who brought to their elected country artisanship, commercial knowledge, entrepreneurial spirit, and, often, liquid capital. Admissions to the freedom of Amsterdam rose from 344 in 1575–79 to 2,768 in 1615–19.[31] For the southern provinces it proved to be a frightening bloodletting; for the northern ones, a powerful tonic. The most famous merchant of the time, the founder and administrator of a great economic empire with headquarters in Amsterdam, Luis de Geer (1587–1652), was a Walloon.[32] At the beginning of the seventeeth century the Walloons were one of the most powerful groups of shareholders within the Dutch East India Company. In 1609–11 the Walloons were the holders of half of the largest bank deposits

---

30. Wilson, *The Dutch Republic,* pp. 15–18.
31. In admitting foreign craftsmen, Amsterdam compromised with guild opposition, found housing for newcomers, and offered inducements to masters deemed capable of starting new industries or improving techniques in those already established. The status of citizen could be acquired at a cost of 8 florins until 1622, when it was raised to 14 florins. Barbour, *Capitalism in Amsterdam,* p. 15–16.
32. On this famous personage, consult Dahlgren, *Louis de Geer.*

in Amsterdam and represented about 30 percent of the citizens in the highest tax brackets.[33] It was the Walloon exiles who introduced new mills for the fulling of woolen cloth at Leyden in 1585 and Rotterdam in 1591.[34]

Vigorous in themselves, strenghtened by the injection of a powerful new dose of vitality and galvanized by the opening of countless new opportunities in oceanic trade, the Northern United Provinces entered into their golden age. Amsterdam became an international market where one could find goods from all over the world —Japanese copper, Swedish copper, Baltic grain, Italian silk, French wines, Chinese porcelain, Brazilian coffee, oriental tea, Indonesian spices, Mexican silver. Amsterdam, in fact, became the main world market for a variety of products—from guns to diamonds, from sugar to porcelain—and the price quotations on the Amsterdam market dictated the prices on the other European markets.[35] The business techniques inherited from the Italians were refined and developed. The stock exchange was born, and what Werner-Sombart described as "Früh Kapitalismus" was replaced by incipient modern capitalism.

As always in such cases, the vigor of a people is by its nature diasporic. What a pope had said of Florentines in the Middle Ages can be applied to the Dutch of the seventeenth century: they were the fifth element in the world. They were to be found everywhere —acting as consultants to the Grand Duchy of Tuscany, reclaiming the Maremma; establishing the first smelting plants for iron cannon in Russia; expanding sugar plantations in Brazil; buying tea, porcelain and silk in China; founding New Amsterdam (later to be called New York) in North America, and, in the Adriatic in 1616–19, protecting with their galleons the once-greatest naval power, Venice, from possible Spanish attacks. The economic development of Sweden in the seventeeth century was the by-product of

---

33. Jeannin, *L'Europe du Nord-Ouest*, pp. 70–71.
34. Van Uytven, *The Fulling Mill*, p. 12.
35. Bulletins of prices quoted on the Amsterdam Commodities Exchange were published from 1585 and circulated throughout Europe. In 1634 these bulletins gave prices of 359 commodities. In 1686 the list increased to 550 commodities.

Dutch activity. When Japan closed its doors to the West for centuries of isolation, an exception was made for the Dutch, who were permitted to maintain a base in Nagasaki.

Just as the vitality of a people knows no geographic frontiers, neither does it know professional boundaries. When between the thirteenth and the fourteenth centuries Tuscany gave Europe her most active merchants and craftsmen, she also produced exceptional poets, writers, and doctors. The northern Low Countries in the seventeenth century were great in shipping as well as in painting, in commercial as well as in philosophical speculation, and in scientific observation. The annual cloth production in Leyden grew from about 30,000 pieces in 1585 to over 140,000 pieces around 1665.[36] At the same time, the University of Leyden became known as the most important center for the study of medicine in Europe. While Huygens made important contributions to both technology and science, in the field of international law Grotius elaborated a theory of international and territorial waters which still rules international relations today.

It is not by chance that Grotius appeared when and where he did. The life and prosperity of the northern Low Countries in their golden age continued to depend upon the freedom of the seas and upon the strength of their fleets. Impressed by the Dutch naval power, contemporaries made the most fantastic estimates about it. Sir Walter Raleigh maintained that the Dutch built a thousand ships a year and that their navy and merchant marine consisted of about twenty thousand units. Colbert estimated in 1669 that "the maritime trade of all Europe is carried out by twenty thousand ships, of which fifteen to sixteen thousand are Dutch, three to four thousand are English, and five to six hundred are French."[37] However, it was a question not only of quantity but also of quality. In 1596 the town council of Amsterdam could write to the States-

---

36. Jeannin, *L'Europe du Nord-Ouest*, p. 75.
37. Clement, *Lettres*, vol. 6, p. 264. For modern estimates of the size of the Dutch fleet, consult Vogel, *Handelsflotten*, pp. 268–334; and Boxer, *The Dutch in Brazil*, pp. 204–5. According to Christensen, *Dutch Trade to the Baltic*, p. 94, a "most reliable calculation from the Dutch States Provincial" of 1636 estimated the size of the Dutch merchant navy trading to the Baltic, Norway, and France at 1,050 ships.

General of the Dutch Republic that "this country in merchant marine and shipbuilding is so much more advanced than the kingdoms of France and England that it is impossible to make a comparison."[38] As R. W. Unger remarked, "Over the following two centuries it was the task of other European shipbuilders to try to equal the technical progress made by Dutch shipcarpenters."[39]

The most dynamic and glamorous sector of the Dutch economy was undoubtedly foreign trade. As Daniel Defoe put it:

The Dutch must be understood as they really are, the Middle Persons in Trade, the Factors and Brokers of Europe. . . . They buy to sell again, take in to send out, and the greatest part of their vast commerce consists in being supply'd from all parts of the world that they may supply all the world again.[40]

It is convenient to divide the Dutch commerce of the sixteenth and seventeenth centuries into two fairly distinct areas, each characterized in general by different techniques of trading, shipping, and finance. On the one hand, there was the long-distance trade overseas—in the East and West Indies, in Brazil, at Canton and Nagasaki. On the other hand there was the trade in home waters of western Europe. Within this latter area it was the Baltic trade in which the Dutch retained their preeminence longest. The composition of the Baltic trade and the overwhelming importance of the Dutch in it is well known because the Danes were able to levy tolls on almost all of the international shipping which passed through the only navigable passage from the Baltic to the North Sea. The records of the tolls at the Sound have survived in great detail from the end of the fifteen century, and, making due allowance for omissions, smuggling, errors of interpretation, and the like, one can derive from them a fairly reliable picture of the Baltic trade patterns. Of the ships which passed through the Sound from 1550 to 1650, the Dutch share fluctuated between 55 and 85 percent. The Dutch share of the imports into the Baltic fluctuated around 50 percent for salt, 60 to 80 percent for herring, more than 80 percent

---

38. Elias, *Het Voorspel*, p. 60.
39. Unger, *Dutch Ship Design*, p. 409.
40. Defoe, *A Plan of the English Commerce,* p. 192.

for Rhine wines. Among exports from the Baltic to the West, grains were a major commodity (about 65 percent of total exports around 1565 and some 55 percent in 1635). The Dutch share of the grain trade fluctuated around a long-run average of about 75 percent.[41] Dutch prosperity however did not rest on mercantile success alone. Agriculture and manufactures developed remarkably in seventeenth-century Holland. As has been said, the Netherlands became the Mecca of European agricultural experts, and it is possible that the Low Countries reached relatively advanced technical levels with yields two or three times above those of the rest of Europe. Manufacturing also developed, greatly favored by the fact that the Dutch were no less successful in harnessing the energy of the wind on land than on the high seas. About 1630 in the province of Holland there were 222 industrial windmills, plus an unknown number of grain mills and drainage mills. Most of these mills were located in the area of Noorder-Kwartier, an area just north of Amsterdam. In this area (approximately 148,000 acres and 85,000 people), the operational distribution of the windmills was as follows:[42]

OPERATION	NUMBER OF MILLS
Saw milling	60
Oil pressing	57
Grain milling	53
Paper production	9
Hemp working	5
Cloth fulling	2
Shell crushing	1
Tanning	1
Buckwheat milling	1
Paint production	1
Dye production	1
Drainage	?

A number of manufactures in the Netherlands were closely linked with international trade insofar as they were concerned with finishing or refining commodities imported in a crude or partly

41. Christensen. *Dutch Trade to the Baltic, passim.*
42. Van der Woude, *Het Noorderkwartier*, vol. 2, p. 320, Table 5.11.

manufactured state.[43] Thus, there were in the northern Low Countries numerous and important concerns for the cutting and wrapping of imported tobacco, for the weaving of imported silk, for the refining of imported sugar. There were three sugar refineries in Amsterdam in 1605 and sixty in 1660. With copper from Japan and Sweden, the foundries of Amsterdam, Rotterdam, and other towns produced guns which were mostly sold to foreign countries —even to the archenemy, Spain. Of French wine, according to Colbert, the Dutch consumed only a third. Two-thirds they re-exported after much manipulation, processing, and blending. As Roger Dion wrote,

Merchants *par excellence,* the Dutch ignored that respect for the integrity of the "cru" which was one of the fundamental principles of high-quality viticulture in France. Even good wines did not escape their manipulations.[44]

Also linked to the development of shipping and international trade were the developments of cartography, shipbuilding, and the making of geometrical and astronomical instruments. Maps and charts by Dutch cartographers invaded Europe and are still a source of delight to map collectors today. Dutch shipyards were the objects of pilgrimages by technicians from every part of Europe anxious to learn skills in building ships. Early in the eighteenth century it was recorded that "there is a greater choice of astronomical, geometrical and other mathematical instruments in Holland than any where else in the world."[45]

Whether one looks at the commercial or at the manufacturing sector, one finds that the Dutch of the seventeenth century had a genius—if not an obsession—for reducing costs. The Dutch succeeded in selling anything to anybody anywhere in the world because they sold at very low prices, and their prices were competi-

---

43. In some cases, the Dutch entrepreneurs found it more convenient to transform the raw materials into finished products at the source where the raw materials were available. De Geer and the Trips operated iron foundries in Sweden. The product, in the shape of iron bars and iron cannon, was imported into the United Provinces: a good deal of it was re-exported, but the pofits of course were retained in Amsterdam.
44. Dion, *Histoire de la vigne,* p. 426–27.
45. Barbour, *Capitalism in Amsterdam,* p. 63n.

tively low because their costs of production were more compressed than elsewhere.

Wages were notoriously high in the United Provinces, where heavy excise taxes burdened all articles of general consumption. But the productivity of Dutch labor more than offset this comparative disadvantage. "The thrifty and neat disposition" of the Dutch craftsmen praised by Nicolaes Witsen (see above, pp. 180–81) was admiringly recognized also by Colbert, who wrote of "l'économie et l'application continuelle au travail" of the Dutch workers.[46] The Dutch relied on cheap money.[47] Moreover, they made extensive use of labor-saving devices. We have already discussed the extensive exploitation of the energy of the wind in the manufacturing sector. In the field of maritime transport, their greatest achievement was the production of the *fluitship* (*fluyt*).

The design of the *fluyt* grew out of experience with the flyboat. As has been aptly said, "the fluyt was the outstanding achievement of Dutch shipbuilding in the era of full-rigged ships, the fulfillment of a long period of improvement in Dutch ship design,"[48] and it became the great cargo carrier of northern Europe in the seventeenth century. Sail area was kept small and masts short relative to carrying capacity; although these features meant a slower ship, such a ship, more importantly, needed a smaller crew, and consequently incurred lower costs. The excellent handling qualities of the ship further helped to reduce the size of the crew, as did the extensive use of pulleys and blocks in controlling the yards and sails. Cheap, light pine was generally used, except for the hull, where oak was needed to withstand exposure to salt water. The lightly built *fluyt* was almost defenseless, and when

---

46. Barbour, *Dutch and English Merchant Shipping,* p. 239.
47. The average rate of interest in Amsterdam was about 3 percent when it was 6 percent in London, and Josiah Child in 1665 considered this as the "causa causans of all the other causes of riches in that people." Compare Wilson, *The Dutch Republic,* pp. 33–34, and Homer, *A History of Interest Rates,* p. 128.
48. Unger, *Dutch Ship Design,* p. 405. In accordance with the character of technological development before the Industrial Revolution, Dutch shipbuilding was "exclusively based on tradition and experience: there was no question of scientific shipbuilding." Compare Van Kampen, *Scheepsbouw,* p. 240.

it carried guns the complement was small; but this too was a calculated risk[49] which further lowered operating costs.

When the Dutch could not reduce costs in any other way, they reduced the quality of the product. In the woollens sector, they produced brightly colored cloths of inferior quality—known as "cloths in the fashion of Holland"—and with them succeeded in cornering a large part of the international market to the detriment of those who continued to produce "cloths of the good old standard."[50] In the wine trade, they dealt in the *"petits vins"* (inferior wines) which had never been considered before in international trade.[51]

In sacrificing quality for the sake of reducing price, the Dutch departed from a tradition that had prevailed in the Middle Ages and the early Renaissance and heralded a principle which was to

The fluyt. This was the masterpiece of the Dutch shipbuilders of the seventeenth century.

49. Defensibility and speed were sacrificed by private shipowners since in most cases their ships could count on the protection of the Dutch navy. For all that precedes, see Unger, *Dutch Ship Design,* pp. 406–8.
50. See above p. 242.
51. Dion, *Histoire de la vigne,* p. 427.

prevail in modern times. The medieval merchant had normally tried to maximize profit per unit of production—thus his insistence on high quality. The Dutch decidedly moved toward mass production. In an increasing number of activities they endeavored to maximize their profit by maximizing the volume of sales. Even Dutch painters produced their masterpieces at low prices and in prolific quantities. The average price of, say, a Salomon Ruisdael landscape or a Steen genre picture was about a quarter of the weekly wage of a Leyden textile worker.[52] The new attitude of the Dutch was prompted by—and their success was linked to—the fact that new, larger social groups were ascending the economic ladder in Europe, and price elasticity of demand was growing for an increasing number of commodities.

The Dutch success evoked admiration among some, envy among others, and great interest everywhere. Holland held all Europe fascinated, but more than anyone else their neighbors across the Channel, the English.

The Rise of England

At the end of the fifteenth century, England was an "underdeveloped country"—underdeveloped not only by comparison with the modern industrialized countries, but also in relation to the standards of the "developed" countries of that time, such as Italy, the Low Countries, France, and Southern Germany.

There were fewer than 4 million inhabitants in England and Wales, while France numbered over 15 million, Italy about 11 million, and Spain between 6 and 7 million. The small size of the English population was not offset by a greater wealth. On the contrary, from both the technological and economic points of view, England was backward compared with most of the Continent. England, however, produced some of the best wool in Europe, and from the fourteenth century onward she moved more and more into the production of woollen cloth. Wool and woollen cloth represented the bulk of English exports in the last centuries of the Middle Ages,

---

52. Price, *Culture and Society in the Dutch Republic.*

Table 10–4

Average Yearly English Exports of Raw Wool and Woollen Cloth,
1361–1500

Years	Raw Wool (bags)	Woollen Cloths (as equivalent to bags of raw wool)
1361–70	28,302	3,024
1371–80	23,241	3,432
1381–90	17,988	5,521
1391–1400	17,679	8,967
1401–10	13,922	7,651
1411–20	13,487	6,364
1421–30	13,696	9,309
1431–40	7,377	10,051
1441–50	9,398	11,803
1471–80	9,299	10,125
1481–90	8,858	12,230
1491–1500	8,149	13,891

SOURCE: Bridbury, *Economic Growth*, p. 32. Data are derived from customs records and therefore must be taken with the reservation of possible underregistration.

As it appears that the underregistration was more accentuated during the Civil War years, the figures for the two decades 1451–70 have been omitted.

and the rise in the proportion of woollen cloth to raw wool among exports can be taken as an index of the increasing weight of manufacturing in the economy. (See Table 10-4 and Fig. 10-2). The transition from a stage characterized by massive exports of indigenous raw materials to a stage increasingly characterized by manufactures made from such raw materials is a typical sequence on the road to economic development.

English products were traditionally exported to markets in the southern Low Countries—first Bruges, then Antwerp—whence they were distributed to various parts of the continent.

In the course of the fifteenth century, the merchants of Nuremberg, Augsburg, Ravensburg, and other cities of southern Germany established closer contacts with Bruges and Antwerp, using as intermediaries the merchants of the Rhineland towns and in the second part of the century, these contacts became more frequent and direct. The development of Portuguese trade in Antwerp was the catalyst; the Portuguese sold ivory, gold, and pepper from West Africa and sugar from Madeira, and were active buyers of those products that the Germans could sell in large quantities, namely, silver, mercury, copper, and weapons.[53] The period 1490–1525 marked the apogee of the southern German merchants' success on the Antwerp market where, among others, economic giants such as the Imhofs, the Welsers, and the Fuggers were very active.[54] On the Antwerp market, the south German merchants found not only the

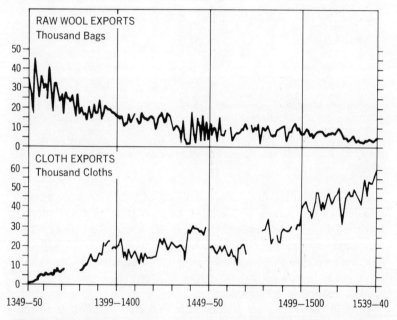

Figure 10–2. Trends in the export of raw wool and cloth from England, 1349–1540.

Source: H. C. Darby (ed.), *A New Historical Geography of England*, p. 219.

53. For the preceding, see Van Houtte, *Anvers au XVe et XVIe siècles*, p. 251.
54. Van der Wee, *Antwerp*, vol. 2, p. 131.

commodities brought there by the Portuguese, but also English textiles.

Traditionally, the merchants of southern Germany obtained their supplies of woollen cloth on the markets of northern Italy (especially Milan, Como, Brescia, and Bergamo)[55] and then redistributed them throughout central and eastern Europe. However, as we have seen above, in the first half of the sixteenth century Italian production collapsed because of the war and the ensuing disasters. As the Italian suppliers were no longer in a position to satisfy the demand of the Germans, the latter availed themselves of cloth made in England and available in Antwerp.

A golden age thus began for English exports, later favored between 1522 and 1550 by the progressive deterioration of the pound which Henry VIII depreciated to finance his extravagant military expenditure. Between 1500 and 1550, the exports of "short cloths" from the Port of London increased by 170 percent (see Table 10-5).

The textile manufacturing sector in England was the first to show the effects of the boom in exports. But in economics the waves travel far, and what happens in one sector never fails to

Table 10–5
Yearly Average Export of Woollen *Shortcloths*
from the Port of London, 1500–50

Years	No. of Cloths (thousands)	Years	No. of Cloths (thousands)
1500–2	49	1527–29	75
1503–5	44	1530–32	66
1506–8	50	1533–35	83
1509–11	58	1536–38	87
1512–14	61	1539–41	103
1515–17	61	1542–44	99
1518–20	66	1545–47	119
1521–23	54	1550	133
1524–26	73		

SOURCE: Fisher, *Commercial Trends and Policy*, p. 153.

---

55. For all this, consult Schulte, *Geschichte des Mittelalterlichen Handels*.

make ripples in others—especially when the expanding sector is a key one in the economy. As Frederick J. Fisher wrote:

On the one hand, there was a marked diversion of national resources into new channels. Arable land was converted to pasture; the textile industry spread over the countryside; the ranks of the merchants were swollen with new entrants. On the other, the growth of exports brought with it a corresponding growth of imports. . . . [Sources bear] witness to a rise in standards of living, a rise that was emphasized by the sumptuary legislation designed to check its most obvious manifestations.[56]

At the middle of the sixteenth century, England looked very different from what she had been half a century earlier. By 1550, England was a prosperous, dynamic country, a country which was lining up with the most advanced countries in Europe of the time. Between 1550 and 1562–64 the export of shortcloths from London fell from about 133,000 to about 61,000 and then leveled off at about 100,000 pieces of cloth a year.[57] The recovery of the Italian textile industry, the stagnation of southern Germany, the war in the southern Low Countries, the ruin of Antwerp, the revaluation of sterling, all contributed to the difficulties of the English exporters. On the basis of these facts, it has been suggested that "the great expansion of trade was over" and that "the maladjustments of the fifties opened a new chapter in English economic history"—a new chapter characterized by a series of depressions if not altogether by a "great depression" which lasted until the end of the century.[58] However, to overgeneralize from the figures on the export of shortcloths would be a serious mistake.

First of all, export does not mean production. If the internal market absorbed progressively greater quantities of textiles, production may not have contracted in proportion to exports. Moreover, Fisher himself suggests that "the value of exports must have fallen less than their volume," and that "it is conceivable that imports and national income were scarcely diminished." But setting aside gratuitous hypotheses of this sort, one must note that the period 1550–1650 was characterized by England's entry precisely

---

56. Fisher, *Commercial Trends and Policy,* pp. 154–155.
57. *Ibid.,* pp. 153 ff.
58. *Ibid.,* pp. 160, 169, 172.

at that time into a new stage in her economic development—a stage in which other manufactures besides woollens began to play a major role in the economy.

The transition from one type of production to another was gradual. Woollen textiles still accounted for about 48 percent of exports (see Table 10-6) at the end of the seventeenth century. But from

Table 10-6
Commodity Composition of English Foreign Trade
1699–1701

	Exports %	Imports %
Wool Manufactures	47.5	31.7
Other Manufactures	8.4	
Foodstuffs	7.6	33.6
Raw Materials	5.6	34.7
Re-exports	30.9	
Total	100.0	100.0

SOURCE: Davis, *English Foreign Trade 1660–1700*, p. 109.

the middle of the sixteenth century, new sectors began to expand and to achieve a progressively greater importance in the economy. The generations of the second half of the sixteenth century were not melancholic generations, gloomily bemoaning the stagnating exports of shortcloth from the harbor of London. They were bold and adventurous generations which, if they encountered some difficulties, looked at new horizons, searched for opportunities, and redirected English development. As usual, the vitality of a people did not manifest itself in one sector only. To the dynamism in trade and navigation corresponded an equal dynamism in the field of technology, culture, and art. At Florence, on the walls of Palazzo Vecchio in the room of the maps, an inscription of the second half of the sixteenth century on England recalls that "the people of this Island, which was described by the ancients as having neither letters nor music, are now seen to be great in both fields." And a Venetian gun founder of good repute, Gentilini, wrote "The English, to say the truth, are judicious people and of great intelligence, and are very ingenious in their inventions."

In order to understand adequately what happened then in England, one must take into account the contribution of the immigrants. As noted previously, religious and political persecutions in France, devastation and persecution by the Spaniards in the southern Low Countries, and economic difficulties in other areas, drove many people to seek peace, tranquillity and employment in more hospitable countries. Walloons and French Huguenots poured into England in increasing numbers after the middle of the century. The development of the "new drapery" was above all the result of "Walloon" immigration. The development of the glass industry, of horology, and of the silk industry was essentially due to French immigrants. Contemporaries were aware of this contribution. Early in the seventeenth century, John Stow wrote:

The making of Spanish needles was first taught in England by Elias Crowse a Germane about the eighth year of Queen Elizabeth. . . . The first making of Venice glasses in England. began at the Crotched Fryers in London, about the beginning of the Reign of Queen Elizabeth, by one Jacob Venaline, an Italian. . . . The cutting of iron bars in a mill for the ready use of smiths to make long rods and all sorts of nayles was brought first into England in the year 1590 by Godfrey Box of the province of Liege. . . . Upon the Dartford River not long before was set up a mill to make white paper by master John Spilman, a German, who was long after knighted by King James; this was the first mill in England wherein fine white paper was made.[59]

W. Cunningham wrote a classic little book on the subject at the end of the last century.[60] It is a pity that the subject has been neglected since then, and that the contribution of immigrants to English economic development between 1550 and 1650 is usually mentioned only in passing and as a factor of secondary importance. The fact that a great deal was owed to immigrants does not detract anything from the English, who wisely accepted the refugees, learned from them, and later perfected new techniques and new trades.

In fact, two features of English society of that time strike even the most casual observer: an extraordinary cultural receptiveness

---

59. Stow, *Annales* pp. 1038–40.
60. Cunningham, *Alien Immigrants.*

and an equally extraordinary ability to react decisively to the difficulties of the moment, making such difficulties the starting points of new developments and new comparative advantages.

Cultural receptiveness was probably sharpened by the fact that, for centuries, the English had lived in close contact with far more highly evolved areas and had, therefore, developed a strong spirit of emulation. While there was no shortage of conservatives, fully satisfied with local culture and traditions, many looked beyond parochial horizons with intense curiosity. The taste for foreign travel and the educational importance attributed to the "Grand Tour," the notion of sending young men to study at foreign universities in Padua or Paris or, later, in Leyden were aspects of a general cultural phenomenon which acquired great vigor between the middle of the sixteenth century and the middle of the seventeenth century.[61] The Italians had displayed similar cultural traits at the times of Dante and Marco Polo, but success breeds presumption and arrogance. Comparing the attitude of the English at the end of the sixteenth century with that of their Italian contemporaries, Fynes Moryson wrote:

[T]he Italians thincke themselves to have so much sweeteness, fruitfullness, and such monuments of arts and fabricks, as they seldome or never travaile into forayne kingdoms, but driven by some necessity ether to followe the warrs or to traffique abroad: this opinion that Italy doth afforde what can be seene or knowne in the world makes them only have home-bred wisdome and the prowde conceete of their own witts.[62]

The Elizabethans were fond of traveling abroad and were accustomed to commend it as a facet of education. "He cannot be a perfect man, not being tried or tutored in the world" says Antonio in *The Two Gentlemen of Verona*. While the craftsmen learned the techniques and trades practiced by the immigrants, travelers imported new ideas.[63] In a number of instances the newly adopted

---

61. Stoye, *English Travellers*, pp. 22 and ff.
62. Moryson, *Itinerary*, p. 419.
63. Henry VIII's quarantine regulations, the "Plague Orders" of Elizabeth, and the College of Physicians at London were all instituted on Italian models. Copeman, *Doctors and Disease*, p. 169; and Clark, *Royal College of Physicians*, vol. 1, pp. 58 ff.

ideas and techniques were actually developed with superior skills. Early in the seventeenth century John Stow wrote, "At this day the best and finest knives in the world are made in London. . . . The Englishmen began to make all sorts of pinnes and at this day they excell all nations."[64] When Henry VIII decided to have work done on the great clock in Nonesuch Palace, he had to invite French clockmakers; Nicholas Cratzer, "deviser of the King's horloges" was a Bavarian; Nicholas Urseau, clockmaker to Queen Elizabeth was of French origin but by 1680 "England has secured an unchallenged preeminence in the horological field, a preeminence which she was to enjoy for about a century."[65]

As Eric Hoffer wrote, "The vigor of a society shows itself partly in the ability to borrow copiously without ill-effects and without impairing its identity."

Not only was there open-mindedness in England at that time, the very fiber of contemporary English society was exceptional. In Toynbian terms, one can say that to the numerous and serious "challenges" which she had to face at that time, England was always able to give positive and innovative "responses" in the same way as a healthy organism reacts to natural abuses and emerges strengthened from them. The destruction of the Spanish Armada is a classic example of the way in which the English took advantage of a few factors favorable to them, and turned an essentially unfavorable situation into a triumph. We saw that in the sector of woollen exports after 1550 the English were faced with increasing competition and difficulties. Instead of admitting defeat, with the aid of the immigrants they swiftly adopted new Dutch methods of production and, abandoning the tradition of having foreign merchants to come to England to buy wool and woollens, they aggressively launched themselves into the conquest of North African and Middle Eastern markets.

In the war-armaments sector, England found herself at a disadvantage when, with the royal finances in ruin, it became increasingly difficult for her to buy the artillery she needed from the continental cannon merchants. The artillery of the time was mostly

64. Stow, *Annales*, p. 1038.
65. Britten, *Old Clocks*, p. 77.

made of bronze, and England lacked copper. Between 1543 and 1545, under the pressure of necessity, a few English technicians, assisted by foreign ones, turned to the raw material which was locally available and successfully developed new techniques for the casting of iron guns. By 1575 England produced annually over 500 tons of iron artillery and, by the end of the century about 1,000 tons. Iron guns were much cheaper than those of bronze and, although inferior to the latter in quality, were more than adequate, especially for the arming of merchant ships and for privateering. In one generation an adverse situation had been turned into an advantageous one.

A similar story is that of energy. England was never a heavily wooded country. What forest heritage there was dwindled rapidly during the course of the sixteenth century, because of a combined expansion of population; building activity and timber consumption for domestic heating; shipbuilding; and production of charcoal, which was the only known fuel for a number of industrial processes. During the sixteenth century a number of Acts of Parliament tried to suppress the cutting of timber for industrial purposes. In 1548–49 the English government ordered an inquiry into the consumption of timber by the iron foundries in Sussex.[66] The governmental action was to little or no avail. English timber reserves were rapidly depleted. About 1580 William Harrison pointed to the fact that a man could often ride ten or twenty miles and find very little wood or even none at all "except where the inhabitants have planted a few elms, oaks, hazels or ashes about their dwellings." In 1611 Arthur Standish pointed to the destruction that had taken place during the preceding twenty or thirty years and urged that trees be replanted. Early in the seventeenth century Edmund Howes wrote:[67]

Such hath been the plenty of wood in England for all bless that, within man's memory, it was held impossible to have any want of wood in England. But contrary to former imaginations such hath beene the great expence of timber for navigation, with infinite increase of building of houses, with the great expence of wood to make household fur-

---

66. Tawney and Power, *Tudor Economic Documents,* vol. 1, pp. 231–38.
67. Stow, *Annales,* p. 1025.

niture, caskes, and othes vessels not to be numbered, and of carts,
wagons and coaches, besides the extreame waste of wood in making
iron, burning of brick and tile, that at this present, through the great
consuming of wood as aforesaid, and the neglect of planting of woods,
there is so great a scarcitie of wood through the whole kingdom. . . .

In 1637 the clothmakers of the town of Cranbrook, in Kent, complained to the Privy Council against John Browne on the ground
that he had caused a rise in the price of wood by burning large
quantities in his furnace.[68] Table 10-7 shows a general price index
and an index of the price of charcoal in England during the period
1560–1670. These figures and any comparison among them must
be subject to many qualifications, but there is justification for
saying that the fuel crisis exploded in all its gravity in the 1630s.[69]

Table 10–7

Indexes of Prices and Charcoal Prices in
England, 1560–1670 (1630 = 100)

Year	General Index	Index of Charcoal Prices
1560	46	60
1610	90	95
1620	87	100
1630	100	100
1640	106	135
1650	133	225
1660	121	220
1670	102	250

SOURCE: Cipolla, *Guns and Sails*, p. 64.

The consequences of the crisis can be clearly observed in the
armament industry. Since the middle of the sixteenth century England had become a manufacturer and exporter of cast-iron ordnance. According to a report of 1573 there were "above 400
tonnes cast yearly and all this will not be sold nor bought to remain
within the Realme"; according to a report of 1607, between 1596
and 1603 more than 2270 tons of iron ordnance were exported
yearly under license, besides an unknown quantity exported

---

68. Nef, *British Coal Industry,* vol. 1, p. 214.
69. See Cipolla, *Guns and Sails*, p. 63.

illegally.[70] By 1630, however, the production of cast-iron ordnance was severely hit by the shortage of fuel, and England was then unable to produce enough guns for her own needs. In 1632 one hears of iron guns made in Sweden shipped to England and by the early 1670s the Marquis de Seignelay reported to Colbert, his father, that the English "not having enough timber for casting all the ordnance they need, import cannon from Sweden, although they esteem that the Swedish iron is not as good as that of England".[71]

England reacted to the energy crisis in two ways. On the one hand she strengthened shipping and trade with Scandinavian countries, where timber was in ample supply. On the other hand, England increasingly resorted to the fuel which was abundantly available in the British Isles. As an Englishman recorded in 1577, "of coalmines we have such plentie in the north and western parts of our Island."

Coal was well known in London in 1228, for in that year there is a definite record of the existence of a "sea-coal lane" which, it is suggested, was then used as a landing place for sea-coal from boats. In the same year fumes of coal allegedly drove Queen Eleanor from Nottingham Castle. In 1257 mention is made of shiploads of coal imported into London. Throughout the Middle Ages, however, the English—like all other Europeans—remained very reluctant to use coal extensively, fearing its fumes which people instinctively regarded as venomous. Early in the seventeenth century, however, under the pressure of necessity, the English put aside all their reservations, and between 1500 and 1700 they resorted extensively to coal not only for domestic heating but also in industrial processes such as the oven-drying of bricks and tiles and of malt for beer, the refining of sugar, the production of glass and soap, and iron-smelting. As early as 1631 Edmund Howes wrote:

> There is so great a scarcitie of wood through the whole Kingdom, that not only the Citie of London, all haven-towns and in very many parts within the land, the inhabitants in generall are constrained to make their fires of sea-coal or pit-coal, even in the

70. Cipolla, *Guns and Sails*, p. 44, n.2.
71. *Ibid.*, p. 64.

chambers of honourable personages, and through necessitie, which is the mother of all arts, they have of very late yeares devised the making of iron, the making of all sorts of glasse and burning of bricke with sea-coal or pit-coal.[72]

From the late sixteenth century onward coal production expanded remarkably as the market, both domestic and industrial, grew and as supplies of wood fuel declined.

British annual total coal production was about 210,000 tons in about 1550; in 1630 it was about 1.5 million ton.[73] In 1650, John Cleveland wrote:

> England's a perfect world
> hath Indies too;
> Correct your maps,
> Newcastle is Peru.

The British coal production was to reach 11 million tons in 1800 and about 60 million tons in about 1850. Development was greater where there was access to water transport. The transport of coal by sea from Newcastle to London increased as follows:

    1549–50: 35,000 tons
    1597–80: 141,000 tons
    1633–40: 409,000 tons
    1697–80: 560,000 tons

This development in turn stimulated shipping and shipbuilding. It was said in seventeenth-century England that the coal trade was "if not the only, yet the special nursery and school of seamen" and "the chiefest in employment of seamen." By 1738 a French traveler wrote that coal was "the soul of all English Industries."

Reacting to serious shortages, England ingeniously developed new techniques which allowed her to utilize those natural resources locally available in relatively ample quantities. Concentrating on iron and coal, England set herself on the road that led directly to the Industrial Revolution. Iron and coal much more than cotton stand as critical factors in the origins of the Industrial Revolution.

---

72. Stow, *Annales*, p. 1025.
73. Nef, *British Coal Industry*, vol. 1, pp. 19–20, 36, 208.

The development of early textile machinery was a major episode in European economic history, but as has been aptly said:

[Early cotton machinery] fits better as an appendage to the evolution of the old industry than in the way it is usually presented as the beginning of the new. . . . Would it have been impossible, if capital could have been raised and if the regular water power of Lancashire had been available, for something very like it to have occurred, say in fifteenth-century Florence? There is continuity between the eighteenth-century development of Lancashire and the West Riding and the pre–Industrial Revolution world. There might have been no Crompton and Arkwright, and still there could have been an Industrial Revolution.[74]

If the increasing use of and reliance on coal and iron were, perhaps, the major development leading to the Industrial Revolution in the form and shape it took, other concomitant factors and developments should not be overlooked. Another process which led directly to the Industrial Revolution was the increase in the size of plants and the concurrent concentration of labor and capital in technical units of production. At iron foundries fixed capital was substantial, but the labor force remained small.[75] In other sectors, however, such as in the production of alum, shipbuilding, and textile manufacture, there was an increasingly large concentration of both capital and labor; plants were worth several million pounds sterling, and hundreds of workers were employed.[76]

Much of what happened in the manufacturing and shipping sectors can hardly be understood if one does not take due account of what was happening at the same time in the commercial sector. In 1706 the Venetian Ambassador in London, Alvise Mocenigo, wrote: "there is no corner of the known world which is accessible by sea, where numerous ships of England are not to be found," and

---

74. Hicks, *A Theory of Economic History*, p. 147.
75. Nef, *The Conquest of the Material World*, p. 125, talks of two hundred workers employed in the cannon foundries of John Browne at the beginning of the seventeenth century. But in all likelihood the number includes charcoal burners and transport workers. (Cipolla, *Guns and Sails*, p. 153). Attendants to the furnaces were always relatively few throughout the seventeenth century.
76. Nef, *The Conquest of the Material World*, pp. 124 ff.; Davis, *The Rise of the Shipping Industry*, p. 389; Coleman, *Naval Dockyards*, pp. 189 ff.

"with sad memory," he commented that England was now what "this same city [Venice] had been in other times." The important role of immigrants stressed above in relation to the development of England's manufactures between 1550 and 1650 was equally in evidence in the development of English foreign trade in the course of the seventeenth and early eighteenth centuries. As Ashton remarked, "Of the 810 merchants who kissed the hand of George III, at least 250 must have been of alien origin. It was one of the merits of the English at this time that they opened their doors to capital and enterprise from all quarters." Table 1-15 shows that between the early seventeenth and the early eighteenth century total exports (exports plus re-exports) increased about six-fold. While these figures, like all statistics of the time, must be taken cautiously, there is no doubt that English foreign trade underwent a most remarkable expansion. In this expansion, extra-European trade and the re-export trade acquired a progressively growing importance (see Table 10-8). Around 1640 re-exports had made up only 3.5 percent of total exports (see Table 1–15). At the end of the century they were about 31 percent (see Table 10–6), and in 1773, about 37 percent.[77] This re-export trade consisted mainly of goods from the East and West Indies. As Phyllis Deane wrote:[78]

The immense importance of the tropical commodities lay in the fact that they increased British purchasing power on the continent of Europe. Britain needed her European imports for vital productive purposes and not merely to meet the upper class demand for wine and brandy. She needed foreign timber, pitch and hemp for her ships and buildings, high-grade bar iron for her metal trade, raw and thrown silk for her textile trades. Her industrial expansion along traditional lines was severely restricted by the fact that the demand for woollen products was inelastic and already near saturation point in traditional markets. Had it not been for the tropical products with their elastic demand and growing markets in temperate regions, it would have been difficult to expand British trade with Europe.

The trade in tropical products also allowed the development of

---

77. Davis, *English Foreign Trade 1700–1774*, p. 109. Compare also Davis, *English Foreign Trade 1660–1700*, pp. 78–98.
78. Deane, *The First Industrial Revolution*, p. 53.

Table 10–8

Geographical Distribution of English Foreign Trade, 1700–50

Total Imports from	1700–1 %	1750–1 %
Europe	66	55
North America	6	11
West Indies	14	19
East Indies and Africa	14	15
Total	100	100
Re-export to		
Europe	85	79
North America	5	11
West Indies	6	5
East Indies and Africa	4	5
Total	100	100
Domestic Exports to		
Europe	85	77
North America	6	11
West Indies	5	5
East Indies and Africa	4	7
Total	100	100

SOURCE: Deane, *The First Industrial Revolution*, p. 56.

altogether new industries, such as sugar refining. The pivotal point of the wide, intricate, multilateral network of world trade that grew up during the eighteenth century was London with its wide sheltered anchorages, its vast wharves and warehouses, its rich city banks, its specialists in marine insurance and its world-wide mercantile contacts.[79] As shown in Table A-1 the population of London grew from about 250,000 people around 1550; to about 450,000 around 1650; to about 600,000 in 1700. London was, then, the largest, busiest, and wealthiest metropolis in the world.

The resources which allowed the English to develop their foreign trade were mainly (a) a relatively abundant stock of good sailors and able merchants; (b) a relatively abundant supply of both physi-

---

79. *Ibid.*, p. 57.

Table 10–9

Size of the English Merchant Navy, 1572–1686

| | | Number of Ships | |
| | Total | | 200 Tons |
Years	Tonnage	100–199 Tons	and Over
1572	50,000	72	14
1577		120	15
1582	67,000	155	18
1629	115,000	>178	>145
1686	340,000		

SOURCE: Davis, *The Rise of the English Shipping Industry*, pp. 7, 15, 25, 27.

cal capital (e.g., see Table 10-9) and financial capital; (c) a well-developed organizational structure of credit, commercial, and insurance organizations; (d) a government deeply aware of and intelligently favorable to the aspirations of the merchant class; and (e) the extension of diplomatic offices and the strength of the Royal Navy. For its part, international trade contributed considerably to general economic development. To define such a contribution precisely is not easy because, besides direct effects which one can detect but not always measure, there were also important indirect effects, especially on economic organization, opportunities, training, value systems, and the like which are difficult to isolate. By way of rough classification one can say, however, that the notable development of international trade.

a. contributed to the expansion of demand for the products of British industry

b. gave access to raw materials which both widened the range and lowered the price of the products of British industry

c. provided the underdeveloped countries with the purchasing power to buy English goods

d. favored an accumulation of capital which helped to finance industrial expansion and agricultural improvement

e. stimulated the development of insurance and transport activities

f. helped to create an institutional structure and a business ethic which was to prove effective in promoting both internal activity and foreign trade

g. proved to be a great school of entrepreneurship for all those who, directly or indirectly, participated in international trade

h. was the prime cause of the growth of large towns and industrial centers.[80]

It would be difficult to overestimate the importance of the various factors mentioned so far. Ultimately, however, human events can be understood only in human terms. I referred above to the presence on the English scene of a large class of capable merchants and to the intelligent action of the public administration in relation to trade. But one should go farther than that. Admittedly, most of the human qualities which ultimately determine the success or the failure of a society can hardly be defined and least of all be measured. But this fact does not detract from their relevance. When one reads the writings of Sameul Pepys, John Graunt, William Petty, Isaac Newton; when one observes their endeavors and the activity of the Royal Society, one distinctly perceives pervasive traits of systematic, enlighted, logical rationalism which seems to have characterized increasingly larger strata of English society in the seventeenth century and perhaps represented its most valuable asset.

During the seventeenth century the English came to a full realization of their power. Vigor harbors the seed of aggressiveness. The English brought forward their theory of *Mare Clausum* in opposition to the Dutch theory of *Mare Liberum*. A Swedish diplomat who attempted to mediate between the two nations wrote from London to Queen Christine of Sweden in June 1653 that the English were "intolerably arrogant and it may be that God will punish them for their pride." But God was busy with other things.

---

80. *Ibid.*, pp. 66–68.

Epilogue

Between 1780 and 1850 an unprecedented and far-reaching revolution changed the face of England. From then on the world was no longer the same. Historians have often used and abused the word "revolution" to mean a radical change, but no revolution has been as dramatically revolutionary as the Industrial Revolution.[1] The Industrial Revolution opened the door to a completely new world, a world of new and untapped sources of energy such as coal, oil, electricity, and the atom; a world in which man found himself able to handle huge masses of energy to an extent inconceivable in the preceding bucolic world. From a narrow technological and economic point of view, the Industrial Revolution can be defined as the process by which a society acquired control over vast sources of inanimate energy. But such a definition does not do justice to the phenomenon, in terms of either its distant origins or its economic, cultural, social, and political implications.

Crescenzi in the thirteenth century and the agronomists of the fifteenth and sixteenth centuries could still usefully refer to the agronomical treatises by the ancient Romans. The ideas of Hippocrates and Galen continued to form the basis of official medicine well into the eighteenth century—two centuries after the revolt of Paracelsus. It did not seem absurd to Machiavelli to refer to Roman

---

1. On the origins and history of the term "Industrial Revolution," consult Bezançon, *The Early Use of the Term Industrial Revolution*. On the Industrial Revolution see, among many others, apart from the classic works of Mantoux and Ashton, the volumes of Beales, *The Industrial Revolution;* Deane, *The First Industrial Revolution;* Mathias, *The First Industrial Nation;* Fohlen, *Qu'est-ce que la Revolution Industrielle*; Crouzet, *Capital Formation in the Industrial Revolution;* Musson, *Science, Technology and Economic Growth;* Drake, *Population in Industrialization*.

military arrangements when he planned an army for his times. At the end of the eighteenth century Catherine II of Russia had transported an enormous stone from Finland to St. Petersburg, to set it at the base of the monument dedicated to Peter the Great. The method of transporting the colossal stone was much the same as that used thousands of years earlier by the ancient Egyptians when they built their pyramids. As Cederna wrote,

From the Pharaohs to Baron Hausmann certain things in the architecture of the past have remained constant and immutable even through a thousand stylistic variations: the materials—stone, lime, bricks—and certain fundamental relations between supporting and supported, wall and roof, column and arch, pillar and vault, and so on. It is easy to give examples of monuments literally born out of existing ones. The travertine of the Colosseum served excellently in the building of St. Peter's in the Vatican in the 16th century.[2]

A basic fundamental continuity characterized the preindustrial world, even through grandiose changes, such as the rise and fall of Rome, the triumph and decline of Islam, the Chinese dynastic cycles. As C. H. Waddington has observed:

If a Roman of the Empire could be transported some eighteen centuries forward in time, he would have found himself in a society which he could, without too great difficulty, have learned to comprehend. Horace would have felt himself reasonably at home as a guest of Horace Walpole and Catullus would soon have learned his way among the sedan chairs, the patched-up beauties and the flaring torches of London streets at night.[3]

This continuity was broken between 1780 and 1850. If, at the middle of the nineteenth century, a general studied the organization of the Roman army, if a physician concerned himself with the ideas of Hippocrates and Galen, if an agronomist read Columella, they did it purely out of historical interest or as an academic exercise. Even in far-away, unchanging China, it was becoming painfully evident to the most enlightened among the scholar-officials of the Celestial Empire that the ancient classical texts and values which had given continuity to Chinese history through invasions and

2. Cederna, *I Vandali*, p. 8.
3. Waddington, *The Ethical Animal*, p. 15.

dynastic cycles were no longer valid for survival in the contemporary world. By 1850 the past was not merely past—it was dead.

On the other hand, if in the course of three generations the Industrial Revolution had created a dramatic discontinuity in the course of history, its roots nevertheless reached deep into the preceding century. In Chapter 4 I tried to show that the origins of the Industrial Revolution go back to that profound change in ideas, social structures, and value systems that accompanied the rise of the urban communes in the eleventh and thirteenth centuries. In Chapter 6 I stressed that the technological changes that we identify with the Industrial Revolution were the extrapolation of the technological innovations of the western Middle Ages. The Industrial Revolution occurred in England because there a series of historical circumstances brought about—as W. S. Jevons once wrote—"the union of certain happy mental qualities with material resources of an altogether peculiar character." From England the Industrial Revolution soon spread to the rest of Europe. To date the beginning of the Industrial Revolution in any country is as arbitrary as to date the beginning of the Middle Ages or the modern age. Within the same country geographical areas, social groups, and economic sectors move to different tempos; new activities and new forms of life develop while a number of traditional activities and old institutions manage to survive. In broad terms, however, one may assert that by 1850 the Industrial Revolution had penetrated into Belgium, France, Germany, and Switzerland. By 1900 it had extended to Northern Italy, Russia and Sweden.

That the Industrial Revolution was essentially and primarily a sociocultural phenomenon and not a purely technological one, becomes patently obvious when one notices that the first countries to industrialize were those which had the greatest cultural and social similarities with England.

The Industrial Revolution gave Europe a tremendous technological and economic advantage over the rest of the world, and the nineteenth century saw Europe proudly asserting her worldwide predominance.

If one pauses and ponders over all that Europe accomplished in the nine centuries of her ascent, one cannot avoid being filled with amazement and admiration. Undoubtedly there were dark and bloody pages, but there was, above all, an endless series of superb accomplishments in all fields of human activity. The medieval cathedrals; the paintings of the Renaissance; the music of Mozart, Beethoven, and Bach; the poetry of Dante; the prose of Boccaccio and Chaucer; the tragedies of Shakespeare, the philosophy of Saint Thomas, Descartes, and Kant; the wit of Montaigne and Voltaire; the medieval clocks; the drawings of Leonardo da Vinci; the innumerable technological innovations of the Middle Ages and the Renaissance; the steam engine; the microscope; the discoveries of microbiology, the miracles of chemistry; the Suez canal; the business techniques, from the check to the stock exchange; the condemnation of torture; the assertion of the principle of human freedom and rights; the parliamentary system—there is no end to the list of Europe's accomplishments in the period A.D. 1000–1900. Moreover, technology and the Industrial Revolution in Europe irrevocably changed the course of history, not only in Europe's own territories, but all over the world. The history of any remote corner of the world after 1500 cannot be properly understood without taking into account the impact of European culture, economy, and technology. Henri Pirenne once wrote that *Sans Mahomet Charlemagne est inconcevable*. We can paraphrase him by saying that *Sans l'Europe l'histoire moderne est inconcevable*.

"La Belle Epoque" was the apogee of the European saga. The great International Expositions in London, Paris, and Vienna were the proud and optimistic celebrations of Europe's success. The Eiffel Tower was the monument to her economic and technological achievements. But within, the germ of decay was already operating. The reaction against rationalism had been voiced already by Rousseau, and it gained ground in the course of the nineteenth century, favoring nationalism and a whole series of other "isms." The latent crisis eventually exploded in the brutal form of a war which the westerners labeled the "First World War," but which to a perceptive Asian historian looked more like "the European Civil War." It was the beginning of a rapid end. Within less than half a century a major economic crisis and a second major war gave Europe the final coup. The Spenglerian vision of the Decline of the West acquired day by day clearer tones of reality. The dawn of the twentieth century had seen Britannia ruling the waves and both England

and continental Europe ruling the world. "At the beginning of the twentieth century there were six world powers and they were all located in Europe. If one mentioned the United States or Japan it was merely to make a show of geographical knowledge." At the end of the twentieth century Europe seems to be struggling for survival.

Paradoxically, Europe is on the retreat at a moment when the industrial way of life, which was originally developed by Europe, is taking over the whole world. The agony of Europe equally finds echoes around the globe. After the optimism of the 1950s and the early 1960s evidences of anxiety are to be found in most nations. A sense of unease and foreboding is blanketing mankind. As the future of Europe looks more uncertain than ever, a question plagues increasing number of people: is there any hope for the kind of civilization which Europe developed and broadcast all over the world?

APPENDIX TABLES

Table A–1

Approximate Population of Selected European Cities, 1300–1700 (thousands)

Country	City	c. 1300	c. 1400	c. 1500	c. 1550	c. 1600	c. 1650	c. 1700
Italy	Asti					9		10
	Bergamo				18	24		25
	Bologna			55	55	63	58	63
	Brescia			50	40	50	40	35
	Como					11	9	
	Cremona		10		37	40	17	
	Ferrara					33	25	27
	Florence	95	55	70	60	80	70	80
	Genoa					63	70	
	Lucca					25	25	
	Mantua			27	35	31	15	20
	Milan			100	50	110	95	100
	Modena			18	20	18		18
	Naples				210	250		215
	Padua	30		27	32	35	25	
	Palermo			50	80	100		100
	Parma			16	20	25	20	30
	Pavia			18	13	18	19	20
	Perugia					20	16	16
	Piacenza				27	30		
	Pistoia	11	4		8	8		8
	Rome			50	45	110	126	135
	San Gimignano		3		5			3

Table A–1 continued on pps. 282–83

Table A–1 (Continued)

Approximate Population of Selected European Cities, 1300–1700 (thousands)

Country	City	c.1300	c.1400	c.1500	c.1550	c.1600	c.1650	c.1700
Italy	Siena			15	10	19	16	16
	Turin		4		14	20		42
	Venice			115	160	150	120	140
	Verona		20	40	46	55	25	
	Vicenza					35	25	26
Germany	Hamburg	7	20	20		19		
	Augsburg		30	18			20	
	Cologne		10		35			
	Frankfurt							25
	Leipzig				7			22
	Nuremberg		20	50				
	Vienna		20			60		
France	Angers					25	32	27
	Besançon			8		11		17
	Lyon	100			70			90
	Paris					300		500
	Rouen		40			80		65
	Strasbourg					25		27
	Toulouse		23	35			42	43
Low Countries	Amsterdam			15	35	100	135	180

	Antwerp	35						
	Bruges						57	
	Leyden						34	
	Liège		11				66	55
	Ypres			8			50	12
England	London		35	70	80	250	450	600
Switzerland	Geneva		5	13				17
	Zurich			5		7		
Sweden	Stockholm							50
Spain	Barcelona				100		64	
	Madrid					150	75	
	Sevilla						125	

Table A–2

Crude Birth and Death Rates in Selected European Cities, 1551–1699

City	Years	Births	Deaths
		(per thousand inhabitants)	
Antwerp	1696–99	30	
Bologna	1581	38	
	1587	38	
	1595	36	
	1600	35	18
	1605		46
	1606	36	43
	1615		11
	1617	35	
	1619		46
	1620		49
Florence	1551	41	
	1559	36	
	1561	47	
	1562	42	
	1622	39	
	1630	45	
	1632	43	
	1633	44	
	1642	48	
	1657	48	
	1660	49	
	1661	48	
	1668	50	
London	1696–99	38	37
Louvain	1635–44	44	
Pavia	1640–49	46	30
	1650–59	40	41
	1690–99	52	44
Parma	1505–9	41	
	1545–49	45	
	1590–94	42	
	1650–54	42	

Table A–2 continued on p. 285

Table A–2 (Continued)

Crude Birth and Death Rates in Selected European Cities, 1551–1699

City	Years	Births	Deaths
		(per thousand inhabitants)	
Venice	1581	34	33
	1624	31	35
	1642	37	30
	1696	31	32
Zurich	1631–50	37	36

Table A–3

Infant Mortality Rate (Died in First Year of Life,
per Thousand Christened) in Fiesole (Tuscany), 1621–99

Years	Deaths	Years	Deaths
1621	141	1647	118
1622	238	1648	363
1623	119	1649	514
1624	258	1650	296
1625	177	1651	223
1626	278	1652	236
1627	216	1653	222
1628	148	1654	355
1629	186	1655	273
1630	164	1656	411
1631	140	1657	310
1632	228	1658	496
1633	224	1659	736
1634	243	1660	162
1635	213	1661	303
1636	257	1662	167
1637	319	1663	230
1638	193	1664	358
1639	315	1665	199
1640	322	1666	388
1641	205	1667	377
1642	192	1668	383
1643	287	1669	212
1644	224	1670	245
1645	369	1671	277
1646	234	1672	301

Table A–3 (Continued)

Infant Mortality Rate (Died in First Year of Life,
per Thousand Christened) in Fiesole (Tuscany), 1621–99

Years	Deaths	Years	Deaths
1673	183	1687	360
1674	115	1688	567
1675	339	1689	393
1676	145	1690	259
1677	364	1691	341
1678	423	1692	298
1679	515	1693	396
1680	184	1694	392
1681	302	1695	277
1682	362	1696	468
1683	492	1697	252
1684	565	1698	370
1685	459	1699	229
1686	430		

Table A–4

Characteristics of a Typical Preindustrial Population: Sweden, 1778–82

Phenomenon	Value
Total population	2,104,000 inhabitants
Population under 15 years of age	31.9 percent
Population between 15 and 64 years	63.2 percent
Population 65 years and over	4.9 percent
Dependency ratio	58.3 percent
Crude birth rate	34.5 per thousand
Crude death rate	25.9 per thousand
Crude rate of natural increase	8.6 per thousand
Intrinsic birth rate (females)	31.2 per thousand
Intrinsic death rate (females)	25.3 per thousand
Intrinsic rate of natural increase (females)	5.9 per thousand
Infant mortality	211.6 per thousand

Age—specific Death Rates:

Age 1-4 (males)	45.9 per thousand
Age 1-4 (females)	44.3 per thousand
Age 50-54 (males)	20.8 per thousand
Age 50-54 (females)	16.1 per thousand

Table A–4 continued on p. 287

Table A–4 (Continued)

Characteristics of a Typical Preindustrial Population: Sweden, 1778–82

Phenomenon	*Value*
Life Table Values:	
Probability of dying in first year	
Males	0.1974
Females	0.1768
Survivors to the age of 50 per one hundred births:	
Males	41
Females	45
Life expectancy at birth:	
Males	36 years
Females	39 years
Life expectancy at 1 year:	
Males	44 years
Females	46 years
Life expectancy at 50 years:	
Males	19 years
Females	20 years
Average age of women at procreation	32 years
General fertility rate	145.2 children per 1000 women
Gross reproduction rate	2.2 female children per woman

SOURCE: Keyfitz and Flieger, *Population*, pp. 100–3.

Bibliography

The existing bibliography of the economic and social history of pre-industrial Europe has reached colossal proportions and is still expanding at an accelerated rate, so that it is increasingly difficult to keep up with what is written and published. As in every sector of the industrial society, quality is not always proportionate to quantity. Learned contributions, however, are not lacking, and our knowledge has progressed considerably in recent decades.

The list that follows does not claim to be and must not be taken as a complete bibliographical repertoire. An entire volume of considerable dimensions would be necessary for the purpose. Essentially, the list that follows aims at providing the full titles of works cited in shortened version in the preceding pages, although it also contains a few additional titles. The readers who wish to obtain further bibliographical information may consult the bibliographies published in the *Cambridge Economic History of Europe* and the *Fontana Economic History of Europe*. I also recommend the classic works by W. Sombart, *Der Moderne Kapitalismus*, Munich/Leipzig, 1924; and by J. Kulischer, *Allgemeine Wirtschaftsgeschichte des Mittelalters und der Neuzeit*, Munich/Berlin, 1928, which are irreplaceable mines of historical and bibliographical information. Such works suffer from the fact that they were written over half a century ago, but if today they are seldom quoted and even less read, this is due to fashion and not to their obsolescence. No author after these has produced anything even remotely comparable to works so powerful in erudition, sharpness of perception, and originality of thought.

Abel, W., *Agrarkrisen und Agrarkonjunktur in Mitteleuropa vom 13. bis zum 19. Jahrhundert*, Berlin, 1966.

Abel, W., *Die Wüstungen des ausgehenden Mittelalters*, Jena, 1943.

Abel, W., *Massenarmut und Hungerkrisen in vorindustriellen Deutschland*, Göttingen, 1972.

Alberi, E. (ed.), *Relazioni degli Ambasciatori veneti al Senato*, Florence, 1840.

Albion, R. G., *Forests and Sea Power*, Cambridge, Mass., 1926.

Aleati, G., "Una dinastia di magnati medievali: gli Eustachi di Pavia," *Studi in onore di A. Sapori*, vol. 2, Milan, 1957.

Allison, K. J., "An Elizabethan Village Census," *Bulletin of the London University Institute of Historical Research*, vol. 36 (1963).

Allix, A., *L'Oisans au Moyen Age. Étude de géographie historique en haute montagne*, Paris, 1929.

Amburger, E., *Die Familie Marselis. Studien zur russischen Wirtschaftsgeschichte*, Giessen, 1967.

Amodeo, D., *A proposito di un antico bilancio di previsione del Vicereame di Napoli*, Naples, 1953.

Andreades, A.M., "The Economic Life of the Byzantine Empire," in N. H. Baynes and H. L. B. Moss (eds.), *Byzantium*, Oxford, 1948.

Annali della Fabbrica del Duomo di Milano, Milan, 1877.

Antero, Maria di S. Bonaventura, *Li Lazzaretti della Città e Riviere di Genova del 1657*, Genoa, 1658.

Arnould, M. A., *Les dénombrements des foyers dans le comté de Hainaut (XIV–XVI siècles)*, Brussells, 1956.

Ashton, T. S., *The Industrial Revolution*, London, 1948.

Ashtor, E., "Che cosa sapevano i geografi arabi dell'Europa occidentale?," in *Rivista storica italiana*, vol. 81 (1969).

Ashtor, E., *Les métaux précieux et la balance des payements du Proche-Orient a la Basse Époque*, Paris, 1971.

Atkinson, G., *Les nouveaux horizons de la Renaissance française*, Paris, 1935.

Attman, A., *The Russian and Polish Markets in International Trade 1500–1650*, Göteborg, 1973.

Baasch, E., *Holländische Wirtschaftsgeschichte*, Jena, 1927.

Balbi, E., *L'Austria e le primarie potenze*, Milan, 1846.

Baratier, E., *La démographie provençale du XIIIᵉ au XVIᵉ siècle*, Paris, 1961.

Barbour, V., "Dutch and English Merchant Shipping to the Seventeenth Century," in E. M. Carus-Wilson (ed.), *Essays in Economic History*, vol. 1, London, 1961.

Barbour, V., *Capitalism in Amsterdam in the Seventeenth Century*, Ann Arbor, 1963.

Barnett, G. E. (ed.), *Two Tracts by Gregory King*, Baltimore, 1936.

Barrow, J., *Travels in China*, Philadelphia, 1805.

Basini, G. L., *Finanza pubblica ed aspetti economici negli Stati Italiani del Cinque e Seicento*, Parma, 1966.

Basini, G. L., *L'uomo e il pane*, Milan, 1970.

Battara, P., *La popolazione di Firenze alla metà del Cinquecento*, Florence, 1935.

Bautier, R. H., "Les foires de Champagne," in *Recueil Jean Bodin*, vol. 5, Brussells, 1953.

Beales, H. L., *The Industrial Revolution, 1752–1850*, London, 1958.

Bean, J. M. W., "Plague, Population and Economic Decline in Later Middle Ages," *The Economic History Review*, ser. 2, vol. 15 (1963).

Beloch, K. J., *Bevölkerungsgeschichte Italiens*, Berlin, 1937–1961.

Beltrami, D., "La composizione economica e professionale della popolazione di Venezia nei secoli XVII e XVIII," *Giornale degli economisti*, n.s., vol. 10 (1951).

Beltrami, D., *Storia della popolazione di Venezia dalla fine del secolo XVI alla caduta della Repubblica*, Padua, 1954.

Beltrami, D., *Saggio di storia dell'agricoltura nella Repubblica di Venezia durante l'età moderna*, Venice/Rome, 1955.

Bennassar, B., "L'alimentation d'une ville espagnole au XVIe siècle. Quelques données sur les approvisionnements et la consommation de Valladolid," *Annales. E.S.C.*, vol. 16 (1961).

Berengo, M., *Nobili e mercanti nella Lucca del Cinquecento*, Turin, 1965.

Bergier, J. F., *Problèmes de l'histoire économique de la Suisse*, Berne, 1968.

Bergier, J. F., *Naissance et croissance de la Suisse industrielle*, Berne, 1974.

Bergier, J. F., and L. Solari, "Histoire et élaboration statisque. L'exemple de la population de Genève au XVe siècle," in *Mélanges Antony Babel*, Geneva, 1963.

Beretta, R., *Pagine di storia briantina*, Como, 1972.

Besta, G. F., *Vera narratione del successo della peste*, Milan, 1578.

Beveridge, W., *Prices and Wages in England from the Twelfth to the Nineteenth Century*, London, 1939.

Bezançon, A., "The Early Use of the Term Industrial Revolution," *The Quarterly Journal of Economics*, vol. 36 (1922).

Bianchini, L., *Della Storia delle Finanze del Regno di Napoli*, Palermo, 1839.

Bilanci generali della Repubblica di Venezia, Venice, 1912–1972.

Bloch, I., *Die Prostitution*, Berlin, 1912–1925.

Bloch, M., *Les caractères originaux de l'histoire rurale française*, Paris, 1931.

Boas, M., *The Scientific Renaissance: 1450–1630*, New York, 1966.

Bodmer, W., *Der Einfluss der Refugianten-einwanderung von 1500–1700 auf die Schweizerische Wirtschaft*, Zurich, n.d.

Boutruche, R., *La crise d'une societé; seigneurs et paysans du Bordelais pendant la Guerre de Cent Ans*, Paris, 1947.

Boutruche, R., "La dévastation des campagnes pendant la guerre de Cent Ans et la reconstruction agricole de la France," *Publications de la Faculté des Lettres de l'Université de Strasbourg*, vol. 3, Paris, 1947.

Boutruche, R. (ed.), *Bordeaux de 1453 à 1715*, Bordeaux, 1966.

Boutruche, R., *Signoria e feudalesimo*, Bologna, 1971.

Bowden, P. J., *The Wool Trade in Tudor and Stuart England*, London, 1962.

Boxer, C. R., *The Dutch in Brazil*, Oxford, 1957.

Boxer, C. R., *Two Pioneers of Tropical Medicine: Garcia d'Orta and Nicolás Monardes*, London, 1963.

Boxer, C. R., *The Dutch Seaborne Empire, 1600–1800*, London, 1965.

Brading, D. A., H. E. Cross, "Colonial silver mining: Mexico and Peru," *The Hispanic American Historical Review*, vol. 52 (1972).

Braudel, F., *Civilisation matérielle et capitalisme*, Paris, 1967.

Bridbury, A. R., *Economic Growth: England in the Later Middle Ages*, London, 1962.

Britten, F. J., *Old Clocks and Watches and Their Makers*, ed. by G. H. Baille, C. Clutton, and C. A. Ilbert, New York, 1956.

Brossolet, J., "L'influence de la peste du Moyen Age sur le thème de la danse macabre," *Pagine di storia della medicina*, vol. 13 (1969).

Brown, M., *On the Theory and Measurement of Technological Change*, Cambridge, 1966.

Brucker, G. A., *Florentine Politics and Society, 1343–1378*, Princeton, 1967.

Brucker, G. (ed.), *Two Memoirs of Renaissance Florence: The Diaries of Buonaccorso Pitti and Gregorio Dati*, New York, 1967.

Brulez, W., "The Balance of Trade in the Netherlands in the Middle of the 16th Century," *Acta Historiae Neerlandica*, vol. 4 (1970).

Bücher, K., *Die Bevölkerung von Frankfurt am Main im 14. und 15. Jahrhundert*, Tübingen, 1886.

Buffini, A., *Ragionamenti intorno all'ospizio dei trovatelli*, Milan, 1844.

Burke, P., *Economy and Society in Early Modern Europe*, New York, 1972.

Caizzi, B., *Il Comasco sotto il dominio spagnolo*, Como, 1955.

Calegari, M., Legname e costruzioni navali nel Cinquecento, in VV.AA. *Guerra e Commercio nell'evoluzione della marina genovese*, vol. 2, Genoa, 1973.

Capmany y de Montpalau, *Memorias históricas sobre la marina, comercio y artes de Barcelona*, Madrid, 1779.

Carabellese, F., *La peste del 1348 e le condizioni della Sanità Pubblica in Toscana*, Rocca San Casciano, 1897.

Carande, R., *Carlos V y sus banqueros*, Madrid, 1964.

Carbone, S., *Provveditori e Sopraprovveditori alla Sanità della Repubblica di Venezia*, Rome, 1962.

Carletti, F., *Ragionamenti del mio viaggio intorno al mondo (1594–1606)*, in M. Guglielminetti (ed.) *Viaggiatori del Seicento*, Turin, 1967.

Carmona, M., "Sull'economia toscana del Cinquecento e del Seicento," *Archivio storico italiano*, vol. 120 (1962).

Carpentier, E., "Famines et épidemies dans l'histoire du XIVe siècle," *Annales E.S.C.*, n.s., vol. 6 (1962).

Carus-Wilson, E. M., *An Industrial Revolution of the Thirteenth Century*, in E. M. Carus-Wilson (ed.), *Essays in Economic History*, vol. 1, London, 1954.

Carus-Wilson, E. M. (ed.), *Essays in Economic History*, vol. 1. London, 1954.

Carus-Wilson, E. M., *The Merchant Adventurers of Bristol in the XVth Century*, Bristol, 1962.

Carus-Wilson, E. M. and O. Coleman, *England's Export Trade 1275–1547*, Oxford, 1963.

Casoni, G., "Note sull'artiglieria veneta," in *Venezia le sue lagune*, vol. 1, part 2, Venice, 1847.

Catellacci, D., "Ricordi del Contagio di Firenze del 1630," *Archivio storico italiano*, ser. 5, vol. 20 (1897).

Cederna, A., *I vandali in casa*, Bari, 1956.

Cernovodeanu, P., *England's .Trade Policy in the Levant (1660–1714)*, Bucharest, 1972.

Chaloner, C. W., "Sir Thomas Lombe and the British Silk Industry," in *People and Industries,* London, 1963.

Chambers, J. D. and G. E. Mingay, *The Agricultural Revolution (1750–1880)*, London, 1966.

Chaudhuri, K. N., "Treasure and Trade Balances: The East India Company's Export Trade 1660–1720," *The Economic History Review*, ser. 2, vol. 21 (1968).

Cherubini, G., "La proprietà fondiaria di un mercante toscano del Trecento," *Rivista di storia dell'agricoltura*, vol. 5 (1965).

Christensen, A. E., "Der handelsgeschichte Wert der Sundzollregister," *Hansische Geschichtblätter*, vol. 59 (1934).

Christensen, A. E., *Dutch Trade to the Baltic about 1600*, Copenaghen/ The Hague, 1941.

Cipolla, C. M., "Per una storia del lavoro," *Bollettino Storico Pavese*, vol. 5 (1944).

Cipolla, C. M., "Comment s'est perdue la propriété ecclésiastique dans l'Italie du Nord," *Annales. E.S.C.*, n.s., vol. 2 (1947).

Cipolla, C. M., "Per la storia della popolazione lombarda nel secolo XVI," in *Studi in onore di G. Luzzatto*, Milan, 1949.

Cipolla, C. M. "The Decline of Italy: the Case of a Fully Matured Economy," *The Economic History Review*, ser. 2, vol. 5 (1952).

Cipolla, C. M., "Note sulla storia del saggio di interesse," *Economia internazionale*, vol. 5 (1952).

Cipolla, C. M., *Money, Prices and Civilization*, Princeton, N.J., 1956.

Cipolla, C. M., *Prezzi, salari e teoria dei salari in Lombardia alla fine del Cinquecento*, Rome, 1956.

Cipolla, C. M., "Per la storia delle epidemie in Italia, *Rivista storica italiana*, vol. 75 (1963).

Cipolla, C. M., "Currency Depreciation in Medieval Europe," *The Economic History Review*, ser. 2, vol. 15 (1963).

Cipolla, C. M., "Four Centuries of Italian Demographic Development," in D. V. Glass and D. E. C. Eversley (eds.), *Population in History*, London, 1965.

Cipolla, C. M., *The Economic History of World Population*, 6th ed., Harmondsworth, 1974.

Cipolla, C. M., *Guns and Sails in the early Phase of European Expansion*, London, 1965.

Cipolla, C. M., *Clocks and Culture*, London, 1967.

Cipolla, C. M., *Literacy and Development in the West*, Harmondsworth, 1969.

Cipolla, C. M. (ed.), *The Economic Decline of Empires*, London, 1970.

Cipolla, C. M., *Cristofano and the Plague*, London, 1973.

Cipolla, C. M., "The Professions—the Long View," *The Journal of European Economic History*, vol. 2 (1973).

Cipolla, C. M., "The Plague and the pre-Malthus Malthusians," *The Journal of European Economic History*, vol. 3 (1974).

Cipolla, C. M., *Public Health and the Medical Profession in the Renaissance*, Cambridge, 1975.

Clamageran, J. J., *Historie de l'impôt en France*, Paris, 1867–68.

Clark, G. N., *A History of the Royal College of Physicians of London*, Oxford, 1964.

Clément, P. (ed.), *Lettres, instructions et mémoires de Colbert*, Paris, 1859–82.

Coleman, D. C., "Naval Dockyards," *The Economic History Review*, ser. 2, vol. 6 (1953).

Coniglio, G., *Il Viceregno di Napoli nel secolo XVII*, Rome, 1955.

Connell, K. H., *The Population of Ireland: 1750–1845*, Oxford, 1950.

Connell, K. H., "The Potato in Ireland," *Past and Present*, vol. 23 (1962).

Contamine, P., "Consommation et demande militaires en France et en Angleterre, XIII–XV siècles," in Istituto Intern. di Storia Economica F. Datini, *Sesta Settimana di Studio*, Prato, 1974.

Conti, E., *La formazione della struttura agraria moderna nel contado fiorentino*, Rome, 1965.

Cooper, J. P., "The Social Distribution of Land and Men in England, 1436–1700," in R. Floud (ed.), *Essays in Quantitative Economic History*, Oxford, 1974.

Copeman, W. C. S., *Doctors and Disease in .Tudor Times*, London, 1960.

Coppola, G., "L'agricoltura di alcune pievi della pianura irrigua milanese nei dati catastali della metà del secolo XVI," *Contributi dell'Isituto di storia economica e sociale* (dell'Università Cattolica di Milano), Milan, 1973.

Corradi, A., *Annali delle epidemie occorse in Italia dalle prime memorie fino al 1850*, Bologna 1867–92.

Coryat, T., *Crudities*, London, 1786.

Coulton, G. C., *The Black Death*, London, 1929.

Craeybeckx, J., *Un grand commerce d' importation: les vins de France aux anciens Pays-Bas*, Paris, 1958.

Creighton, C., *A History of Epidemics in Britain*, Cambridge, 1891–94.

Crosby, A. W., *The Columbian Exchange: Biological and Cultural Consequences of 1492*, Westport, Conn., 1973.

Crouzet, F. (ed.), *Capital Formation in the Industrial Revolution*, London, 1972.

Cunningham, W., *Alien Immigrants to England*, London, 1897.

Curschmann, H. W. F., *Hungersnöte im Mittelalter*, Leipzig, 1900.

Curtin, P. D., *The Atlantic Slave Trade: a Census*, Madison, Wis., 1969.

Dahlgren, E. W., *Louis de Geer*, Uppsala, 1923.

D'Orta, G. and Monardes, N., *Dell'Historia de i semplici aromati et altre cose che vengono portate dall'Indie pertinenti all'uso della medicina*, Venice, 1582.

Dallington, R., *Survey of Tuscany*, London, 1605.

Dallington, R., *The View of France (1605)* (ed. by W. P. Barnett), Oxford, 1936.

D'Ancona, A., See Montaigne.

Darby, H. C. (ed.), *A New Historical Geography of England*, Cambridge, 1973.

Dati, G., *Il libro segreto,* ed. by G. Gargiolli, Bologna, 1869 (see also Brucker).

Davidsohn, R., *Storia di Firenze*, Florence, 1956.

Davidsohn, W. D., "The History of the Potato and Its Progress in Ireland," *Journal of the Department of Agriculture*, vol. 34.

Davis, D., *A History of Shopping*, London, 1966.

Davis, R., "England and the Mediterranean 1570–1670," in F. J. Fisher (ed.), *Essays in the Economic and Social History of Tudor and Stuart England*, Cambridge, 1961.

Davis, R., *The Rise of the English Shipping Industry*, London, 1962.

Davis, R., *A Commercial Revolution: English Overseas Trade in the Seventeenth and Eighteenth Centuries*, London, 1967.

Davis, R., "English Foreign Trade 1660–1700," in W. E. Minchinton (ed.), *The Growth of English Overseas Trade in the Seventeenth and Eighteenth Centuries*, London, 1969.

Davis, R., "English Foreign Trade 1700–1774," in W. E. Minchinton (ed.), *The Growth of English Overseas Trade in the Seventeenth and Eighteenth Centuries*, London, 1969.

Davis, R., *The Rise of the Atlantic Economies*, London, 1973.

Daviso di Charvensod, M. C., *I pedaggi delle Alpi occidentali nel Medio Evo*, Turin, 1961.

Deane, P., "The Implications of Early National Income Estimates for the Measurement of Long-term Economic Growth in the United Kingdom," *Economic Development and Cultural Change* (1955).

Deane, P., *The First Industrial Revolution*, Cambridge, 1967.

Deane, P., "Capital Formation in Britain before the Railway Age," in F. Crouzet (ed.), *Capital Formation in the Industrial Revolution*, London, 1972.

Deane, P. and Cole, W. A., *British Economic Growth (1688–1959)*, Cambridge, 1967.

Defoe, D., *A Plan of the English Commerce*, London, 1728.

Del Panta, L., *Una traccia di storia demografica della Toscana nei secoli XVI–XVIII*, Florence, 1974.

Delumeau, J., *Vie économique et sociale de Rome dans la seconde moitié du XVIe siècle*, Paris, 1957.

De Maddalena, A., "Il mondo rurale italiano nel Cinque e nel Seicento," *Rivista storica italiana*, vol. 76 (1964).

De Muinck, B. E., "A Regent's Family Budget about the Year 1700," *Acta Historiae Neerlandica*, vol. 2 (1967).

De Mussis, J., "Chronicon Placentinum," *Rerum Italicarum Scriptores*, vol. 16.

Derlange, M., "Cannes," *Cahiers de la Méditerranée*, vol. 5 (1972).

De Roover, R., "Aux origines d'une technique intellectuelle: la formation et l'expansion de la comptabilité à partie double," *Annales d'histoire économique et sociale*, vol. 9 (1937).

De Roover, R., *L'évolution de la lettre de change*, Paris, 1953.

De Roover, R., "The Development of Accounting prior to Luca Pacioli," in *Studies in the History of Accounting*, London, n.d.

De Roover, R., *The Rise and Decline of the Medici Bank 1397–1494*, New York, 1966.

Devèze, M., *La vie de la forêt française au XVIe siècle*, Paris, 1961.

Devèze, M., *Histoire des forêts*, Paris, 1965.

Devèze, M., *L'Europe et le monde à la fin du XVIIIe siècle*, Paris, 1970.

De Vries, J., *The Dutch Rural Economy in the Golden Age, 1500–1700*, New Haven, Conn., 1974.

Di Capua, L., *Parere divisato in otto Ragionamenti*, Naples, 1689.

Dietz, F. C., "English Government Finance 1485–1558," *University of Illinois Studies in the Social Sciences*, vol. 9 (1920).

Dijksterhuis, E. J., *The Mechanisation of the World Picture*, Oxford, 1961.

Dion, R., *Histoire de la vigne et du vin en France dès origines au XIXe siècle*, Paris, 1959.

Di Simplicio, O., "Due secoli di produzione agraria in una fattoria del Senese, 1550–1751," *Quaderni storici*, vol. 21 (1972).

Doehaerd, R., *L'expansion économique belge au Moyen Age*, Brussells, 1946.

Dollinger, P., *La Hanse, XIIe–XVIIe siècles*, Paris, 1964.

Doren, A., *Storia economica dell'Italia nel Medio Evo*, Padua, 1937.

Doria, G., *Uomini e terre di un borgo collinare dal XVI al XVIII secolo*, Milan, 1968.

Drake, M. (ed.), *Population in Industrialization*, London, 1969.

Drummond, J. C. and Wilbraham, A., *The Englishman's Food. A History of Five Centuries of English Diet*, London, 1939.

Dublin, L., A. Lotka, and M. Spiegelman, *Length of Life. A Study of the Life Table*, New York, 1949.

Duby, G., *L'économie rurale et la vie des campagnes dans l'Occident médiéval*, Paris, 1962.

Duby, G., *Guerriers et paysans*, Paris, 1973.

Duncan, D., *Avis salutaire contre l'abus des choses chaudes et particulierment du café, du chocolat et du thé*, Rotterdam, 1705.

Durand, J. D., *The Modern Expansion of World Population*, in C. B. Nam (ed.), *Population and Society*, Boston, 1968.

East, G., *Géographie historique de l'Europe*, Paris, 1939.

Eden, F. M., *The State of the Poor*, London, 1797.

Edler de Roover, F., "Early Example of Marine Insurance," *Journal of Economic History*, vol. 5 (1945).

Ehrman, J., *The Navy in the War of William III*, Cambridge, 1952.

Elias, J. E., *Het Voorspel van den Eersten Engelschen Oorlog*, The Hague, 1920.

Elliott, J. H., *Imperial Spain 1469–1716*, New York, 1963.

Elsas, M. J., *Umriss einer Geschichte der Preise und Löhne in Deutschland*, Leiden, 1949.

Elton G. R., "An early Tudor Poor Law," *The Economic History Review*, ser. 2, vol. 6 (1953).

Elvin, M., *The Patterns of the Chinese Past*, London, 1973.

Endres, R., "Zur Einwhonerzahl und Bevölkerungsstruktur Nürnbergs im 15/16. Jahrhundert," *Mitteilungen des Vereins für Geschichte der Stadt Nürnberg*, vol. 57 (1970).

Ennen, E., "Les différents types de formation des villes européennes," *Le Moyen Age*, ser. 4, vol. 11 (1956).

Eulenburg, P., "Städtische Berufs und Gewerbestatistik im 16. Jahrhundert," *Zeitschrift für die Geschichte des Oberrheins*, n.s., vol. 11 (1896).

Faber, J. A., "Cattle-plague in the Netherlands during the Eighteenth Century," *Medelingen van de Landbouwhogeschool te Wegeningen*, vol. 62 (1962).

Fanfani, A., *Storia del lavoro in Italia dalla fine del secolo XV agli inizi del XVIII*, Milan, 1943.

Feller, G., *Geschichte Berns*, Berne, 1953.

Felloni, G., *Gli investimenti finanziari genovesi in Europa tra il Seicento e la Restaurazione*, Milan, 1971.

Ferrario, G., *Statistica medica di Milano*, Milan, 1838–40.

Finch, M. E., *The Wealth of Five Northamptonshire Families 1540–1640*, Northamptonshire Record Society, vol. 19, 1956.

Finley, M. I., "Technical Innovation and Economic Progress in the Ancient World," *The Economic History Review*, ser. 2, vol. 18 (1965).

Fiochetto, G. F., *Trattato della peste*, Turin, 1720.

Fisher, F. J., "Commercial Trends and Policy in Sixteenth-Century England," in E. M. Carus-Wilson (ed.), *Essays in Economic History*, vol. 1, London, 1961.

Fisher, H. E. S., *The Portuguese Trade*, London, 1971.

Fiumi, E., "Fioritura e decadenza dell'economia fiorentina," *Archivio storico italiano*, vols. 115–17 (1960).

Fiumi, E., "La popolazione del territorio volterrano-sangimignanese ed il problema demografico dell'età comunale, in *Studi in onore di A. Fanfani*, Milan, 1962, vol. 1.

Fiumi, E., "Popolazione, società ed economia volterrana dal catasto del 1428–29," *Rassegna volterrana*, vols. 36–39 (1972).

Flamma, G., "Opusculum," *Rerum Italicarum Scriptores*, vol. 12.

Fohlen, C., *Qu'est-ce que la Révolution industrielle*, Paris, 1971.

Foss, M., *The Art of Patronage: The Arts in Society 1660–1750*, London, 1972.

Fourastié, J., *Machinisme et bien-être*, Paris, 1962.

Fourquin, G., *Histoire économique de l'Occident mediéval*, Paris, 1969.

Frank, J. P., *System einer vollständingen medizinischen Polizey*, Vienna, 1786.

Frankel, S. H., *The Economic Impact on Underdeveloped Societies*, Oxford, 1953.

Franklin, A., "La vie privée d'autrefois," vol. 14: *L'hygiène*, Paris, 1890.

Franz, G., *Der Dreissigjährige Krieg und das deutsche Volk*, Jena, 1943.

Frumento, A., *Imprese lombarde nella storia della siderurgia italiana*, Milan, 1963.

Gade, J. A., *The Hanseatic Control of Norwegian Commerce during the Late Middle Ages*, Leyden, 1951.

Galassi, N., *I rapporti sociali nella campagna imolese dal sec. XVI al sec. XIX*, Imola, n.d.

Gallagher, L. J. (ed.), *The Journals of Matthew Ricci*, New York, 1953.

Gargiolli, G., see Dati.

Garosi, A., *Siena nella storia della medicina (1240–1555)*, Florence, 1958.

Gascon, R., *Grand commerce et vie urbaine au XVIe siècle—Lyon et ses marchands*, Paris, 1971.

Geanakoplos, D. J., "A Byzantine Look at the Renaissance," *Greek and Byzantine Studies*, vol. 1, (1958).

Genicot, L., "On the Evidence of Growth of Population from the 11th to the 13th Century," in S. L. Thrupp (ed.), *Change in Medieval Society*, New York, 1964.

Gilbert, M. and ass., *Comparative National Products and Price Levels*, Paris, 1958.

Glamann, K., *Dutch-Asiatic Trade, 1620–1740*, The Hague, 1958.

Glass, D. V., "Graunt's Life Table," *Journal of the Institute of Actuaries*, vol. 76 (1950).

Glass, D. V., "Two Papers on Gregory King," in D. V. Glass and D. E. C. Eversley (eds.), *Population in History*, London-Chicago, 1965.

Glass, D. V. and D. E. C. Eversley (eds.), *Population in History*, London, 1965.

Gnoli, D., "Roma e i Papi nel Seicento," in *La vita italiana nel Seicento*, Milan, 1895.

Godinho Magalhães, V., *A Expansao Quatrocentista Portuguesa*, Lisbon, 1945.

Goubert, P., *Beauvais et le Beauvaisis de 1600 à 1730*, Paris, 1960.

Gould, J. D., *Economic Growth in History*, London, 1972.

Graf, A., *Attraverso il Cinquecento*, Turin, 1888.

Grasby, R., "The Rate of Profit in Seventeenth-Century England," *The English Historical Review*, vol. 84 (1962).

Grierson, P., "Commerce in the Dark Ages: a Critique of the Evidence," in *Transactions of the Royal Historical Society*, ser. 5, vol. 9 (1959).

Gualdo Priorato, G., *Relatione della città di Firenze e del Gran Ducato di Toscana*, Cologne, 1668.

Guicciardini, F., "Relazione di Spagna (1512–13)," in *Opere* (ed. by R. Palmarocchi), Bari, 1936.

Guicciardini, L., *Descrittione di tutti i Paesi Bassi*, Antwerp, 1567.

Haeser, H., *Bibliotheca epidemiographica*, Greifswald, 1969.

Hajnal, J., "European Marriage Patterns in Perspective," in D. V. Glass and D. E. C. Eversley (eds.), *Population in History*, London, 1965.

Hall, A. R., *The Scientific Revolution*, Boston, 1956.

Halley, E., *Degrees of Mortality of Mankind (1693)*, Baltimore, 1942.

Hamilton, E. J., *American Treasure and the Price Revolution in Spain, 1501–1650*, Cambridge, Mass., 1934.

Hare, R., *Pomp and Pestilence*, London, 1954.

Harrison, M. and O. M. Royston, *How They Lived*, Oxford, 1965.

Hart, S., "Amsterdam Shipping and Trade to Northern Russia in the Seventeenth Century," *Mededelingen van de Nederlandse Vereniging voor Zeegeschiedenis*, vol. 26 (1973).

Hartwell, R. M. (ed.), *The Causes of the Industrial Revolution*, London, 1967.

Haudricourt, A. G., "De l'origine de l'attelage moderne," *Annales d'histoire économique et sociale*, vol. 8 (1936).

Haudricourt, A. G. and L. Hédin, *L'homme et les plantes cultivées*, Paris, 1944.

Haudricourt, A. G. and M. J. Bruhnes Delamarre, *L'homme et la charrue*, Paris, 1955.

Heaton, H., "Financing the Industrial Revolution," in Crouzet, F. (ed.), *Capital Formation in the Industrial Revolution*, London, 1972.

Hecksher, E. F., *An Economic History of Sweden*, Cambridge, Mass., 1954.

Heidemann, H., "Bevölkerungszahl und Beruflische Gliederung Münster in Westfalia am Ende des 17. Jahrhundert," *Münsterische Beitrage zur Geschichtsforschlung*, vol. 37, Münster, 1917.

Helleiner, K. F., "The Vital Revolution reconsidered," in D. V. Glass and D. E. C. Eversley (eds.), *Population in History*, London, 1965.

Hémardinquer, J. J., (ed.), *Pour une histoire de l'alimentation*, Paris, 1970.

Henry, L., *Anciennes familles genevoises*, Paris, 1956.

Herlihy, D., "Treasure Hoards in the Italian Economy, 960–1139," *The Economic History Review*, ser. 2, vol. 10 (1957).

Herlihy, D., *Medieval and Renaissance Pistoia*, New Haven, Conn., 1967.

Hernandez, F., *Rerum medicarum Novae Hispaniae Thesaurus*, Rome, 1651.

Hicks, J., *A Theory of Economic History*, Oxford, 1969.

Hilf, R. B., *Der Wald*, Potsdam, 1938.

Hill, C., *Puritanism and Revolution*, London, 1965.

Hobsbawm, E. J., "The Crisis of the Seventeenth Century," *Past and Present*, vols. 5–6 (1954).

Hodgen, M. T., "Domesday Water Mills," *Antiquity*, vol. 13 (1939).

Hollingsworth, T. H., *A Demographic Study of British Ducal Families*, in D. V. Glass and D. E. C. Eversley (eds.), *Population in History*, London, 1965.

Homer, S., *A History of Interest Rates*, New Brunswick, N.J., 1963.

Honig, G. J., "De Molens van Amsterdam," *Jaarboek van het Genootschap Anstëlodamum*, vol. 27 (1930).

Howes, E. (ed.), see Stow, J.

Hudson, G. F., *Europe and China*, London, 1961.

Hull, C. H. (ed.), *The Economic Writings of Sir William Petty together with the Observations upon the Bills of Mortality by John Graunt*, New York, 1963.

Imberciadori, I., "Spedale scuole e chiesa in popolazioni rurali dei secoli XVI–XVII," *Economia e storia*, vol. 6 (1959).

Irigoin, J., "Les débuts de l'emploi du papier à Byzance," *Byzantinische Zeitschrift*, vol. 46 (1953).

James, M. K., *Studies in the Medieval Wine Trade*, ed. by E. M. Veale, Oxford, 1971.

Jeannin, P., *L'Europe du Nord-ouest et du Nord aux XVIIe et XVIIIe siècles*, Paris, 1969.

Johnsson, J. W. S., *Storia della peste avvenuta nel borgo di Busto Arsizio 1630*, Copenhagen, 1924.

Jones, E. L. (ed.), *Agriculture and Economic Growth in England 1650–1815*, London, 1967.

Jones, R. F., *Ancients and Moderns: Study of the Rise of the Scientific Movement in Seventeenth-Century England*, St. Louis, 1961.

Jordan, W. K., *Philanthropy in England 1480–1660*, London, 1959.

Karmin, O., *Vier Thesen zur Lehre von der Wirtschaftskrisen*, Heidelberg, 1905.

Keller, A. G., "A Byzantine Admirer of Western Progress: Cardinal Bessarion," *Cambridge Historical Journal*, vol. 11 (1953–55).

Kennedy, C. and A. P. Thirlwall, "Technical Progress: A Survey," *Economic Journal*, vol. 82 (1972).

Kenyon, G. H., *The Glass Industry of the Weald*, Leicester, 1968.

Kerridge, E., *Agrarian Problems in the Sixteenth Century and After*, London/New York, 1969.

Keyfitz, N. and W. Flieger, *Population*, San Francisco, 1971.

Kiechle, F., "Probleme der Stagnation des technischen Fortschritts im Altertum," *Geschichte in Wissenschaft und Unterricht*, vol. 16 (1965).

King, G., "Natural and Political Observations," in G. E. Barnett (ed.), *Two Tracts by Gregory King*, Baltimore, 1936.

Kirchner, W., *Commercial Relations between Russia and Europe 1400 to 1800*, Bloomington, Indiana, 1966.

Kirsten, E., E. W. Buchholz, and W. Köllmann, *Raum und Bevölkerung in der Weltgeschichte*, Würzburg, 1956.

Kjoczowski, J., "La population écclesiastique des villes du Bas Moyen Age," in Istituto Internaz. di Storia Economica F. Datini, *Sesta Settimana di Studio*, Prato, 1974.

Knoop, D. and G. P. Jones, *The Medieval Mason*, Manchester, 1967.

Knowles, D., *The Religious Orders in England*, Cambridge, 1948–59.

Kuznets, S., *National Income. A Summary of Findings*, New York, 1946.

Kuznets, S., *Economic Growth*, Glencoe, Ill., 1959.

Labarge, M. Wade, *A Baronial Household of the Thirteenth Century*, New York, 1965.

Labrousse, C. E., *La crise de l'économie française à la fin de l'ancien régime*, Paris, 1944.

Lambros, S. P., "Ipomnina tou Kardinaliou Vissarionos," *Neos Hellenomnemon*, vol. 3 (1906).

Landry, A., *Traité de démographie*, Paris, 1945.

Lane, F. C., "The Economic Meaning of the Invention of the Compass," *American Historical Review*, vol. 68 (1963).

Lane, F. C., *Venice, a Maritime Republic*, Baltimore, 1973.

Langer, W. L., "The Next Assignment," *American Historical Review*, vol. 63 (1958).

Lantbertus, "Vita Heriberti," *Monumenta Germaniae Historica, Scriptores*, vol. 4.

Lastri, M., *L'osservatore fiorentino sugli edifizi della sua patria* (ed. by G. Del Rosso), Florence, 1821.

Le Comte, L., *Empire of China*, London, 1737.

Le Goff, J., *La Civilisation de l'Occident médiéval*, Paris, 1964.

Leighton, A. C., *Transport and Communication in Early Medieval Europe*, Newton Abbot, 1972.

Leonard, E. M., *Early History of English Poor Relief*, Cambridge, 1910.

Leonardo di Capua, see Di Capua.

Le Roy Ladurie, E., *Les paysans de Languedoc*, Paris, 1966.

Le Roy Ladurie, E., *Historie du climat depuis l'an Mil*, Paris, 1967.

Letwin, W., *The Origins of Scientific Economics*, London, 1963.

Lilley, S., *Men, Machines and History*, London, 1965.

Lilley, S., "Technological Progress and the Industrial Revolution," in *The Fontana Economic History of Europe*, vol. 3, London, 1973.

Lombardini, G., *Pane e denaro a Bassano tra il 1501 e il 1799*, Vicenza, 1963.

Lopez, R. S., "Venezia e le grandi linee dell'espansione commerciale nel secolo XIII," in *La civiltà veneziana del secolo di Marco Polo*, Venice, 1955.

Lopez, R. S., *The Commercial Revolution*, Englewood Cliffs, N. J., 1971.

Lopez, R. S. and I. W. Raymond (eds.), *Medieval Trade in the Mediterranean World: Illustrative Documents*, New York, 1955.

Lucas, H. S., "The Great European Famine of 1315, 1316 and 1317, in E. M. Carus-Wilson (ed.), *Essays in Economic History*, vol. 2, London, 1962.

Lütge, F., *Deutsche Sozial- und Wirtschaftsgeschichte*, Berlin, 1960.

Luzzatto, G., "Sull'attendibilitá di alcune statistiche economiche medievali," *Giornale degli Economisti*, ser. 4, vol. 69 (1929).

Luzzatto, G., *Storia economica dell'età moderna e contemporanea*, Padua, 1938.

Luzzatto, G., *Studi di storia economica veneziana*, Padua, 1954.

Luzzatto, G., *Storia economica di Venezia dall'XI al XVI secolo*, Venice, 1961.

Malowist, M., "Poland, Russia and Western Trade, in the 15th and 16th Centuries," *Past and Present*, vol. 13 (1958).

Malowist, M., *Croissance et regression en Europe XVIe–XVIIe siècles*, Paris, 1972.

Marshall, D., "The Old Poor Law, 1662–1795," in E. M. Carus-Wilson (ed.), *Essays in Economic History*, vol. 1, London, 1954.

Massa, P., *Un'impresa serica genovese della prima metà del Cinquecento*, Milan, 1974.

Mathias, P., *The First Industrial Nation*, London, 1969.

Mazzaoui, M. F., "The Emigration of Veronese Textile Artisans to Bologna in the XIIIth Century," *Atti e Memorie dell'Accademia di Agricoltura, Scienze e Lettere di Verona*, vol. 149 (1967–68).

Meiss, M., *Painting in Florence and Siena after the Black Death*, Princeton, N.J., 1951.

Melis, F., *Storia della ragioneria*, Bologna, 1950.

Melis, F., *Aspetti della vita economica medievale*, Siena, 1962.

Melis, F. (ed.), *Guida alla Mostra internazionale della storia della banca*, Siena, 1972.

Meroni, U., *Cremona fedelissima*, Cremona, 1951–57.

Mignet, M., *Rivalité de François I et de Charles-Quint*, Paris, 1886.

Mill, C., *Puritanism and Revolution*, London, 1965.

Minchinchton, W. E. (ed.), *The Growth of English Overseas Trade in the Seventeenth and Eighteenth Centuries*, London, 1969.

Mira, G., *Aspetti dell'economia comasca all'inizio dell'età moderna*, Como, 1939.

Mira, G., *Vicende economiche di una famiglia italiana dal XIV al XVII secolo*, Milan, 1940.

Mira, G., "Le entrate patrimoniali del Comune di Perugia," in *Annali della Facoltà di economia e commercio dell'Università di Cagliari*, 1959–60.

Mollat, M. (ed.), *Les pauvres dans la société médiévale*, Paris, 1973.

Mollat, M., "La mortalité à Paris," in *Le Moyen Age*, vol. 69 (1963).

Mollat, M., *Le rôle du sel dans l'histoire*, Paris, 1968.

Mollat, M., *Etudes sur l'histoire de la pauvreté*, Paris, 1974.

Mols, R., *Introduction à la démographie historique des villes d'Europe du XIVe au XVIIIe siècle*, Louvain, 1954.

Montaigne, M. de, *Journal de voyage en Italie, 1580–81* (ed. by A. D'Ancona), Città di Castello, 1859.

Monter, W., *Calvin's Geneva*, New York, 1967.

Moritz, L. A., *Grain-mills and Flour in Classical Antiquity*, Oxford, 1958.

Morris, C., "The Plague in Britain," *The Historical Journal*, vol. 14 (1971).

Morse, H. B., *The Chronicles of the East India Company Trading to China, 1635–1834*, Cambridge, Mass., 1926.

Moryson, F., *Itinerary* (ed. by C. Hughes), London, 1903.

Mullet, C. F., *The Bubonic Plague and England*, Lexington, Ky., 1956.

Muendel, J., "The Horizontal Mills of Medieval Pistoia," *Technology and Culture*, vol. 15 (1974).

Muratori, L. A., *Della carità cristiana*, Modena, 1723.

Musson, A. E. (ed.), *Science, Technology and Economic Growth in the Eighteenth Century*, London, 1972.

Nadal, J., *Historia de la población española*, Barcelona, 1966.

Narducci, E. (ed.), "Tre prediche inedite del B. Giordano da Rivalto," *Giornale Arcadico di scienze, lettere ed arti*, vol. 146 (1857).

Needham, J., *Science and Civilisation in China*, Cambridge, 1954–1973.

Nef, J. U., *Rise of the British Coal Industry*, London, 1932.

Nef, J. U., *The Conquest of the Material World*, Chicago/London, 1964.

Noel, R., "La population de la paroisse de Laguiole d'après un recensement de 1691," *Annales de démographie historique*, 1967.

Oakeshott, M., *Political Education*, Cambridge, 1951.

Ozanam, J. A. F., *Histoire médicale générale et particulière des maladies épidémiques contagieuses et épizootiques qui ont régné en Europe*, Paris, 1817.

Pach, Z. P., "The Role of East-Central Europe in International Trade (16th and 17th Centuries)," *Etudes Historiques*, Budapest, 1970.

Parenti, G., *La popolazione della Toscana sotto la Reggenza lorenese*, Florence, 1937.

Parenti, G., *Prime ricerche sulla rivoluzione dei prezzi in Firenze*, Florence, 1939.

Parenti, G., *Prezzo e mercato del grano a Siena (1546–1765)*, Florence, 1942.

Paschetti, B., *Lettera*, Genoa, 1580.

Passerini, L., *Storia degli stabilimenti di beneficenza*, Florence, 1853.

Patzelt, E., *Karolingische Renaissance*, Vienna, 1924.

Pazzagli, C., *L'agricoltura toscana nella prima metà dell'800*, Florence, 1973.

Petty, W., "Verbum Sapienti," in *The Economic Writings* (ed. by C. M. Hull), vol. 1, New York, 1963.

Phelps Brown, E. H. and S. V. Hopkins, "Wage-rates and Prices," *Economica*, vol. 24 (1957).

Phelps Brown, E. H. and S. V. Hopkins, "Seven Centuries of Building Wages," in E. M. Carus-Wilson (ed.), *Essays in Economic History*, vol. 2, London, 1962.

Phelps Brown, E. H. and S. V. Hopkins, "Seven Centuries of the Prices of Consumable Compared with Builder's Wage-rates," in E. M. Carus-Wilson (ed.), *Essays in Economic History*, vol. 2, London, 1962.

Pini, A. I., "Problemi demografici bolognesi del Duecento," *Atti e Memorie della Deputazione di Storia Patria per le Provincie di Romagna*, n.s., vols. 16–17 (1969).

Pini, A. I., "La Viticultura Italiana nel Medioevo," *Studi Medievali*, ser. 3, vol. 15 (1974).

Piponnier, F., *Costume et vie sociale. La Cour d' Anjou, XIVᵉ–XVᵉ Siècle*, Paris, 1970.

Pirenne, H., *Histoire de Belgique*, Brussells, 1900–1932.

Pirenne, H., *A History of Europe*, New York, 1936.

Pirenne, H., *Histoire économique et sociale du Moyen Age* (ed. by H. van Wervecke), Paris, 1963.

Pirenne, H., *Medieval Cities*, Princeton, N.J., 1952.

Pitti, B., *Cronica* (ed. by A. Bacchi della Lega), Bologna, 1905 (see also Brucker).

Pleket, H. M., "Technology and Society in the Greco-Roman World," *Acta Historiae Neerlandica*, vol. 2 (1967).

Pollard, J., "Fixed Capital in the Industrial Revolution in Britain," *Journal of Economic History*, vol. 24 (1964) (reprinted in Crouzet, F. (ed.), *Capital Formation in the Industrial Revolution*, London, 1972).

Poni, C., "Archéologie de la fabrique: la diffusion des moulins à soie 'alla bolognese' dans les Etats vénitiens du XVIᵉ au XVIIIᵉ siècle," *Annales. E.S.C.*, vol. 27 (1972).

Porisini, G., *La proprietà terriera nel Comune di Ravenna dalla metà del secolo XVI ai giorni nostri*, Milan, 1963.

Postan, M. M., "Credit in Medieval Trade," in E. M. Carus-Wilson (ed.), *Essays in Economic History*, vol. 1, London, 1954.

Postan, M. M., "Investment in Medieval Agriculture," *The Journal of Economic History*, vol. 27 (1967).

Posthumus, N. W., *Geschiedenis der Leidsche Lakenindustrie*, La Haje, 1908–39.

Power, E., *The Wool Trade in English Medieval History*, Oxford, 1941.

Presotto, D., "Genova 1656—Cronache di una pestilenza," in *Atti della Societá Ligure di Storia Patria*, vol. 79 (1965).

Price, J. L., *Culture and Society in the Dutch Republic during the Seventeenth Century*, London, 1974.

Priuli, G., "Diarii," *Rerum Italicarum Scriptores*, vol. 24.

Pullan, B. (ed.), *Crisis and Change in the Venetian Economy*, London, 1968.

Pullan, B., "Wage-earners and the Venetian Economy: 1550–1630," in B. Pullan (ed.), *Crisis and Change in the Venetian Economy*, London, 1968.

Ramazzini, B., *Le malattie dei lavoratori* (ed. by O. Rossi), Turin, 1933 (English translation by W. C. Wright, New York, 1940).

Ramsay, J. H., *A History of the Revenue of the Kings of England, 1066–1399*, Oxford, 1925.

Redlich, F., "An Eighteenth-Century German Guide for Investors," *Bulletin of the Business Historical Society*, vol. 26 (1952).

Redlich, F., "De Praeda Militari," *Vierteljahrschrift für Sozial- und Wirtschaftsgeschichte*, vol. 39 (1956).

Reinhard, M. R., A. Armengaud, and J. Dupaquier, *Histoire générale de la population mondiale*, Paris, 1968.

Renouard, Y., *Etudes d'histoire médiévale*, Paris, 1968.

Rey, M., *Les finances royales sous Charles VI—Les causes du deficit 1388–1413*, Paris, 1965.

Richet, D., "Croissance et blocage en France du XV au XVIII siècle," *Annales E.S.C.*, vol. 23 (1968).

Romani, M. A., *La gente, le occupazioni e i redditi del Piacentino*, Parma, 1969.

Romani, M. A., *Aspetti dell'evoluzione demografica parmense nei secoli XVI e XVII*, Parma, 1970.

Romano, R., "A Florence au XVIIᵉ siècle. Industries textiles et conjoncture," *Annales. E.S.C.*, vol. 7 (1952).

Romano, R., "Economic Aspects of the Construction of Warships in Venice in the Sixteenth Century," in B. Pullan (ed.), *Crisis and Change in the Venetian Economy*, London, 1968.

Rondinelli, F., *Relazione del Contagio stato in Firenze l'anno 1630 e 1633*, Florence, 1634.

Rörig, F., *The Medieval Town*, Berkeley, 1967.

Rosen, E., "The Invention of Eyeglasses," *Journal of the History of Medicine*, vol. 11 (1956).

Rossi, P., *I filosofi e le macchine*, Milan, 1962.

Rotelli, C., "Rendimenti e produzione agricola nell'Imolese dal XVI al XIX secolo," *Rivista storica italiana*, vol. 79 (1967).

Rotelli, C., *L'economia agraria di Chieri attraverso i catasti dei secoli XIV–XVI*, Milan, 1967.

Rubinstein, N., "Some Ideas on Municipal Progress and Decline in the Italy of the Communes," in *Fritz Saxel* (ed. by D. J. Gordon), London, 1957.

Ruiz Martin, F., "Demografia eclesiástica hasta el siglo XIX," in *Diccionario de Historia Eclesiástica de España*, vol. 2, Madrid, 1972.

Russell, J. C., "The Clerical Population of Medieval England," *Traditio*, vol. 2 (1944).

Russell, J. C., *British Medieval Population*, Albuquerque, N.M., 1948.

Salaman, R. N., *History and Social Influence of the Potato*, Cambridge, 1949.

Samuelson, P. A., "A Fallacy in the Introduction of Pareto's Law of Alleged Constancy of Income Distribution," *Rivista Internazionale di Scienze Economiche*, vol. 12 (1965).

Saraceno, P., *La produzione industriale*, Venice, 1965, p. 16.

Sapori, A., "L'attendibilitá di alcune testimonianze cronistiche dell' economia medievale," *Archivo Storico Italiano*, ser. 7, vol. 12 (1929).

Sapori, A., *Le marchand italien au Moyen Age*, Paris, 1952.

Sapori, A., "Le compagnie mercantili toscane del Dugento," in *Studi di storia economica*, vol. 2, Florence, 1955.

Sayous, A., "Les débuts du commerce de l'Espagne avec l'Amerique," in *Révue Historique*, vol. 2 (1934).

Scavia, M., *L'industria della carta in Italia*, Turin, 1903.

Scavizzi, P., "Considerazioni sull'attività edilizia a Roma nella prima metà del Seicento," *Studi storici*, vol. 9 (1968).

Schaube, A., *Handelsgeschichte der romanischen Völker des Mittelmeergebiets bis zum Ende der Kreuzzüge*, Munich/Berlin, 1906.

Schiavoni, C., "Introduzione allo studio delle fonti archivistiche per la storia demografica di Roma," *Genus*, vol. 27 (1971).

Schmitz, H. J., *Faktoren der Preisbildung für Getreide und Wein in der Zeit von 800 bis 1350*, Stuttgart, 1968.

Schöffer, I., "Did Holland's Golden Age Coincide with a Period of Crisis?," *Acta Historiae Neerlandica*, vol. 1 (1966).

Schollier, E., *De Levensstandaard in de 15 en 16 Eeuw te Antwerpen*, Antwerp, 1960.

Schubert, H. R., *History of the British Iron and Steel Industry*, London, 1957.

Schulte, A., *Geschichte des mittelalterlichen Handels und Verkehrs zwischen Westdeutschland und Italien mit Auschluss von Venedig*, Leipzig, 1900.

Schumpeter, E. B., *English Overseas Trade Statistics 1697–1808*, Oxford, 1960.

Schumpeter, J. A., "The Creative Response in Economic History," *The Journal of Economic History*, vol. 7 (1947).

Sclafert, T., *Cultures en Haute-Provence*, Paris, 1959.

Scott Thomson, G., *Life in a noble Household: 1614–1700*, Ann Arbor, Mich., 1959.

Segni, G. B., *Trattato sopra la carestia e fame*, Bologna, 1602.

Sella, D., "La popolazione di Milano nei secoli XVI e XVII," in *Storia di Milano*, vol. 12 (1959).

Sella, D., *Commerci e industrie a Venezia nel secolo XVII*, Venice/ Rome, 1961.

Sella, D., "The Rise and Fall of the Venetian Woolen Industry," in B. Pullan (ed.), *Crisis and Change in the Venetian Economy*, London, 1968.

Sella, D., *Salari e lavoro nell'edilizia lombarda durante il sec. XVII*, Pavia, 1968.

Sella D., "Industrial Production in 17th-century Italy," in *Explorations in Entrepreneurial History*, vol. 6 (1969).

Sestan, E., "La città comunale italiana dei secoli X–XII," *XI Congrés International des Sciences Historiques*, vol. 3, Stockholm, 1960.

Sevcenko, I., "The Decline of Byzantium Seen through the Eyes of Its Intellectuals," *Dumbarton Oaks Papers*, vol. 15 (1961).

Shrewsbury, J. F. D., *A History of Bubonic Plague in the British Isles*, Cambridge, 1970.

Siegfried, A., *Itinéraires de contagions: épidémies et idéologies*, Paris, 1960.

Simons, F. J., *Eat not This Flesh*, Madison, Wis., 1961.

Sivori, G., "Il tramonto dell'industria serica genovese," *Rivista Storica Italiana*, vol. 84 (1972).

Slicher van Bath, B. H., "Accounts and Diaries of Farmers before 1800," *Afdeling Agrarische Geschiedenis Bijdragen*, vol. 8 (1962).

Slicher van Bath, B. H., "Yield Ratios 810–1820," *Afdeling Agrarische Geschiedenis Bijdragen*, vol. 10 (1963).

Slicher van Bath, B. H., *The Agrarian History of Western Europe 500– 1850*, London, 1963.

Smith, C. T., *An Historical Geography of Western Europe before 1800*, New York/Washington, 1967.

Smith, J., *Old Scottish Clockmakers*, Edinburgh, 1921.

Snape, R. H., *English Monastic Finances in the Late Middle Ages*, London, 1968.

Soltow, L., "Long-run changes in British income inequality," *The Economic History Review*, ser. 2, vol. 21 (1968).

Spengler, J. J., "The Population Problem," *The Southern Economic Journal*, vol. 27 (1961).

Sprandel, R., *Das Eisengewerbe im Mittelalter*, Stuttgart, 1968.

Stella, A., "La proprietà ecclesiastica nella Repubblica di Venezia dal secolo XV al secolo XVII," *Nuova rivista storica*, vol. 42 (1958).

Stone, L., "Elizabethan Overseas Trade," *The Economic History Review*, ser. 2, vol. 2 (1949).

Stone, L., *La crisi dell'aristocrazia*, Turin, 1972.

Stouff, L., *Ravitaillement et alimentation en Provence au XIVe et XVe siècles*, Paris/The Hague, 1970.

Stow, J., *Annales*, continued and augmented by E. Howes, London, 1631.

Stoye, J. W., *English Travellers Abroad*, London, 1952.

Strachey, L., *Portraits in Miniature*, New York, 1962.

Strauss, G., *Nuremberg in the 16th Century*, New York, 1966.

Supple, B. E., *Commercial Crisis and Change in England 1600–1642*, Cambridge, 1959.

Sutherland, I., "John Graunt: A Tercentenary Tribute," *Journal of the Royal Statistical Society*, ser. A, vol. 126 (1963).

Svenskt Biografiskt Lexikon, Stockholm, 1918.

Tadino, A., *Raguaglio dell'origine et giornali successi della gran peste*, Milan, 1648.

Tagliaferri, A., *L'economia veronese secondo gli estimi dal 1409 al 1635*, Milan, 1966.

Tagliaferri, A., *Consumi e tenore di vita di una famiglia borghese del 1600*, Milan, 1968.

Talbot, C. H., *Medicine in Medieval England*, London, 1967.

Tawney, A. J. and R. H. Tawney, "An Occupational Census of the Seventeenth Century," *The Economic History Review*, vol. 5 (1934–35).

Tawney, R. H. and E. Power, (eds.), *Tudor Economic Documents*, London/New York/Toronto, 1953.

Tawney, R. H., *Business and Politics under James I*, Cambridge, 1958.

Taylor, E. G. R., "Mathematics and the Navigator in the 13th Century," *Journal of the Institute of Navigation*, vol. 13 (1960).

Tissot, S. A., *De la santé des gens de Lettres*, Lausanne, 1768.

Titow, J. Z., *English Rural Society 1200–1350*, London, 1969.

Titow, J. Z., *Winchester Yields. A Study in Medieval Agricultural Productivity*, Cambridge, 1972.

Trenard, L., "Le charbon avant l'ere industrielle," in *Charbon et Sciences Humaines* (col. Université de Lille), Paris/The Hague, 1966.

Trevor-Davies, R., *Spain in Decline, 1621–1700*, London/New York, 1965.

Trexler, R. C., "Une table florentine d'espérance de vie," *Annales. E. S. C.*, vol. 26 (1971).

Trow-Smith, R., *A History of British Livestock Husbandry to 1700*, London, 1957.

Tucci, U., "L'industria del ferro nel Settecento in Val Trompia," in *Ricerche storiche ed economiche in memoria di C. Barbagallo*, Naples, 1970.

Ullyett, K., *British Clocks and Clockmakers*, London, 1947.

Unger, R. W., "Dutch ship design in the 15th and 16th Centuries," in *Viator*, vol. 4 (1973).

United Nations, *The Determinants and Consequences of Population Trends*, New York, 1953.

Unwin, G., *Studies in Economic History*, London, 1927.

Urlanis, T. S., *Rost naselenija v Evropi*, Moscow, 1941.

Usher, A. P., *The Early History of Deposit Banking in Mediterranean Europe*, Cambridge, Mass., 1943.

Usher, A. P., *A History of Mechanical Inventions*, Boston, 1959.

Vandenbroeke, C., "Cultivation and Consumption of the Potato in the 17th and 18th Century," in *Acta Historiae Neerlandica*, vol. 5 (1971).

Van der Wee, H., *The Growth of the Antwerp Market and the European Economy*, The Hague, 1963.

Van der Wee, H., "Anvers et les innovations de la technique financière aux XVIᵉ–XVIIᵉ siècles," *Annales E. S. C.*, vol. 22 (1967).

Van der Wee, H., "The Economy as a Factor in the Start of the Revolt in the Southern Netherlands," *Acta Historiae Neerlandica*, vol. 5 (1971).

Van der Woude, A.M., "Het Noorderkwartier," in *Afdeling Agrarische Geschiedenis Bijdragen*, vol. 16 (1972).

Van Houtte, J. A., "La genèse du grand marché international d'Anvers à la fin du Moyen Age," *Revue belge de philologie et d'histoire*, vol. 19 (1940).

Van Houtte, J. A., "Anvers aux XVᵉ et XVIᵉ siècles. Expansion et apogée," *Annales. E. S. C.*, vol. 16 (1961).

Van Houtte, J. A., *Economische en Sociale Geschiedenis van de Lage Landen*, Antwerp, 1964.

Van Kampen, S. C. *De Rotterdamse particuliere Sheepsbouw in de tijd van de Republiek*, Assen, 1953.

Van Linschoten, J. H., *The Voyage to the East Indies* (ed. by A. C. Burnell and P. A. Tiele), London, 1885.

Van Uytven, R., "The Fulling Mill: Dynamics of the Revolution in Industrial Attitudes," *Acta Historiae Neerlandica*, vol. 5 (1971).

Vauban, S. La Preste de, *Project de dixme royal*, Paris, 1707.

Ventura, A., *Nobiltà e popolo nella società veneta del '400 e '500*, Bari, 1965.

Verdenius, W. J., "Science grecque et science moderne," *Revue philosophique*, vol. 152 (1962).

Vicens Vives, J., *Manual de historia economica de España*, Barcelona, 1959.

Vilar, P., *Oro e moneta nella storia*, Bari, 1971.

Violante, C., "I Vescovi dell'Italia centro-settentrionale e lo sviluppo dell'economia monetaria," in *Vescovi e Diocesi in Italia nel Medio-Evo*, Padua, 1964.

Vogel, W., "Zur Grosse der Europäischen Handelsflotten im 15., 16. und 17. Jahrhundert," *Festschrift Dietrich Schäfer*, Jena, 1915.

Waddington, C. H., *The Ethical Animal*, Chicago, 1960.

Walford, C., "The Famines of the World, Past and Present," *Journal of the Statistical Society*, vols. 41–42 (1878–79).

Walker, P. G., "The Origins of the Machine Age," *History Today*, vol. 16 (1966).

Waters, D. W., *The Art of Navigation in England in Elizabethan and Early Stuart Times*, London/New Haven, Conn., 1958.

Wertime, T., *The Coming of the Age of Steel*, Leyden, 1961.

White, L., *Medieval Technology and Social Change*, Oxford, 1962.

White, L., "What Accelerated Technological Progress in the Western Middle Ages," in A. C. Crombie (ed.), *Scientific Change*, New York, 1963.

White, L., "Cultural Climates and Technological Advance in the Middle Ages," *Viator*, vol. 2 (1971).

White, L., "The Expansion of Technology 500–1500," in *The Fontana Economic History of Europe*, vol. 1, London, 1972.

Wilson, C., *England's Apprenticeship, 1603–1763*, Oxford, 1965.

Wilson, C., *The Dutch Republic*, London, 1968.

Woodward, G. W. O., *The Dissolution of the Monasteries*, London, 1966.

Wolff, P., *Commerce et marchands de Toulouse (1350–1450)*, Toulouse, 1954.

Wolff, P., "Prix et marché," *Méthodologie de l'histoire et des sciences humaines*, Toulouse, 1973.

Working, H., "Statistical Laws of Family Expenditure," *Journal of the American Statistical Association*, vol. 38 (1943).

Wrigley, E. A., *Population and History*, New York, 1969.

Youings, Y., *The Dissolution of the Monasteries*, London, 1971.

Young, A., *Political Arithmetic*, London, 1774.

Young, A., *Travels in France during the Years 1787, 1788, 1789*, London, 1912.

Zanetti, D., *Problemi alimentari di una economia preindustriale*, Turin, 1964.

Zanetti, D., "Note sulla Rivoluzione dei prezzi," *Rivista storica italiana*, vol. 77 (1965).

Zanetti, D., *La demografia del patriziato milanese*, Pavia, 1973.

Ziegler, P., *The Black Death*, London, 1969.

Zinsser, H., *Rats, Lice and History*, New York, 1935.

Index